CAR TROUBLE

Other volumes in the
World Resources Institute Guides to the Environment

*The Greenhouse Trap: What We're Doing to the Atmosphere and
How We Can Slow Global Warming*
Francesca Lyman with Irving Mintzer, Kathleen Courrier, and
James MacKenzie

Trees of Life: Saving Tropical Forests and Their Biological Wealth
Kenton Miller and Laura Tangley

CAR TROUBLE

Steve Nadis and James J. MacKenzie

with Laura Ost

Beacon Press
Boston

World Resources Institute is deeply grateful to the Florence and John Schumann Foundation and the Geraldine R. Dodge Foundation, whose generous financial support made this book possible. WRI's gratitude extends also to the Nathan Cummings Foundation; the Joyce Foundation; the Joyce Mertz-Gilmore Foundation; the William Penn Foundation; and the Public Welfare Foundation, Inc., for their support of WRI's work on transportation issues.

Beacon Press
25 Beacon Street
Boston, Massachusetts 02108

Beacon Press books
are published under the auspices of
the Unitarian Universalist Association of Congregations.

99 98 97 96 95 94 93 92   8 7 6 5 4 3 2 1

Library of Congress Cataloging-in-Publication Data

Nadis, Steven J.
  Car trouble / Steve Nadis and James J. MacKenzie, with Laura Ost.
    p.   cm. — (World Resources Institute guide to the environment)
  Includes index.
  ISBN 0-8070-8522-7 (cloth).—ISBN 0-8070-8523-5 (pbk.)
    1. Automobiles—Motors—Exhaust gas—Environmental aspects.
  2. Transportation, Automotive—Environmental aspects.
  3. Automobiles—Social aspects—United States.   I. MacKenzie, James J.
  (James John), 1939–   .   II. Ost, Laura.   III. Title.
  IV. Series.
  TD886.5.N3 1993
  363.73'1—dc20   92-28303
                                                              CIP

CONTENTS

ABOUT WRI GUIDES
TO THE ENVIRONMENT

If the novelty of environmental issues has begun to wear off in the 1990s, their importance is just beginning to sink in. Whether as on-lookers or victims, most Americans have gradually figured out that waste, pollution, congestion, land degradation, and the like are not iso-lated mishaps that time will cure, but are byproducts of the way we live. And with this recognition has come another: that we have choices to make—the sooner, the better.

We can't make these choices, of course, without a firm fix on the facts and some sense of what's economically and politically possible in our own lifetimes. And we also need a shared understanding of how our productive, big-spending, and still widely emulated country shapes the planet's environmental future—and of how economic and social choices in the rest of the world influence us.

To help Americans grasp the big picture, the World Resources In-stitute created *WRI Guides to the Environment*. These books—*The Greenhouse Trap, Trees of Life,* and now *Car Trouble*—were written to dispel confusion about our most pressing environmental concerns and bring new facts and ideas to light. They reflect the belief that even the most scientifically complex environmental issues can be clearly ex-plained, that there is plenty that can be done about them, and that Americans are ready to try.

Kathleen Courrier
Series Editor

FOREWORD

Cars are central to the American dream, as tied to our culture as owning a home or getting ahead in the world. Learning to drive is a rite of passage for young Americans, and so is buying one's first set of wheels. Since the 1950s, we've built a 44,000-mile interstate highway system that some have called "the eighth wonder of the world." Two percent of our land, more than we use for housing, is given over to roads and to the care and feeding—repairing, fueling, parking—of automobiles. The American landscape is chockablock with drive-in restaurants and banks—and in some Western states, drive-in churches and funeral parlors, too. In traditional small-town America, fast-food strips flourish along the highways leading out of town, while Main Street dwindles. The romance of the open road—and the quick getaway—comes up over and over in popular songs and movies.

The reality is that over 80 percent of all the driving we do takes us no farther than 10 miles from home. But we do a lot of it. All told, Americans drive more than 2 trillion miles a year, logging as many miles behind the wheel as all the world's other drivers put together. Getting to work or school, buying groceries, visiting family and friends, going out to dinner or taking in a show—most daily activities seem nearly unthinkable without a car.

For many Americans, though, the country's long love affair with the automobile has gone sour. According to a recent *Washington Post* article, 25 percent of Americans are "road haters" who don't enjoy driving. Another 15 percent consider cars a necessary evil but take little interest in style, color, or upkeep. Forty percent of American drivers may be disenchanted, but except for those living in cities with good public transportation, driving remains the only reasonable way to get around.

There's no mystery about why the car is king: it's a matter of public policy. Since the 1940s we have made motor vehicles ever more central to our transportation system, while letting the train and trolley lines that once moved most workers and goods deteriorate. By the 1960s, for instance, once-thriving trolley lines had been dismantled in 45 American cities. Given our public policy tilt toward the automobile, it's also not surprising that the U.S. Department of Transportation now spends five times as much on highway construction and repair as on mass transit.

What is our addiction to automobiles costing us? For openers, it translates into an addiction to Persian Gulf oil, with all the attendant national security risks. In 1989, we imported 220 million barrels of oil from Iraq and Kuwait—the same amount that would be saved if the U.S. auto fleet were three miles per gallon more efficient. Making big gains in gas mileage can't wipe out our dependence on foreign oil, though, because such gains are continually outpaced by the rising number of cars on the road and miles driven.

Gasoline is as cheap in real dollars as it's been for 50 years, so people have every reason to use lots of it. Most commuters who drive solo have access to free or subsidized parking, so they have little incentive to consider carpooling or public transit. Meanwhile, new highways intended to relieve traffic gridlock often clog within weeks. Many cities contend with rush-hour traffic all day and into the night, and in the past five years 30 to 50 percent of Americans lived in places where air quality failed at least one federal standard. Yet even as more and more of us are choked by smog or trapped for hours in traffic, we keep buying into the promise of mobility and ease associated with owning a car.

The American dream of a car—or two or three of them—in every garage is beginning to look like a nightmare for our planet. Besides their role in making the smog and acid rain that damage forests, crops, and aquatic life over vast regions, motor vehicles are driving two other global problems. In America, air conditioners installed in cars are the single largest source of the CFCs that destroy the protective ozone layer in the stratosphere. Motor vehicles account for 53 percent of U.S. carbon monoxide emissions and much of the harmful ground-level ozone—a greenhouse gas and the chief ingredient of smog. Most damaging of all—because hardest to curtail—they account for 25 percent of U.S. emissions of the leading greenhouse gas, carbon dioxide.

Fortunately, as the authors of *Car Trouble* point out, it's not too late to change. We can get the economic incentives right, starting with a raise in energy taxes to make gasoline prices reflect more fully the social, environmental, and defense-related costs of gasoline use that are currently hidden. Such a move would encourage greater fuel efficiency, thereby reducing our need for imported oil and our greenhouse gas emissions. It would also create a level playing field on which the new and greener automotive technologies of the future could fairly compete. Who knows? If Detroit gets serious about clean cars, maybe it can woo back the American car buyers who have been buying Japanese cars in droves.

We at the World Resources Institute hope that *Car Trouble* will help spur action to protect the environment—and soon. The urgency is real: today's global motor vehicle fleet will likely double to one billion over the next 20 years. If we are to flourish in such a future, we must now start designing greener ways of getting around.

Gus Speth, President
World Resources Institute

ACKNOWLEDGMENTS

Responsibility for the content of *Car Trouble* is ours alone, but credit for the concept, for some of its ideas, for research assistance, and for no-holds-barred reviews must be spread around.

We are particularly indebted to colleagues at the World Resources Institute. Kathleen Courrier, series editor of *WRI Guides to the Environment,* first proposed this book and kept the project moving for close to two years. Clara Rankin helped with the preliminary research. Laurie Milford did a phenomenal job of tracking down documents and references, as well as checking facts. Roger Dower and Jessica Mathews gave invaluable advice on the transportation technologies and fuels explored here, while offering insights into public policies for giving the best of them a fair chance in the market—and on the road. Alan Brewster provided a piercing and most helpful review. Consultant Laura Ost prepared one of the appendices and helped us clarify our thinking on tomorrow's cars, roads, and fuels. Sue Terry cheerfully obtained many of the books, reports, and other references needed to prepare this book. Working under tremendous pressure, Lori Pierelli expertly guided the manuscript through production.

Outside of WRI, many people reviewed sections of the book. Our deepest thanks go to Deborah Bleviss at the International Institute for Energy Conservation; Sarah Campbell, project director of the Surface Transportation Policy Project; and David Burwell, president of the Rails-to-Trails Conservancy. Their careful readings turned up a few blunders and led us to various people and technical reports that we might not otherwise have found.

We also owe thanks to Bob Aglow of ABC News, Andrew Hamilton of the Conservation Law Foundation, James Womack of MIT's International Motor Vehicle Program, and others who took time from busy schedules to share their knowledge with us. Unfortunately, there is not enough space to express our gratitude to everyone who contributed in this way.

Gus Speth, the founder of the World Resources Institute and for ten years its president, deserves special thanks for making WRI the sort of place where people are not only free to pursue their own ideas, but encouraged and helped in every way possible. This book is one of many in which he is the silent partner.

S.N. and J.M.

CAR FACTS

- *Millions of cars and trucks retired from American roads each year: 11*

- *Millions of motor vehicles added to the scrap heap in the United States since 1946: 288*

- *In the U.S., percentage of carbon monoxide polluting the air that comes from motor vehicles: 50+*

- *In the U.S., percentage of nitrogen oxides contributed by motor vehicles: 30*

- *Number of pounds of carbon dioxide produced by burning one gallon of gasoline: 19*

- *Percentage of global carbon dioxide emissions from burning fossil fuel contributed by motor vehicles worldwide: 14*

- *Number of tons of carbon dioxide that a car getting 27.5 mpg emits over 100,000 miles: 35*

- *Percentage of carbon dioxide emissions from burning fossil fuel contributed by motor vehicles in the United States: 25*

- *Percentage of the airborne carcinogen benzene that comes from gasoline: 85*

- *Miles of road in the U.S. Interstate Highway System: 44,000*

- *Number of motor vehicles registered in the United States: 190 million*

- *Millions of barrels of oil used in U.S. transportation each day in 1990: 10.8*

- *Millions of barrels of petroleum produced in the U.S. each day in 1990: 9*

• *Number of days that air pollution in Los Angeles in 1988 rose above health standards: 232*

• *Percentage increase in vehicle miles traveled in California between 1980 and 1989: 61*

• *Millions of cars operating daily in the Los Angeles basin: 8*

• *Percentage of the pollution in Los Angeles contributed by cars: 70–80*

• *Pounds of carbon monoxide released into the atmosphere for every 1,000 miles a new gasoline-powered car is driven: 7*

• *Fraction by which Americans would have to cut oil use to end the need for Persian Gulf imports: 1/8*

• *Increase needed in gas mileage of household vehicle fleet to cut U.S. oil use by 1/8: 12 mpg*

• *Factor by which number of motor vehicles worldwide multiplied between 1950 and 1989: 8*

• *Millions of motor vehicles on the road worldwide in 1989: 556*

• *Percentage of world motor vehicle fleet in developing nations: 15*

• *Number of years before the global motor vehicles fleet is expected to double: 20–30*

• *Average annual percentage increase in U.S. car population: 2*

• *Ratio of bicycles to cars in China: 250 to 1*

• *Ratio of bicycles to cars in the United States: 0.7 to 1*

• *Percentage of oil consumed in the United States for transportation: 64*

- *Percentage of U.S. steel use accounted for by automobiles: 20*

- *Millions of licensed drivers in the United States in 1990: 168*

- *Billions of gallons of motor fuel used in the United States in 1990: 133*

- *Percentage of Americans in 1990 who lived in areas where the air did not meet national air quality standards: 30*

- *Annual losses of wheat, corn, soybean, and peanut crops attributed to ozone pollution: $4 billion*

- *Number of the hottest years of this century that have occurred since 1980: 8*

1

The Age of Invention

The horseless vehicle is the coming wonder . . .
It is only a question of time when the carriages
and trucks in every large city will be run with
motors.

THOMAS A. EDISON, 1895

The American's marriage to the American
automobile is now at an end, and it is only a
matter of minutes to the final pistol shot,
although who pulls the trigger has yet to be
determined.

JOHN KEATS,
The Insolent Chariots (1958)

The nineteenth century gave rise to the telephone, telegraph, electric light, and flush toilet, as well as to many lesser known engineering oddities—the "Combined Plow and Gun," the "Improved Burial Case," and the "Ventilating Rocking Chair." The late 1870s were a particularly industrious time, and several inventions from the period survive to this day. One is the carpet sweeper patented in 1876 by Melville Reuben Bissell of Grand Rapids, Michigan. Bissell invented his contraption to get rid of the sawdust that persistently clung to the carpet of his crockery shop. Devices similar to the original dustbin on wheels are still used in movie theaters and restaurants. In 1877, Chester Greenwood of Farmington, Maine, patented the earmuff; he later invented a machine to mass-produce the aural insulators in a factory. Since that breakthrough, millions of earmuffs have been sold, and Farmington has become the indisputable earmuff capital of the world.

The same year that earmuffs made their debut, Nikolaus August Otto, a young merchant's assistant in Cologne, Germany, succeeded, after 10 years of tinkering, in electrically igniting a gas-air mixture in a model engine. In 1877, Otto received a patent for his motor, a four-stroke compression gas engine, the prototype for today's internal combustion engine (ICE). The basic principles of the ICE—the engine powering nearly all cars on the road today—have remained virtually unchanged in the 100-plus years since Otto's original design.

Carpet sweepers and earmuffs are still with us, but not in the way that Otto's engine is. His invention paved the way for the early motorcars of Karl Benz, Gottlieb Daimler, and Henry Ford. The first cars were novelty items—expensive recreational toys for the rich and famous. At the time, no one knew that these vehicles would soon transform the world—totally, unconditionally, and irrevocably.

Before 1886, when Benz patented the first practical automobile, most people of the world, including those living in Europe and Japan, never traveled more than 20 miles from their homes except when forced to join conquering armies or choosing to accompany bands of religious pilgrims.[1] In this regard, cars have been great liberators, routinely carrying people and their belongings far from home.

For some people the car *is* home. The Ford Motor Company once advertised one of its vehicles as "a living room on wheels."[2] In the United States, the dream of a car in every garage is almost a reality, except that people drive their cars so often that the garage may be vacant most of the time. Automobiles define, in large measure, how we live, where we live, how we get to work, how much money we spend getting to work, and, to some extent, how we spend the money we make at work.

To see how cars gained such influence, a glance at history helps. After Benz launched the horseless carriage in 1886, Daimler immediately introduced a new engine that he tested on various frames—the predecessors to today's Mercedes. In 1893, Henry Ford of Dearborn, Michigan, put his first car on the road. The Daimler motor company produced what some experts have called "the first modern motor car" in 1900, the year Daimler died.[3] In 1901, the company predicted that worldwide car sales would never exceed 1 million because the population at large could not provide more than a million people capable of learning how to drive such vehicles.[4] Daimler underestimated rather dramatically. There are more than 550 million motor vehicles on the world's roads today.

Other historical highlights: In 1903, the first U.S. speed traps were set to catch daredevils surpassing the 20-mile-per-hour limit. In 1905, the first car theft was reported in St. Louis. In 1908, the Ford Motor Company introduced the Model T. In 1914, in Detroit, the first stop sign was erected. In 1921, the first fast-food drive-in opened in Dallas, Texas—Royce Hailey's Pig Stand. In 1933, the first drive-in movie theater opened in Camden, New Jersey.

October 1, 1908, when the Ford Motor Company put its Model T on the market for about $825, is perhaps *the* crucial date in the automobile timeline. The Model T was intended to be, according to Henry Ford, "a car for the great multitude."[5] Mass-production techniques introduced by the company brought per-unit prices down to about $350 by 1916, for the first time making automobiles affordable to the middle class.

Ford's continuous production system, the assembly line, tremendously increased the number of cars that could be cranked out per day. In 1903, the company's first year of operation, 1,700 vehicles were manufactured. This figure rose, gradually, to 10,000 by 1908. Production soon exploded. In 1914, some 300,000 cars rolled off the assembly lines. Production of the Model T in U.S. plants peaked in 1923 at 1.9 million cars. When the line was finally discontinued in 1927, over 15 million models of the famous Ford car had been sold.[6]

By 1929, annual American production of motor vehicles of all makes climbed to 5.3 million—10 times the combined output of the rest of the world. In that year, a total of 26.5 million motor vehicles were registered in the country. Owing to design innovations and advances in manufacturing, "Ford had singlehandedly fashioned the first great transformation in the world industry, very nearly becoming the entire world auto industry in the process," explains auto historian James Flink.[7]

In just two decades, car ownership had grown dramatically. In 1910 there was only one car for every 44 U.S. households; by 1930 there was one car for every 1.3 households.[8]

Henry Ford considered the rise in auto ownership and use the key to economic growth. "We believe that the automobile is, in itself, both directly and indirectly, an important wealth-producing instrument," he said in 1930. "The people of the United States do not own automobiles because they are prosperous. They are prosperous because they own automobiles and use them as tools to increase the range of their abilities."[9]

Although people may have prospered, and automakers certainly did, the manufacturers of horse-drawn carriages did not. The widespread adoption of the automobile diminished the number of horses on city streets and reduced the considerable costs of cleaning up after them. At the turn of the century, an estimated 15,000 dead horses were removed from New York streets each year. On a typical day, these beasts of burden contributed some 2.5 million pounds of manure and 60,000 gallons of urine to the city's thoroughfares, posing a serious health hazard. Cleanup costs and other horse-related expenses in New York were estimated in 1908 to run about $100 million a year.[10]

After surpassing horses as a principal means of conveyance, cars overtook rail transport during the 1920s. In 1922, people traveled four times as many miles by train or trolley as by automobile. However, by 1929 cars accounted for four times as many passenger miles as did rail cars.[11]

Several factors underlie the spectacular rise of the auto. First, cars offered flexibility and freedom unmatched by almost any other mode of transportation. Second, oil supplies were cheap and seemingly limitless; the notion of conserving this resource would not be seriously discussed—and largely ignored—for decades to come.

Consumer preference alone did not make the automobile what it is today, however. Government policies, industry lobbying, and corporate greed were more important factors behind the ascendance of the automobile and the corresponding decline of intercity rail and mass transit. The automakers, tire manufacturers, oil companies, and construction industry fought fiercely for the conversion to an auto-based transportation system. Their actions went beyond mere influence peddling, at times approaching outright sabotage.

Starting in the 1930s, National City Lines, a company backed by General Motors, Standard Oil, Phillips Petroleum, Firestone Tire and Rubber, Mack Truck, and other auto interests, systematically bought up and closed down more than 100 electric trolley lines in 45 cities across the country. In 1949, a federal jury convicted GM and the other companies of conspiring to replace electric transportation systems with buses and to monopolize the sale of buses. (These corporations were fined a trifling $5,000 each for their actions.) But the long-term damage had already been done. In 1947, when the destruction of mass transit was just beginning, 40 percent of U.S. workers relied on public transportation to get to their jobs. In 1963, only 14 percent did.[12] By that time, electric trolley lines were virtually extinct in the United States. The trend has continued: today less than 5 percent of the working population commutes by way of public transportation.

In 1974, antitrust lawyer Bradford Snell testified before Congress on the corporate conspiracy to wreck mass transit. The Big Three automakers—GM, Ford, and Chrysler—"used their vast economic power to restructure America into a land of big cars and diesel trucks," Snell contended. These companies "reshaped American ground transportation to serve corporate wants instead of social need."[13]

Henry Ford's prescription for urban reform also put corporate wealth first. He urged Americans to abandon the slum-ridden cities in favor of auto-dependent suburbs, saying, "We shall solve the city problem by leaving the city." For Ford and others cars offered the ticket to freedom—escape from the tenements for refuge in pastoral suburbia. Writer William Dix laid out his vision in 1904: "Imagine a healthier race of working men, toiling in cheerful and sanitary factories . . . who, in the late afternoon, glide away in their own comfortable vehicles to their little farms or houses in the country or by the sea twenty or thirty miles distant. They will be healthier, happier, more intelligent and self-respecting citizens because of the chance to live among meadows and flowers of the country instead of in crowded city streets."[14]

State and federal policies in effect throughout most of this century have promoted this vision, encouraging road building and housing construction in low-density outlying suburbs. For example, through tax deductions and mortgage guarantees, the federal government has encouraged home ownership and single-family housing—benefits that most urban apartment renters must pass up. Similarly, federal tax laws have given preferential treatment to real estate developers for erecting new structures rather than renovating old ones.

A 1938 Federal Housing Administration document called the Minimum Property Standards laid the groundwork for the postwar housing boom. The planning code, which anyone receiving federal mortgage insurance had to follow, was based on the premise that America's old-fashioned towns, with gridlike street layouts, were not compatible with the automobile. New housing, according to the document, was to be built in isolated enclaves rather than on a continuous network of through streets. Thus began the proliferation of "transit unfriendly" environments—cul-de-sacs and other circuitous routes that were simply inaccessible to buses and rail transit. In these communities, therefore, reliance on the automobile became a virtual necessity.

The Veterans Administration Housing Loan Program started by the federal government after World War II provided money to veterans to purchase housing; veterans accepting these loans were *required* to buy brand new homes, and most new housing was to be found in spread-out suburbs reachable only by cars.

"Because more land is available at the periphery of urban areas than closer in, the vast majority of single-family housing has been built in peripheral regions," explains John Pucher, an urban planner at Rutgers University. "Thus American policies to promote home ownership have also promoted low-density suburbanization and—through lack of co-ordination by land-use controls—sprawl."[15]

The degree to which federal policies spurred the flight to the suburbs is debatable, Pucher says. Personal preference for low-density living was certainly a factor. Indeed, the idea of owning a home with a yard surrounded by trees inhabited by chirping birds is an undeniable fixture of "the American dream." Nevertheless, he maintains, "there can be no question that policies at every governmental level in the United States have at least facilitated and accelerated suburbanization."[16]

The explosive growth in home construction, particularly after World War II, took place in a land-use planning vacuum. This led to decades of uncontrolled urban sprawl—an ungainly legacy that is all too visible today. Development in the United States has proceeded haphazardly, according to Pucher, "as private developers and builders try to maximize their profits without coordination and with little regard, if any, for social and environmental consequences."[17]

This vicious cycle, set in place decades ago, persists to this day. The sales of tens of millions of cars early in this century put pressure on the government to build new roads for motorists. The availability of new roads, in turn, made it easier for people to live farther from cities and to commute to work by private automobile. As more and more people, lured by government housing incentives, chose to live and work farther from city centers, the pressure on the government to provide more and better roads mounted commensurately. The call was not only for surface roads to service the new crop of housing developments, but also for major highways to get people and goods into, out of, and between major cities.

A network of some 27,000 miles of road had been developed as far back as the 1830s. But these roads were crude by today's standards— mostly dirt, cobblestone, or brick.[18] In 1909, fewer than 10 percent of the nation's roads were paved. With the passage of the Federal Aid Road Acts of 1916, the United States embarked on a massive road-building campaign to accommodate the growing numbers of motor vehicles. In 1919, Colorado, New Mexico, and Oregon became the first states to adopt gasoline taxes to finance road construction. By 1929, every state in the country, plus the District of Columbia, had its own gas tax, usually running at about three cents a gallon.[19]

"Who ever heard, before, of a popular tax?" asked the chief collector of Tennessee's gas tax in 1926. "Never before in the history of taxation has a major tax been so generally accepted in so short a period," auto scholar John Burnham noted. He considered it astonishing that Americans "were willing to pay for the almost infinite expansion of their automobility."[20]

In the spirit of "almost infinite expansion," President Franklin Roosevelt endorsed a system of limited-access highways (modeled after the German *autobahn*) connecting major U.S. population centers from coast to coast. He sent his road-building proposal to Congress in 1939. At the time of the request, fewer than half the nation's roads and streets were paved.

A year later, while Congress was deliberating, America's first "superhighway," the Pennsylvania Turnpike, opened for commerce. With four concrete lanes partitioned by a median strip, banked curves and gentle grades, merge lanes, and entrance and exit ramps, the turnpike surpassed existing highways or freeways, providing through passage without the bother of stoplights and crossings.

Final approval of Roosevelt's ambitious proposal, including a financing system for the nationwide highway network, came in 1956 with the passage of the Interstate Highway Act. The bill committed the federal government to construct 44,000 miles of toll-free express highways. The Interstate Highway System created by the act was, at the time, the largest and most costly public works project in human history.

National defense was one of the main selling points of the new highway network and the reason the federal government agreed to pay 90 percent of the costs, leaving 10 percent to local governments. (Under the provisions of the previous 1944 Federal Highway Act, the federal government was responsible for 60 percent of highway funding, local governments 40 percent.) The new highway system, proponents maintained, would make the country less vulnerable to nuclear attack—a compelling argument in the era of nuclear paranoia following World War II. The interstate network would help decentralize the nation's industrial base and, as the argument went, encourage the dispersal of the U.S. population by way of suburbanization—a trend, as we have seen, already well under way.

The 1956 Interstate Highway Act created the Highway Trust Fund to pay for the national system. Money for the fund was derived chiefly from taxes on cars, gasoline, tires, and auto parts and could be used only for highway construction. By funneling all such receipts back into the trust fund, an expanding revenue base for highway construction was assured. Annual federal spending on highways increased steadily to more than $5 billion in 1973. By 1989, a cumulative sum of $220 billion had been poured into the fund.

In 1973, President Nixon boldly challenged the hallowed principle of "nondivertibility" of highway revenues collected from gasoline and other user taxes. He signed a bill that allowed a small fraction of the Highway Trust Fund to be allocated to urban mass transit. By that time, however, the interstate system was 82 percent complete. Even with the compromise engineered by Nixon, highway funding was still favored over public transportation by more than eight to one.

As James Flink notes in *The Automobile Age,* "passage of the 1956

Interstate Highway Act ensured the complete triumph of the automobile over mass-transit alternatives in the United States and killed off, except in a few large cities, the vestiges of balanced public transportation systems that remained in 1950s America.''[21] To be sure, the case for the new roadways made by auto industry lobbyists back in 1956 reflected a kind of circular reasoning with a now familiar ring. The industry argued, in essence, that more highways would be needed to handle the projected increases in urban travel that would result from the new highways. This slippery logic goes a long way toward explaining why so much of this country has been paved over—an area greater than the size of Georgia.[22] More cars beget more roads, which beget more cars and even more roads.

How much longer this pattern can be sustained remains a biting public policy question. Yet, it is clear that a whole way of life is at stake in the current controversy over transportation. The inescapable presence of cars today in almost every aspect of American life is reflected in the numbers. The United States is home to 190 million motor vehicles, automobiles accounting for 145 million of the total.[23] ''The United States could put everybody in a car at the same time (which often seems to be the case at rush hour) and nobody would have to sit in the back seat,'' *Boston Globe* writer Dianne Dumanoski calculated.[24] Americans buy 15 million cars and trucks each year; over 11 million cars and trucks are produced here annually. In 1990, vehicle sales in the United States added up to more than $300 billion.[25] The automobile industry, not surprisingly, is the world's largest manufacturing activity, churning out 50 million new vehicles a year.[26] One out of six jobs in this country is in auto or related industries.[27] Auto sales account for between one fifth and one sixth of all U.S. retail trade.

''Model'' American males, according to social critic Ivan Illich, devote a major chunk of their waking hours to cars—driving them, servicing them, parking them, and searching for them.[28] The typical male devotes another big chunk of his working hours (not counting time spent commuting) paying for the privilege of owning and operating these vehicles. The American Automobile Association (AAA) estimated that a motorist driving 15,000 miles a year paid $5,170 to own and operate a car in 1990.[29]

This money, for the most part, is not spent on joyriding. Only about 10 percent of car trips are taken for vacations, visiting family and

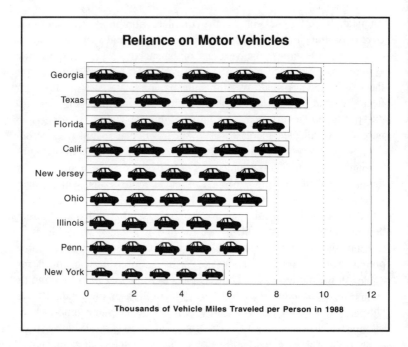

Reliance on Motor Vehicles

Georgia
Texas
Florida
Calif.
New Jersey
Ohio
Illinois
Penn.
New York

0　　2　　4　　6　　8　　10　　12

Thousands of Vehicle Miles Traveled per Person in 1988

friends, or pleasure driving. Over 70 percent are for commuting to work, shopping, or other business-related matters.[30] Ironically, half of all trips to work are five miles or less—an easy bike ride.[31]

Cars, vans, and pickup trucks take 87 percent of the American work force from home to job. These private vehicles account for 82 percent of all the trips made in America, more than four times the combined total from all other sources—walking, biking, buses, trains, airplanes, subways, mopeds, scooters, and skateboards.[32] Public transportation, which carried the majority of Americans to work at the end of World War II, now takes only 4.6 percent of all commuters.[33] Clearly, the automobile has triumphed.

Although cars may have won the battle, our society may have lost the war. Cars might seem like tremendous timesavers, but the evidence suggests otherwise. In the nation's big cities of 200 years ago, when walking was the dominant mode of transportation, most people could walk the mile or two to the center of town in 30 to 60 minutes, typical of today's commuting times.[34]

Ivan Illich estimates that if we divide the total number of miles we travel in cars by all the time spent either in cars or dealing with them (including time spent in gas stations, repair shops, traffic court, or in hospitals as a result of car-related trauma), the average speed works out to only five miles per hour. That's not much faster than walking, and it's considerably slower than bicycling. Despite the prevalence of cars, Illich adds, "modern Americans walk, on the average, as many miles as their ancestors." The difference, of course, is that rather than walking past fields or woods, most of those miles are traversed "through tunnels, corridors, parking lots, and stores."[35]

Americans drive their cars, trucks, vans, and buses over two trillion miles annually—enough to take us to the sun and back more than 10,000 times, and as many miles as the rest of the world combined. With only 5 percent of the Earth's population, we own 34 percent of the total cars and use 26 percent of the world's oil.[36] Our vehicles continue to whittle away at the American population: nearly 47,000 people are killed each year on U.S. roads and highways.

Cars are prodigious consumers of the earth's resources, devouring "20 percent of all the steel, 12 percent of the aluminum, 10 percent of the copper, 5 percent of the lead, 95 percent of the nickel, 35 percent of the zinc, and 6 percent of the rubber used in the U.S.," according to Jeremy Rifkin, author of *Biosphere Politics*. In the 1930s, a zealous booster of the automobile proclaimed: "Think of the results to the industrial world of putting on the market a product that doubles the malleable iron consumption, triples the plate-glass consumption, and quadruples the use of rubber. As a consumer of raw material, the automobile has no equal in the history of the world."[37]

"Here is a machine costing thousands of dollars, intentionally designed to be replaced every 36 to 48 months," Rifkin says. "Between 1900 and 1984, some 647,507,000 automobiles, trucks, and buses were junked in the United States alone."[38] Eleven million cars are retired annually in the United States, many left to sit in junkyards, abandoned lots, or roadsides. An additional 240 million tires are junked each year, joining the 2 to 3 billion already piled up in heaps across the nation, where they pose fire and air pollution hazards and serve as breeding grounds for mosquitoes.[39]

The biggest problems, of course, are the motor vehicles still operating, those not yet consigned to auto graveyards. To make room for these roving machines, some 60,000 square miles of U.S. land have been paved over—about 2 percent of the total surface area. One third to one half of the space of American cities is devoted to automobiles, except in car-saturated regions like Los Angeles, where that figure rises to two thirds.[40] More land in this country is set aside for roads, driveways, ramps, parking lots, and garages than is dedicated to housing.

The car has reshaped the nation's landscape, making it virtually unrecognizable from the unpaved version of the previous century. Car-induced urban sprawl has produced cities without end—one metropolis overlapping with the next, a continuous fabric of developed land. "You can now drive for 500 miles on the Atlantic seaboard from Portland, Maine, to Fredericksburg, Virginia, without ever leaving what the U.S. Census Bureau considers to be a metropolitan area," writes Kevin Kasowski in *Developments,* the newsletter of the National Growth Management Leadership Project. "On the West Coast, you can do the same thing: 600 miles from Chico, California, to San Diego and then south and east."[41] As a result, the proverbial drive in the country is becoming an increasingly elusive challenge. "The tranquility that Americans seek is perpetually retreating another 10 exits down the Interstate," as writer Robert Fishman puts it.[42]

So many of the elements we take for granted in twentieth-century life owe their existence to the automobile. "Eliminate cars and you wipe out McDonald's, the Indy 500, the strip, Holiday Inns, CBs, trailers, carpools, much of the Sun Belt, and many marriages," says *Boston Globe* columnist Steven Stark. "According to a 1960s poll, almost 40 percent of American men proposed in a car."[43] (Birth rates may have been affected too, though we can't blame Henry Ford for a roadside baby boom. Reportedly, he made the seats of the Model T short in a deliberate attempt to discourage the use of his cars for illicit carryings-on.)

Besides their impact on our natural surroundings, city layouts, and population, cars have also made an indelible mark on the places we call home. For example, a standard suburban dwelling, commonly entered through the garage, is often an extension of the street; the garage serves as a buffer zone, so that people need not contact the outside world except from within the confines of their private vehicle. "A domestic or social journey in Los Angeles does not so much end at the door of one's destination as at the off-ramp of the freeway; the mile or two of ground-level streets counts as no more than the front drive of the house,'' British author Reyner Banham wrote in 1971.[44] Architect Daniel Solomon restated this point in 1988, commenting on the style of homes, still prevalent in the 1980s, that appear to be mere extensions of their garages. "The town does not intercede between the freeway and the electric garage door," Solomon wrote. "From the private car to the private landscape, there is no prospect of human encounter.''[45]

The blending of home into garage, garage into street, and street into highway has put a lasting stamp on design. "Buildings are made to look good as you pass by them in a speeding car, not to spend any time in them,'' notes Brad Bellows, an architect based in Cambridge, Massachusetts.

Automobiles and highways also hold a prominent presence in the nation's cultural and social life. Americans invented road movies, and the Beach Boys made a career singing songs about catching rides on waves and freeways. Tailgate parties are still the rage in some circles. Moreover, some people have been known to use the completion of a driveway as a pretext for a party, a so-called "driveway bash." Car washes—a wholesome, recreational activity at which teens can raise money for their high school football team, church group, or favorite charity—have become an American institution.

For the better part of a century, we have been conditioned to believe that cars are essential to maintaining the American way of life; nearly every American who can afford a car has one. Recent events in the Middle East show that if push comes to shove, we'll even go to war to defend the right to drive gas-guzzling vehicles. Without question, cars have brought unprecedented mobility, convenience, and privacy. A family can pile into the station wagon on a moment's notice and head off to the country. A person with a car can easily bring home a full shopping cart's worth of groceries. A parent can rush a sick child off to the doctor's office in any weather at any hour. Friendships and family ties can be maintained across distances that might have been daunting in another era.

But what are the social and environmental costs of all the cars we have today and all the additional ones expected to hit the roads in the near future? That's the crux of "the automotive paradox"—we can't live without cars, and increasingly it seems we can't live with them.

2

Dead End

The car was supposed to give us freedom;
instead it is choking us.

Is it possible, could it be, that while we
concentrated on withstanding the Communist
menace these past 40 years, we were being
done in by our most beloved possession?

In 1989, ads for what appeared to be the environmentally perfect car
began airing on TV. "The car is connected to the road," drones a
sleepy New Age voice. The road, in turn, is connected to the Earth.
The Earth, we learn, is one big ecosystem, which is part of the solar
system, which is part of the Milky Way galaxy, *ad infinitum*. The car
itself is called Infiniti.

Based on the early ads, the car seemed unique—a machine perfectly
attuned to its natural surroundings. That's because there was no car.
The pictures showed only a winding country road, trees rustling in the
wind, water coursing in a bubbling brook, waves washing up on the
seashore—all soft, soothing, and rhythmic.

Months later, when Nissan finally unveiled the Infiniti, the company
had to reveal the mythical chariot of its TV spots. That's when the
magic ended. Behind the hype, we could see it was a car, just like other
cars. It burned gasoline, gave off carbon monoxide, nitrogen oxides,
hydrocarbons, and carbon dioxide, and it contributed to urban smog,
rural air pollution, acid rain, and the buildup of greenhouse gases in
the atmosphere.

There's nothing wrong with the Infiniti that's not wrong with most
cars. Basically, an isolated car cruising down a quiet country lane is
almost harmless. The problem is millions of cars on city streets and

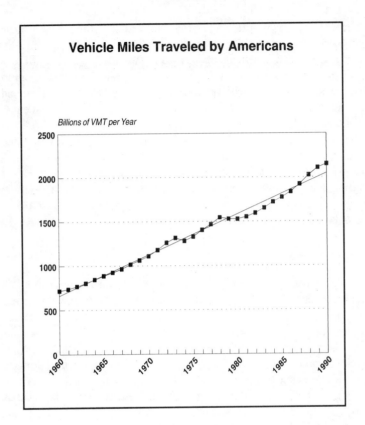

Vehicle Miles Traveled by Americans

Billions of VMT per Year

thoroughfares the whole world over. While the total number of motor vehicles—like the number of hamburgers sold by McDonald's—will never quite reach infinity, there has been a nearly eightfold increase since 1950. And the growth since then (at a rate of about 5.3 percent per year) shows no signs of tapering off.

The combined effects of the world's half-billion vehicles add up to a strikingly different picture than the pastoral vision presented in advertisements for the Infiniti. Instead of being in harmony with the environment, cars are among nature's chief adversaries.

Somehow we have allowed cars—in principle, our servants—to gain the upper hand. We have designed our cities and towns around them, often with seemingly little regard for other considerations. Large tracts of urban areas have been converted into a dense web of underpasses, overpasses, ramps, and interchanges—a nightmare for pedestrians, cyclists, and even for motorists. The price we've paid for the freedom to roam at the turn of a switch is becoming painfully obvious. A broad look at our car-dominated transportation system reveals environmental, economic, and safety problems at every link in the chain—from the extraction of crude oil from the ground to the burning of carbon-based fuels in vehicles that jam our city streets, befoul the air, and not infrequently crash into each other. On top of this, we add the threat of altering the composition of our atmosphere and as a result resetting Earth's thermostat. All for a vehicle that initially promised just an occasional jaunt in the country!

THE FUEL GAUGE

In many ways, oil is a miracle fuel that has made the transportation revolution possible. Alternative fuels are hard pressed to match its energy density and relative ease of use. However, despite the practical advantages of this vital energy source, oil has many drawbacks: risks are incurred in moving it, storing it, burning it, and breathing its combustion products. On top of that, supplies are limited, contributing to episodes of economic havoc in the short run and resource scarcity in the long run. It's like the joke about bad restaurants: "The food is lousy, but the portions are small."

Some of the liabilities become apparent by considering a single week in June of 1990: 260,000 gallons of oil spilled into New York harbor from a British tanker; a Norwegian supertanker carrying 38 million gallons of oil exploded off the coast of Texas, dumping 3 million gallons into the Gulf of Mexico; a cruise ship ran aground near Cape Cod, Massachusetts, spilling 7,500 gallons into Buzzard's Bay; and 75,000 gallons of diesel fuel leaked from a pipeline into the Minnesota River just south of the Twin Cities.

In the first half of 1989, 766 accidents involving tankers, barges, and other vessels occurred, and some 5.8 million gallons of oil were spilled in U.S. waters as a result. That figure does not include the 11 million gallons that leaked off the coast of Alaska from the Exxon *Valdez* in March 1989.[1] However, tanker accidents account for only 20 percent of the oil spilled from marine transportation activities, according to Henry Marcus, head of MIT's Ocean Systems Management Program. Most spilled oil enters the seas through routine operations—fuel loading and unloading, tank flushings, and wastewater discharge.[2]

The intentional, and illegal, dumping of shipboard toxins—such as sludge left over from fuel purification and the thick tarry residues left in tank bottoms—poses a greater threat to the health of oceans and marine life than headline-grabbing oil spills. "Animals killed in big spills get the attention because they look so awful," claims Riki Otts, a marine toxicologist based in Alaska. "But it's these invisible compounds, when dissolved in seawater, that have truly long-term and insidious effects on our marine food chain the world over."[3]

Stormwater runoff from roads is another way oil, gasoline, and other chemicals infiltrate our rivers, lakes, and seas. Used motor oil poured into the ground, sewers, or streets or dumped in landfills eventually winds up in rivers, lakes, and groundwater supplies. Each year, Americans use roughly a billion gallons of motor oil, and about 240 million gallons are discharged into the environment.[4] This single source, according to some estimates, accounts for 40 percent of the pollution of the nation's waterways.[5]

Time bombs are also ticking in storage tanks across the country. Seventeen million gallons of oil have leaked from a single tank in Brooklyn, New York.[6] Even larger underground spills have occurred in California—a 200-million-gallon pool of oil lies beneath a refinery in El Segundo and another 28-million-gallon puddle near San Francisco Bay. There are nearly 6 million underground oil storage tanks scattered around the country, including 2 million large gasoline tanks located at service stations, industrial plants, and airports. These storage vessels are expected to last 30 to 40 years. After that, notes Helga Butler of the Environmental Protection Agency, "they don't have anywhere to go but corrode." Since most of these containers were installed in the 1950s and 1960s, massive leaks in the near future are all but inevitable. In fact, some 500,000 gasoline tanks are believed to be leaking already.[7]

Our heightened reliance on foreign oil raises the risks of oil spills, which are a result of increased barge and tanker traffic. In 1990, imports comprised about 42 percent of the oil consumed in the United States— up from 27 percent in 1985. If trends continue, Americans may be importing 69 percent in the year 2010, according to the Department of Energy.[8]

Half of the oil that Americans use powers motor vehicles, and two thirds is devoted to transportation. Increased driving is the principal force behind increased oil demand. American motorists are logging more miles than ever before. In the past 50 years, total vehicle miles have increased sevenfold.[9] Between 1980 and 1989, the number of miles driven per vehicle grew by 16 percent, while total miles traveled rose by more than 40 percent.

Over the same time period, fuel economy slipped as motorists began returning to bigger, more powerful vehicles. From 1988 to 1992, the average fuel economy of new cars in the United States dropped by 4 percent, according to EPA statistics.[10] Performance, rather than frugality, has become the rage again. "I've yet to have someone come in and say, 'Give me a good, fuel-efficient car,' " said Barry Wishengrad, general sales manager of West Valley Toyota in Canoga Park, California.[11] More and more consumers are ordering options that reduce fuel efficiency, such as air conditioning, power accessories, and four-wheel drive. From 1980 to 1987, fuel economy dropped from first place to eighth place as a consumer priority. Zero-to-sixty miles per hour acceleration times—a measure of how powerful a car is—have dropped every year since 1982, according to a report by the Office of Technology Assessment.[12]

Spending a few hundred dollars extra to make cars lighter and more efficient "doesn't necessarily make sense to the guy in the showroom, [with gasoline] at a dollar a gallon and no threat of oil shortages on the horizon," explains Chrysler engineer Floyd Allen.[13] Indeed, there is little incentive to save fuel these days, explains Jeffrey Zupan, planning director of the New Jersey Transit Authority, because low gas prices, coupled with the fuel economy gains made prior to 1988, have made it about five times cheaper to drive now than during the height of the oil embargo.[14]

To make matters worse, growing numbers of Americans are driving light trucks, vans, and jeeps, even though the biggest load they are likely to haul is a week's worth of groceries. Between 1970 and 1985, light-truck miles tripled, while auto miles grew by only 38 percent.[15] One third of the passenger vehicles sold in the United States today are light trucks, vans, or jeeps.[16] These conveyances, on average, obtain only 21 miles per gallon, compared to 28 miles per gallon for a new car.[17] "It wasn't *his* driving that caused the Alaska oil spill," said a Greenpeace ad, referring to the skipper of the Exxon *Valdez.* "It was *yours.*"[18]

America's increased dependence on imported oil makes us more vulnerable to supply interruptions and sudden price hikes like those experienced in the 1970s and again in 1990 following Iraq's invasion of Kuwait. Ironically, the amount of oil imported from the Persian Gulf has more than doubled since the oil embargo of 1973. The tens of billions of dollars spent on foreign oil, year after year, add nothing to our long-term energy security. Instead, the expenditure contributes to America's critical balance-of-payments problem. In 1990, we paid $60.7 billion for imported oil, which accounted for 60 percent of the nation's trade deficit. Our oil import bill (which was 24 percent higher in 1990 than in the previous year) is expected to double in the next decade, according to Department of Energy projections.[19]

Further problems stem from the volatile nature of global oil markets. Genuine or perceived threats to world supplies can quickly translate into price hikes, setting off economic tremors at home. In 1990, for example, the confrontation in Iraq drove crude oil prices up from $16 per barrel in July to more than $33 per barrel in October. At the time, some analysts expected prices to continue to rise to $60 or even $100 per barrel, though they eventually stabilized at prewar levels.[20]

Underlying these periodic crises is a simple fact: oil is a nonrenewable fuel. Every gallon pumped out of the ground and burned is a gallon lost forever. Someday, inevitably, supplies will grow scarce. Continued attempts at recovery will cost more and produce less, and oil prices will rise accordingly. We will never totally "run out" of the stuff, because at some point it will become too expensive to wring additional oil out of the ground.

Domestic crude oil production in the lower 48 states, which peaked in 1970, has been declining for more than two decades and is now at a 40-year low.[21] The Organization of Petroleum Exporting Countries (OPEC) controls over three quarters of the world's proven oil reserves. Two thirds of the world's reserves lie in the politically unstable Persian Gulf.[22] We pay a great deal in military expenditures to protect our

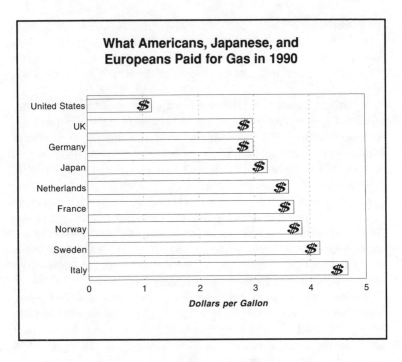

What Americans, Japanese, and Europeans Paid for Gas in 1990

Dollars per Gallon

access to these precarious energy supplies—anywhere from $15 billion to $54 billion in 1989, according to Harold Hubbard of Resources for the Future.[23] Of course, those figures don't include the exorbitant costs—estimated at about $61 billion (or $1.4 billion per day of combat)—of an all-out military engagement such as Operation Desert Storm.

The average price of gasoline at the pump in 1991 was about $1.15 a gallon, but, as we have seen, the true cost—including road construction and repair, subsidies, free parking, the expense of maintaining a military presence in the Middle East, climate risks, health and environmental cleanup costs—could exceed several dollars a gallon.[24] Over the course of a year, these "hidden" energy subsidies could amount to between $100 billion and $300 billion, Hubbard claims.[25] The World Resources Institute figures that auto-related subsidies—including road construction, tax deductions, and employer-provided parking, plus military expenditures to keep gasoline prices low—add up to more than $300 billion a year, equivalent to an additional gas tax of $2 per gallon.[26]

Despite lip service to energy conservation and the development of alternative fuels, the United States has made little progress in reducing its vulnerability to oil shortages. Farsighted thinking about energy, unfortunately, has never been an American strength; instead, the pattern has been a flurry of proposals unleashed in the wake of an energy crisis. These ideas are debated vigorously, then shelved once oil prices begin to drop, only to be resurrected again when the next crisis arrives. The country has never had bold energy planning that departs significantly from a business-as-usual approach.

What we have had is de facto energy policy ruled largely by stalemate. John Sawhill, president of the Nature Conservancy and a former energy official in the Nixon, Ford, and Carter administrations, summed up the dilemma this way: "There are proponents, mostly in industry, in favor of expanding production in this country. And there are strong proponents, among environmentalists and elsewhere, to reduce consumption. The two sides are about equal. As a result, nothing gets done."[27]

SOMETHING IN THE AIR

Although astute observers may have sensed something funny in their air prior to 1950, that was the first time a scientific case was made linking cars to pollution in general and to the thick haze hovering over the Los Angeles basin in particular. In that year, Arie Jan Haagen-Smit, a chemist at the California Institute of Technology, proposed a theoretical mechanism for smog formation in which automobile exhaust and sunlight play central roles. His findings were hotly contested by the oil and auto industries. At a 1952 meeting of the American Petroleum Association, Vance Jenkins, research supervisor for the Union Oil Company of California, called the theory "unproved speculation" that could have dangerous repercussions for the business world. Within a few years, however, Haagen-Smit's "speculation" had earned virtually unanimous support among scientists.[28]

In the four decades since Haagen-Smit first promulgated his theory, much has been learned about the automobile's contribution to dirty air.

In the United States, motor vehicles contribute about 53 percent of the carbon monoxide, 30 percent of the nitrogen oxides, and 27 percent of the hydrocarbons emitted to the air.[29] Ozone, the chief ingredient of smog, is produced when hydrocarbons from cars and other sources (including trees) and nitrogen oxides react in the presence of sunlight. (Ground-level ozone, which is a pollutant, should be distinguished from the natural ozone in the upper atmosphere, which screens Earth from harmful ultraviolet radiation.) Over the course of its lifetime, a typical new car equipped with pollution-control devices will spew out some 300 pounds of smog-forming compounds and 34 tons of carbon dioxide. Greater Los Angeles, home of Haagen-Smit's research, stands out in this respect, with tailpipes from eight million cars and trucks supplying 70 to 80 percent of the area's noxious fumes.[30] Massachusetts Commissioner of Environmental Protection Daniel Greenbaum estimates likewise that 75 percent of his state's air pollution comes from cars and trucks.[31]

Auto emissions and gasoline vapors contain a host of toxic and carcinogenic pollutants. For example, motor vehicles are responsible for about 85 percent of the benzene and 30 percent of the formaldehyde released to the air—chemicals that the Environmental Protection Agency considers probable human carcinogens.[32] Other carcinogenic vapors are given off when cars are on the road or at the gas station. Some brake linings contain asbestos—yet another source of potential carcinogens.

Despite these dire figures, American cars today are far cleaner than the pollution machines of the 1960s. After emission standards were first imposed in 1968, and then tightened further with the 1970 Clean Air Act, carbon monoxide and hydrocarbon emissions in new cars dropped by 96 percent, while nitrogen oxides emissions were slashed by 76 percent.[33] These reductions came about largely through the adoption of the catalytic converter, which turns hazardous exhaust gases into less harmful ones. Engine modifications and the introduction of lead-free gasoline also helped.

Before the Clean Air Act was adopted in 1970, industry leaders lobbied furiously against the new emission limits, claiming that pollution reductions would be technically impossible to achieve as well as economically ruinous. "This bill is a threat to the entire American economy and to every person in America," Lee Iacocca, then vice president

of Ford Motor Company, claimed in 1970. Despite these patriotic pro-
testations, Detroit did help cut pollution dramatically and later trum-
peted these improvements as evidence of the automakers' "can-do"
record and their dedication to a cleaner environment. "In a way, we
made liars out of ourselves because we sincerely believed we couldn't
pull a rabbit out of the hat," Greg Terry, a GM spokesman, recently
admitted.[34]

Unfortunately, the impressive reductions in tailpipe emissions did not
end pollution. In fact, air quality in many American cities has stayed
the same or worsened. From 1987 to 1989, according to tests conducted
by the Environmental Protection Agency, 119 U.S. cities exceeded federal standards for ozone or carbon monoxide,[35] up from 64 cities that
failed to comply between 1985 and 1987.[36] Since 1986, anywhere from
30 to 50 percent of all Americans have lived in areas where federal air
quality standards were violated at least occasionally. Much of this pollution is due to motor vehicles.

The Los Angeles region, not surprisingly, has the poorest record.
There, air quality standards are exceeded an average of 137.5 days a
year.[37] On bad days, ozone levels in the city are three times the federal
limit.[38] 1988 was a particularly bad year; federal limits were breached
on 232 days. Houston, the second worst city, violated standards on 30
days in 1988.[39] Air pollution–related illnesses, according to estimates
made by the American Lung Association, cost the nation tens of billions of dollars per year in health-care expenses and lost productivity.[40]

Of course the United States is not alone in its air pollution problems.
Many other countries are worse off. In metropolitan Athens, for instance, the death rate jumps 500 percent on the most polluted days.[41]
Mexico City, with perhaps the world's dirtiest air, routinely exceeds
ozone limits set by the World Health Organization by a factor of three
or more. A record was established on March 17, 1992, when ozone
reached four times the health standard.[42] While emissions from the
city's 36,000 factories and other airborne contaminants are also culprits,
by far the biggest source of filth is the three million vehicles that clog
the streets, burning five million gallons of low-quality fuel daily and
emitting over 80 percent of the pollutants.[43] "It appears that Mexico
City exceeds our federal ozone standard every day of the year," claims
former EPA official Michael Walsh.[44]

Other cities—among them, Bangkok, New Delhi, and Santiago—

face similarly immense air quality challenges. The situation in developing countries is comparable, at least in one respect, to that faced in the United States some three decades ago: the catalytic converter and other pollution control technologies are scarce where they exist at all.

A big part of the problem stems from a lack of money. Howard Applegate, an environmental engineer at the University of Texas at El Paso, has met repeatedly with officials at Mexico's environmental agency, SEDUE. They agree that vehicles are the principal source of the region's bad air, but add, "It all costs money, and we don't have it." A good tune-up, for example, can cut down on pollution significantly, Applegate notes, "but in Mexico, buying a set of points and a set of plugs for a six-cylinder car costs a week's wages."[45]

In Mexico City, as in most major cities around the world, the problem is simple: *too many dirty cars,* which clutter the streets and cloud the skies. But the obvious solution—driving fewer cars, cleaner cars, fewer miles overall—is far from simple to bring about. Although American assembly lines began turning out lower-emission vehicles in the 1970s, resultant gains were partly offset by the number of cars on the road and the number of miles they travel—both of which have risen dramatically.

A growing auto population, for example, has kept New York City from meeting standards set for certain pollutants by the federal government. What's more, says Eric Goldstein of the Natural Resources Defense Council in New York, "if traffic keeps increasing, we may never achieve national health standards."[46]

Further emission reductions can be achieved, to be sure. The new Clean Air Act, signed into law by President Bush on November 15, 1990, calls for lowering the emission limits on hydrocarbons by 40 percent and on nitrogen oxides by 60 percent in all new cars by 1996. Beginning in 1992, oil companies are required to sell cleaner-burning gasoline in the cities where carbon monoxide pollution is worst. In March 1992, President Bush announced that the EPA would not require automakers to install on-board canisters—conditionally required by the 1990 amendments to the Clean Air Act—to trap smog-forming compounds that would otherwise escape during refueling. EPA waived the canister requirement in favor of vapor collector systems to be installed at gas pumps.[47] Finally, under a trial program, new "alternative-fuel" vehicles (including electric cars and vans) will gradually hit the streets in California. The California Air Resources Board will require that 2 percent of the new cars sold in the state by 1998 will have zero emissions. By 2002 that figure will rise to 5 percent, and by 2003 up to 10 percent. By 2010, according to an estimate made by the South Coast Air Quality Management District, 17 percent of passenger cars and light trucks in Los Angeles will be powered by electricity.[48]

The auto industry fought tooth and nail against the 1990 bill, resurrecting many of the same arguments used two decades before. "We can't squeeze much more out of the catalytic converter," complained the device's inventor, Dick Klimisch, now General Motors' director of environmental activities. Former EPA official Michael Walsh has a different perspective. The industry's "public posture is always much more pessimistic than technical reality," he says. "When you give them a challenge, they meet it."[49]

Truly coming to grips with motor vehicle air pollution means addressing two critical issues. First, clean air regulations pertain almost exclusively to new cars, but older, poorly maintained cars are the biggest offenders; 10 percent of the cars on the road spew out about half of the pollutants, the EPA claims.[50] Inspection and maintenance programs aimed at older cars have not been as successful as the EPA had hoped.

Second, increased driving—the result of ever more vehicles being driven more—will probably offset much of the hard-earned cut in emissions from individual cars. Federal standards set limits on the amount of pollutants a car can release per mile, but not on the number of miles Americans can drive. Until we gain control over the number of vehicles on the road and the total miles they travel, we just can't win the battle against pollution.

GLOBAL CHANGE

Emissions from cars, trucks, and buses are both a local concern and a problem of global dimensions. With half a billion motor vehicles on the world's roads, the potential now exists for irrevocably altering the composition of the atmosphere, thereby changing the climate of the entire planet.

Wayne Stayskal for the Tampa Tribune © 1990. Reprinted with permission.

It is well established scientifically that water vapor, carbon dioxide, methane, and certain other atmospheric gases are responsible for maintaining temperatures in the range that supports life on this planet. These gases act somewhat like the panes of glass in a greenhouse, allowing sunlight to reach the ground but preventing some fraction of the infrared heat radiated by the Earth from escaping into space.

Without this warming effect, our planet would be about 60° F (33° C) colder, and life as we know it would be impossible. But human activities—in transportation, industry, agriculture, and forestry—are increasing the atmospheric concentrations of natural greenhouse gases, as well as adding new and very powerful infrared-absorbing gases to the mix. According to an emerging scientific consensus, if current trends continue, our benign atmospheric "greenhouse" is likely to turn into a progressively warmer "greenhouse trap."

Carbon Dioxide

Catalytic converters and other high-tech control devices greatly reduce automotive pollution, but they do nothing to prevent the emission of carbon dioxide to the atmosphere because there is no way to burn oil (or coal or natural gas, for that matter) without releasing carbon dioxide. For every gallon of gasoline consumed by an automobile—whether a sleek sports car or a run-down city clunker—about 19 pounds of carbon dioxide spew out the tailpipe and into the air. If you fill up with 15 gallons of unleaded and drive off into the orange, smog-enhanced sunset, nearly 300 pounds of the gas will be released by the time your tank runs dry. Over a year, the typical American car pumps almost 5 tons of carbon dioxide into the atmosphere.

Globally, motor vehicles produce 14 percent of the carbon dioxide given off in fossil fuel combustion. In the United States, 25 percent of the carbon dioxide emissions come from our 190 million cars, trucks, and buses. Global carbon-dioxide concentrations have grown by 25 percent since preindustrial times, with half of this increase occurring over the past three decades. Unless ambitious countermeasures are taken, the concentration of greenhouse gases in the atmosphere could double by the year 2030 compared to levels in preindustrial times.

Scientists don't yet know the precise consequences of this doubling. According to the most reliable computer models, the average global temperature would eventually rise by 3°–8° F (1.5°–4.5° C).[51] But even the best models are riddled with uncertainties. The interactions between the oceans, clouds, vegetation, and other factors that regulate the climate "machine" are so complex that nobody is expecting any clearcut answers in the next decade.

Chlorofluorocarbons

CFCs, first developed in 1928, have been used in aerosol spray cans, in air conditioning and refrigeration applications, as blowing agents for plastic foams, and as solvents in the electronics industry. Worldwide, about 28 percent of the CFCs are used in vehicular air conditioners and in servicing such units. In the United States, vehicle air conditioners make up the single largest use of CFCs, accounting for about 20 percent of the total consumption, and eventual emissions, of these substances.

These long-lived artificial gases were once held responsible for one fourth of the greenhouse warming threat. However, recent evidence suggests that the net contribution of CFCs to global warming is substantially less than originally thought. Although these chemicals are indeed greenhouse gases, their primary (and most deadly) impact stems from their ability to deplete quantities of an important component of the atmosphere, the ozone that resides in the stratosphere some 9 to 30 miles above the Earth's surface. The net result is that the greenhouse warming that has been expected from CFCs appears to be offset by the cooling effect caused by ozone destruction in the lower stratosphere.

This is no cause for jubilation because the assault on the Earth's ozone layer is unquestionably a major environmental disaster. This layer has existed for hundreds of millions of years, absorbing most of the sun's lethal ultraviolet radiation. Life on Earth would not be possible without it.

Ironically, CFCs came into widespread use because they seemed so safe. They are nontoxic, stable, and cause no direct harm to living creatures. Scientists have since discovered a negative side to this stability. Years after CFCs are released to the environment, they drift up to the stratosphere, where the sun's harsh ultraviolet light breaks them apart, freeing up chlorine atoms that can destroy ozone through a series of complex chemical reactions.

In 1985, British scientists announced their discovery of a "hole" in the ozone layer above Antarctica—40 percent of the ozone normally there had been lost over recent years. The hole forms every spring, when sunlight returns to the region. At times, half of the ozone that once shielded the continent of Antarctica is gone.

More recent studies have indicated that a significant loss of ozone could also occur over the Northern Hemisphere. Measurements taken in January 1992 revealed that conditions were then ripe for ozone depletion—with a 20 to 30 percent loss of ozone possible. Scientists believe these conditions could occur once every several years. Year-round ozone thinning is also occurring more rapidly than had been expected throughout the hemisphere, putting populations in Asia, Europe, and North America at risk.

As the ozone layer deteriorates, more ultraviolet radiation reaches the Earth. We can expect, as a consequence, more cases of skin cancer,

On the Fastrack

Reprinted with special permission of King Features Syndicate, Inc.

cataracts, and immune system damage. There is also a growing concern for potential damage to wildlife, crops, forests, and marine plankton. "For every 1 percent decrease in ozone overhead, you get roughly a 2 percent increase in the incidence of skin cancer," says Harvard University atmospheric chemist James Anderson.[52] The EPA predicted that expected ozone losses could cause 12 million additional cases of skin cancer and 200,000 deaths in this country over the next 50 years.[53] And these estimates were formulated in 1991, before more pessimistic observations came to light.

Government leaders, first alerted to the ozone crisis in the 1970s, have made sporadic progress in responding. In 1978, after considerable public debate, the United States, Canada, Norway, and Sweden banned the use of CFCs in spray cans. But total CFC use still grew globally as other applications were developed. In September 1987, the United Nations adopted the Montreal Protocol, which called for a 50-percent cut in CFC production by the year 2000. Under the amended protocol signed by 90 nations in June 1990, CFCs will be banned in industrialized countries by the year 2000 and in developing countries by 2010. In February 1992, the United States announced it would cease producing CFCs by the end of 1995.

These are encouraging steps. The bad news is that the chlorine released to the stratosphere by CFCs will go on destroying ozone for decades, regardless of whether a CFC production ban has been imposed 10 miles below on Earth. That means that even under the best of circumstances—even if all parties to the Montreal Protocol live up to their commitments—it will take until well into the next century before the ozone layer is fully repaired.

Ozone

Ironically, while air conditioners in cars have been releasing CFCs that eat ozone in the stratosphere, the vehicles themselves have also been contributing to the production of that same molecule, ozone, in the lower atmosphere (the troposphere), where it is the main ingredient of smog. Besides damaging crops, trees, and other plants, ozone is a major health hazard. Persons exposed to ozone suffer eye irritation, coughing and chest discomfort, headaches, upper respiratory illness, increased asthma attacks, and reduced pulmonary function. Tropospheric ozone also makes up about 8 percent of the greenhouse gases introduced into the atmosphere by human activity. In short, we are producing ozone in the lower atmosphere where we don't want it and destroying the same molecule in the upper atmosphere where we need it.

Carbon Monoxide

This odorless, colorless gas is a menace to human health. For people who run their cars in garages or sit in idling vehicles with leaky exhaust systems, carbon monoxide can be lethal. Even at low levels of exposure, the gas impairs hand-eye coordination, visual sensitivity, and vigilance, thereby making it harder to perform such tasks as driving. People breathing carbon monoxide–polluted air may experience chest pains while exercising. The elderly and those suffering from coronary heart disease are especially at risk.

In the United States, over 50 percent of carbon monoxide emissions come from motor vehicles. Globally, over 90 percent of all man-made carbon monoxide comes from transportation sources, industrialized nations accounting for 75 percent of the total.

Carbon monoxide contributes to global warming in two ways. First, it plays an important role in producing ground-level ozone, a pollutant and a greenhouse gas. Second, through a chain of chemical reactions, it indirectly contributes to the buildup of methane, another very potent greenhouse gas whose atmospheric concentration has doubled since preindustrial times. (A methane molecule traps nearly 30 times as much infrared heat as a carbon dioxide molecule does.)

What can be done to avert the threat of global warming, or at least push the day of reckoning further into the future? Advances in pollution control can further reduce emissions of carbon monoxide and the gases responsible for ground-level ozone formation, hydrocarbons and nitrogen oxides. But no existing or conceivable pollution control technology can stop, or even slow, the carbon dioxide buildup. Efficiency improvements and fuel substitutions are the only answers here. For example, a car that gets 55 miles per gallon, twice the current U.S. average for new cars, would release half as much carbon dioxide per mile traveled. Even so, carbon dioxide emissions will probably keep rising as long as the population of automobiles and the number of miles they rack up do.

Between 1970 and 1989, the average fuel economy of American cars improved by 50 percent (from 13.5 mpg to 20.3 mpg) while total vehicle miles increased by 62 percent. From 1988 to 1992, moreover, new-car fuel economy declined rather than improved. Simply put, we're losing ground in the carbon dioxide crusade. Even if automakers resume efficiency improvements at the pre-1987 rate, the four million cars and trucks added to the nation's roads each year could easily cancel out gains made in fuel economy. If the growth rate continues, Congress could mandate efficiency improvements in new cars of 1 percent a year for the next 20 years, and total carbon dioxide output would still expand by several percentage points.[54]

Globally, the picture looks even more dismal. Since 1950, the world's vehicle fleet has swelled from 70 million to more than 550 million, with no end to this growth in sight. Worldwide, motor vehicles expel at least two-thirds more carbon dioxide into the atmosphere than they did 20 years ago. If nothing is done to retard the explosive growth in vehicle numbers, these emissions could increase another 20 to 50 percent by 2010.

Certainly, any workable solution must include not only efficiency improvements in motor vehicles, but also measures to stem growth in vehicle numbers by relying more on car pools, buses, and trains and, over time, on alternative vehicles that don't run on fossil fuels. Global

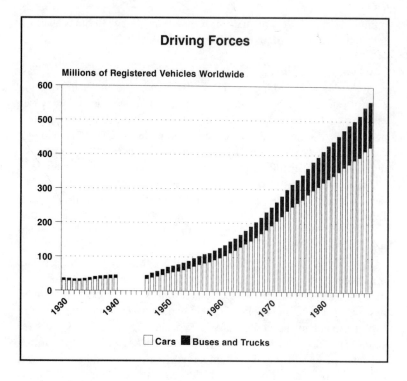

warming, by definition, is not a problem that the United States (or any single country) can solve alone, but any positive initiatives taken by the world's most die-hard motorists can only help. And why shouldn't the nation that almost single-handedly led the world into the automotive morass take the lead in discovering a way out?

Although climate models abound with uncertainties, we cannot afford a cautious, wait-and-see approach. The continued warming of the earth's atmosphere, the inundation of coastal cities, the loss of wetlands and other ecosystems, altered rainfall patterns, and the like are all changes to be avoided at any reasonable cost. If we hold off until scientists can confidently predict exactly what is going to happen, a task that could take decades, the eventuality we fear may be upon us.

The prudent thing to do under the circumstances is to cut down on the use of fossil fuels. "Not in any panicky way," explains writer Robert Silverberg,

> but with a calm, clear-eyed resolve, based on the understanding that it's a dumb idea for any creature to foul its own nest. The junk we're putting into the atmosphere can't possibly do us any good, and there's a reasonable chance that it can do us great harm. Therefore, we should clean up our act.[55]

ROADWAY CONGESTION

> If someone were to tell you he had seen strings of noxious gases drifting among the buildings of a city, black smoke blotting out the sun, great holes in the major streets filled with men in hard hats, planes circling overhead, unable to land, and thousands of people choking in the streets, pushing and shoving in a desperate effort to get out of the city . . . you would be hard-pressed to know whether he was talking about a city at war or a city at rush hour.[56]

Former U.S. transportation secretary Alan Boyd's dramatic remarks underscore what many Americans have already figured out for themselves: that our overcrowded streets are becoming impassible and the lives of many commuters impossible. Even if we develop fuel-efficient cars that run on nonpolluting, carbon-free fuels, will we be able to go anywhere if road congestion continues its fitful march to gridlock?

In the past three decades, traffic growth has vastly outstripped U.S. highway capacity. The Conservation Law Foundation calculates that total vehicle mileage increased 168 percent from 1960 to 1987, while new highway miles rose by only 9 percent.[57] As a result, the number of cars per mile of U.S. road almost doubled during these years, and travel delays roughly tripled. Americans now waste eight billion hours a year idling in traffic, claims a 1991 Department of Transportation study.[58]

During the 1980s, traffic in California increased 55 percent while miles of new roads grew by less than 2 percent, according to a report by the group Californians for Better Transportation.[59] In Los Angeles, congestion rose 15 percent per year throughout the decade, doubling every five years.[60] In San Francisco, traffic grew at the more rapid annual clip of 25 percent during the early 1980s.

California is not alone. Traffic problems have worsened in virtually every city in the country. In Atlanta, for example, congestion doubled during the last half of the 1980s.[61] Nevertheless, based on a "roadway congestion index" computed by the Texas Transportation Institute, Los Angeles and San Francisco still rank number one and two in the congestion derby. The rest of the top ten, in descending order, are: Washington, Chicago, Miami, Seattle, Houston, San Diego, Boston, and New York and Atlanta (tied for tenth).[62] However, a report by the Federal Highway Administration (FHWA) says that traffic is heading south. According to FHWA projections, such Sun Belt cities as Charlotte, Dallas, and San Antonio will crack the traffic top ten by 2005.[63]

Among a host of other unpleasant effects, bumper-to-bumper driving exacerbates pollution. Carbon monoxide and hydrocarbon emissions are highest at low speeds, especially those below 40 miles per hour.[64] Emissions also go up during acceleration, deceleration, and idling—the basic conditions of stop-and-go driving—by (roughly) a factor of three.[65] Traffic jams also eat up prodigious amounts of fuel. American motorists now spend 1.6 billion hours a year on the road without budging an inch,[66] wasting 2.2 billion gallons of gasoline in the process. Tying up workers and goods in interminable traffic jams is not ideal from a business point of view, either. The practice, in fact, is credited with productivity losses totalling $40 billion a year, and there's no relief on the horizon.[67]

The U.S. Department of Transportation recently estimated that vehicle delays on the nation's highways could rise fourfold by the year 2000.[68] Heightened traffic on major arteries, the agency predicts, could in turn increase delays on other roads more than threefold.[69] Overall, that could add up to the equivalent of about four million "person work years" wasted each year by 2005.

In some places, people view traffic as the number one problem in life. A 1988 survey of Sacramento residents identified road congestion as the most pressing issue facing them from among a list of 17 candidates; inadequate transportation services were cited as the fourth most urgent problem.[70] In Charlotte, North Carolina, crime and drugs were considered the top problem; traffic ran a close second, according to

Terry Lathrop, assistant director of Charlotte's transportation department.[71]

Of course, suburbia has not been spared the urban affliction; changing metropolitan growth patterns have brought big-time traffic jams and attendant pollution to the suburbs, undermining the very conditions that lured residents there in the first place. "People moved to the suburbs for mobility and privacy," says architect and city planner Peter Calthorpe. "What they got was gridlock and isolation."[72]

Traffic management experts used to regard a city as the hub of a wheel, with the spokes carrying most of the flow into the center during the morning commute and out to the rim of the wheel late in the day. But now the configuration has changed. Although the traditional morning suburb-to-city commute has not gotten any easier, the number of vehicles driving in other directions, such as from suburb to suburb or from city to suburb, has increased even more.

Traffic patterns are following population shifts. As people go, so go their cars—or is it the other way around? Eighty-six percent of U.S. population growth since 1950 has occurred in suburban regions,[73] and two thirds of the jobs created between 1960 and 1980 were in suburbia—a trend that has since accelerated. For every 70 jobs created in the suburbs of Washington, D.C., in 1986, only 10 were added in the city.[74]

Thanks to this demographic shift, suburb-to-suburb drives now make up the largest fraction of the nation's daily work trips, constituting an estimated 40 percent of all commutes. The suburb-to-city commute has fallen to third place (10 percent), with city-to-city trips capturing second (33 percent).[75] "Congestion has lost its directional bias," explains transportation specialist C. Kenneth Orski. "People commuting from one suburb to another or driving from their suburban homes to a shopping center are just as likely to run into heavy traffic as are commuters on their way downtown."[76]

These traffic jams are being caused in part by suburban "megacenters"—vast complexes of offices, hotels, restaurants, movie theaters, medical and dental centers, and a variety of service establishments—suburbia's answer to downtown. Tysons Corner, Virginia, is an oft-cited example. Twenty-five years ago, it was a quiet intersection west of Washington, D.C., with little more than a gas station and a small grocery store. Today this once dreamy hamlet is one of the biggest "edge cities" in the nation, with 70,000 employees and more office space than downtown Miami. Yet it is only one of 13 megacenters in the Washington metropolitan area. Horrendous traffic in the vicinity of Tysons Corner is reportedly one reason the American Automobile Association (AAA) moved its headquarters from there to the comparatively tranquil setting of Orlando, Florida.[77]

Apparently traffic can get bad enough to influence some people's choices about where to live and work and how to get around. It's clear that if you put enough cars on the roads, and throw in a few accidents for good measure, no one will be able to move. At the point of total paralysis, people would surely abandon their vehicles because even walking would be faster, but the question no one can answer is how much most people, ultimately, will put up with. How much lower must driving speeds dip before large numbers of motorists will seek alternatives to cars?

Evidence suggests that conditions will have to get downright dismal before drivers consider something drastic like not driving. Average speeds on some London streets during rush hour get as low as eight miles per hour; cars creep along even more slowly in Tokyo.[78] Every morning, 1.3 million commuters crawl into Paris at a painfully sluggish six miles per hour.[79] That's also the average vehicle speed on New York City cross streets—slower than bicycles and roller blades, as well as last century's mainstay, the horse and buggy.[80]

City driving may become like the game of limbo: how low can you go? "Twenty years ago, if someone had told me that the average speed driving across Manhattan would be allowed to get down to 1.5 miles per hour, I would say no, it'll never happen. But you don't know what people will stand for," says Michael Oppenheimer, senior scientist at the Environmental Defense Fund.[81]

They won't stand for much more, maintains architect Daniel Solomon. People "have survived pollution and the despoliation of the landscape," he says. "And they have gotten used to the sheer ugliness of everything around them. But take away mobility, take away freedom, take away the great joy of driving, and there is big trouble. Comes gridlock; comes the revolution."[82]

Pack enough people onto a roadway, with no room to move and no way out, and stress is inevitable. Stress, like water, has to spill over somewhere. "Aggressive behavior and physiological reactions have been linked to exposure to congested traffic conditions," concludes a study by the U.S. General Accounting Office.[83] In 1987, more than 100 incidents of random freeway shootings and rock throwing were reported in California alone.[84]

Freeway aggression may be facilitated by the anonymity and the lack of social contact characteristic of driving. "The car can be a private bubble that allows the Mr. Hyde in all of us to emerge when we are crossed," notes Raymond Novaco, a professor of social ecology at the University of California at Irvine.[85]

Tempting as it may be, cracking open the window and taking a potshot at an irritating driver won't necessarily get you to your destination any faster. As comedian Jay Leno put it: "It's bumper-to-bumper. You get angry. You kill the guy in front of you. You're still stuck in traffic. Except now you've got to wait for a tow truck."[86]

Some commuters let out their murderous impulses in psychoanalysis. T. Byron Karasu, a New York City psychiatrist, claims that some of his patients spend most of their $200-per-hour sessions talking about the difficulties they had commuting to those sessions rather than dealing with whatever traumas or neurotic symptoms brought them there in the first place. Eventually, Karasu says, traffic-born tension can lead to high blood pressure, neck and back pain, and ulcers.[87]

What can we do about this no-win situation, apart from finding a good, affordable health plan? The traditional response, laying down more roads, is not the answer. In these days of budget cutbacks, new freeway construction, especially in urban areas, can cost $100 million per mile.[88] Space is also at a premium in cities, making it all but impossible to build our way out of the traffic problem. "In some places, we have built our last mile of highway," says G. Sadler Bridges, associate director of the Texas Transportation Institute.[89]

The fact is, roads can't be created fast enough to meet rising demand. Even when the funds are found for proposed thoroughfares and environmental approval is secured, new roads fill up as fast as they can be built. Paraphrasing a line from the movie *Field of Dreams,* Northeastern University economist Steven Morrison explained why highway construction as a proposed traffic solution is doomed to failure: "If you build it, they will come."[90]

Long-term relief means going beyond road building and traffic controls. Measures that speed up the flow of traffic can trim commuting times, but this doesn't address the central issue: finding ways to entice people out of gasoline-powered cars. To do that, we need cleaner alternative vehicles and attractive modes of public transportation, plus a new strategy for urban planning that makes most car trips unnecessary.

This approach will take more ingenuity than the old standby of two parts asphalt and one part cheap gasoline. Before trying to build more roads, doesn't it make sense to pause long enough to see where we ought to be going in the first place? With average speeds on highways and surface arteries dropping fast, we should have plenty of time to think about our long-range destination and the best way of getting there.

3

The Drive for Better Cars

This is the story of how to build a better car and
why, once again, it is not being built in Detroit.

PETER JENNINGS,
"ABC World News Tonight"

In 1980, a group of scientists and engineers in Columbus, Ohio, set
out to design the car of the future. They envisioned a safe, roomy
automobile that could go 100 miles on a gallon of gas in city driving.
The group was assembled by Sherwood Fawcett, then chairman of the
Battelle Memorial Institute, the largest nonprofit research laboratory in
the world. Fawcett, a physicist who has since retired, was not interested
in a novelty car that might win a race or a beauty contest. He wanted
to spur the development of affordable, highly efficient vehicles that
could significantly reduce America's dependence on imported oil,
thereby enhancing our national security.

Fawcett started worrying about military skirmishes over oil long before the Kuwait-Iraq war of 1990–1991, and even before the Arab oil
embargo of the early 1970s. "The chances of World War III being
fought over oil are very real," he predicted. "As a nation, if we allow
that to happen, we're almost as guilty as the Germans were in allowing
the Nazis to arise."[1]

Fawcett appointed Jim Swain, Battelle's top automotive engineer, to
head the research effort. In six months, Swain's team came up with a
detailed, computer-tested blueprint for a mid-sized car known as Pertran
(short for "personal transportation vehicle") that would sell for about
$6,500. The diesel-fueled version would obtain 105 miles per gallon in
city driving; the gasoline-powered model was calculated to get about
85 mpg.

To achieve such a high fuel efficiency (at least on paper), Pertran
incorporated many innovative features, but no technologies that
couldn't be bought in 1980. For example, Pertran would weigh slightly
more than 1,000 pounds, less than half the weight of a comparable

sedan, because it would have a smaller engine and a frame constructed of aluminum, plastics, and fiberglass. A "supercharging" system would provide intermittent bursts of power to the down-sized engine as needed. A "continuously variable transmission," offering a virtually unlimited number of gears, would allow the engine to operate at its most efficient speed. The car would be streamlined, reducing aerodynamic drag to less than half that of a typical vehicle. A flywheel system would recover energy normally wasted in braking.

Many of Pertran's key features have since found their way into other cars, particularly those of foreign make. Progress, however, is barely evident in the new crop of cars sold in the United States. Overall, the 1992 domestic and imported models have an average fuel efficiency of only 27.5 miles per gallon—one fourth that estimated for the diesel Pertran, and a 4-percent drop from the 1988 average. Although Pertran was predicated on 1980 technology, the goals embodied in its revolutionary design are as distant as ever. A dozen years after it was conceived on Battelle drawing boards, Pertran remains the car of the future.

Fawcett tried to interest the Big Three automakers—General Motors, Ford, and Chrysler—in building six prototype vehicles, "but they laughed at me." He was told, in essence, that "you can't make a car like this because if you could, we would have already done it."[2] Battelle's chairman collided head-on with a longstanding prejudice in Detroit against energy-efficient vehicles. The basic thinking is that energy-efficient vehicles mean small vehicles, and small vehicles mean small profits. In general, it's true that large cars are more profitable to build than small ones. According to auto expert James Flink, material costs for a standard-sized car run only about $500 above those for a subcompact, but the larger car may be sold for thousands of dollars more.[3] This line of reasoning, however, had nothing to do with Pertran, which was specifically designed to be an efficient standard-sized model, not a small car.

Fawcett got an entirely different reaction from executives at the Japanese manufacturer Mitsubishi: "We know you can do this; we can do it too. But we have such a big lead over Americans in fuel efficiency [that] we can afford to wait."[4]

Fawcett found a champion in his congressman, Bob Shamansky, who introduced a bill offering incentives to manufacturers to build a car meeting Pertran's specifications. Alaska Senator Ted Stevens intro-

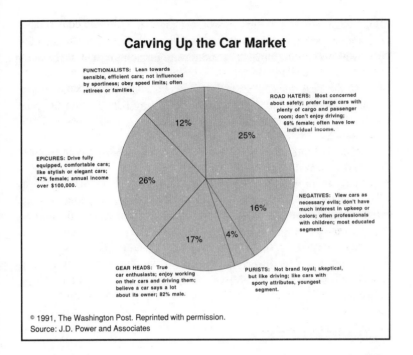

Carving Up the Car Market

FUNCTIONALISTS: Lean towards sensible, efficient cars; not influenced by sportiness; obey speed limits; often retirees or families.

ROAD HATERS: Most concerned about safety; prefer large cars with plenty of cargo and passenger room; don't enjoy driving; 69% female; often have low individual income.

EPICURES: Drive fully equipped, comfortable cars; like stylish or elegant cars; 47% female; annual income over $100,000.

NEGATIVES: View cars as necessary evils; don't have much interest in upkeep or colors; often professionals with children; most educated segment.

GEAR HEADS: True car enthusiasts; enjoy working on their cars and driving them; believe a car says a lot about its owner; 82% male.

PURISTS: Not brand loyal; skeptical, but like driving; like cars with sporty attributes; youngest segment.

12% 25% 26% 16% 17% 4%

© 1991, The Washington Post. Reprinted with permission.
Source: J.D. Power and Associates

duced an identical bill in the Senate, but the idea met with ridicule in Congress. Dan Glickman, chairman of the House Subcommittee on Transportation, responded to Fawcett's 1981 testimony by asking, "Are you serious?" Republican Representative Jim Dunn from Michigan suggested an alternative to Pertran: a car with a sail attached to the roof that could get 100 mpg provided there was a strong tailwind.[5]

The Reagan administration was not much more helpful, maintaining that government had no business promoting one kind of car over another. If Pertran was going to succeed, it would have to do so on its own merits, in the marketplace. Laissez-faire is fine, so far as it goes, Fawcett says. "What bothers me is that the public has never had a choice. They've been offered incremental improvements; they've never been offered a car that can get 100 mpg in city driving. Sometimes the market will just create an opening if something really new and different comes along."[6]

What went wrong with an idea that sounded so right? For one thing,

Jim Swain admits, the timing was not exactly perfect. When Battelle researchers began assembling their hypothetical car on paper, fuel economy was not a burning issue. People were more interested in regaining some of the acceleration capacity that had been stripped away from cars in the past decade. Still, Swain says, "there hasn't been a good window of opportunity before or since. It may take another 20 years before the world is thinking in the terms we were back in 1980." And that, he adds, is "kind of frustrating."[7]

The shortsighted mentality that dominates transportation planning is frustrating not only for Swain, but for anyone trying to make intelligent decisions about the nation's transportation future. To alleviate the problems catalogued at great length in the preceding chapter, two things have to happen. First, people simply have to drive less, a notion that runs contrary to a prolonged and pervasive trend. (Ways of accomplishing this are taken up in chapters 5 and 6.) Second, since cars probably aren't going to be abolished anytime soon, we must take great pains to make sure that the cars we drive are as fuel efficient and nonpolluting as possible.

TRIMMING THE FAT

If Pertran was a tantalizing idea that never moved beyond the design stage, several automobile prototypes on the road today are proof positive that high fuel economy can be readily achieved. Renault's Vesta, for example, attained 124 mpg in testing.[8] Going to extremes, a modified Audi 100 luxury sedan averaged a dazzling 133 mpg in a 3,000-mile trek through Europe. To get such extraordinary mileage, engineers ripped out its backseat to cut down weight, and professional drivers turned off the Audi's engine while going downhill.[9]

Peugeot, to cite another example, regards its high-mileage ECO 2000 as a "crisis car" that could be placed on the assembly line in the event of another oil crisis. The flaw in that reasoning is that oil shortages or supply dislocations can materialize suddenly, without notice. Meanwhile, it normally takes about 5 years to bring a new model car into production and another 10 or more to replace most of the fleet of less efficient cars already on the road.[10]

Volvo has no plans to market the LCP 2000, another prototype that gets 100 miles to the gallon in highway driving, even though it appears ready for mass production. Engineers estimate that the car could be manufactured at costs competitive with today's average subcompact.[11] But the company is holding back for the same reason that Pertran never got out of the starting block—the low cost of oil. Manufacturers aren't making cars like the LCP 2000 for a simple reason: they're afraid no one will buy them.

Consumer interest in fuel economy remains low, despite the recent war with Iraq, which, contrary to official denials, obviously had something to do with oil. "The war has had essentially no impact, either on production or on consumption trends," notes Christopher Flavin of the Worldwatch Institute. "We seem to be pretty much back on the path that we've been on since 1986, which is a path of rapidly rising oil imports."[12] That observation squares with the less formal research of Jack Pohanka, a car dealer in Marlow Heights, Maryland, who says his customers couldn't care less about fuel economy. "They walk right past the stickers that show the miles per gallon. They're really not interested in fuel efficiency, and they don't even want to talk about it."[13]

Going against the prevailing tide, Honda is considering producing its two-seater EP-X ("efficient personal experimental"), a prototype that gets about 100 miles to the gallon. The curtain was raised on the EP-X for the first time at the Tokyo Motor Show in October 1991. This 1400-pound car owes its extreme fuel efficiency in part to its lightweight aluminum body.[14]

Honda had already created waves earlier in the same year, when it unveiled its 1992 model Civic VX. The new car gets about 59 miles per gallon in combined city and highway driving—a 44 percent improvement over the 1991 Civic DX.[15] Added draws: the VX has a more powerful engine than the DX and can accommodate five passengers. Environmentalists touted the development. "We've said all along that you can make a fuel-efficient car without making a tiny little itsy-bitsy car," commented Dan Becker, a lawyer for the Sierra Club.[16]

Several factors underlie Honda's advance. The new Civic VX is more streamlined than its predecessor. It has lightweight wheels and narrow tires that create less friction. The real breakthrough, though, is a "lean-burn" engine that keeps fuel consumption down by mixing

The Car of the Future? The experimental Side FX, brainchild of
UC–Davis students, set the world mileage record in June 1991
with 3,313 miles per gallon.

more than the usual amount of air with the gasoline. The new
VTEC-E engine uses a sophisticated computerized control mechanism
(developed in Honda racing cars) to coordinate the opening and closing
of the piston valves, which creates an optimum mix of air and gas.

"This is the car that Detroit said could not be built," Ned Potter
reported on ABC News. "American carmakers have argued that if you
want an efficient car, you'll have to give up power, safety, and size.
They say if you really want small, we already sell it."[17] General Motors, for example, points to its Geo Metro—currently the most fuel-
efficient American-made car on the market. The Geo Metro gets
roughly the same mileage as the Civic VX, but it is smaller, shorter,
and has one-third less power.

With the introduction of the Civic VX and the ultra–high mileage
EP-X, Honda is making an aggressive push toward fuel economy—a
goal shared, at least on the research level, by other Japanese companies
such as Toyota, Nissan, and Mitsubishi. It remains to be seen whether
the Civic VX will win consumers' hearts. Nevertheless, the example
does reflect a telling attitude toward innovation. U.S. car manufacturers
tend to resist, sometimes vociferously, efforts to raise efficiency standards for new cars. Japanese automakers have no gripe with U.S. efficiency requirements so long as domestic companies are held to the
same standards as they are. "The Japanese say, Tell us what kind of

fuel economy you want us to get, and we'll get there,'' explains Senator Richard Bryan of Nevada, whose legislative efforts to boost fuel economy standards of new cars sold in the United States have met fierce opposition. ''The American automobile industry's response is, We're going to fight you every inch of the way.''[18]

Efficient Engines

In July 1991, around the same time Honda presented its new VTEC-E engine, Mitsubishi announced that it, too, would employ lean-burn engines on 1992 subcompacts sold in Japan. The Mitsubishi engine is expected to boost mileage about 20 percent over comparable models by using proportionately more air and less fuel in combustion. The engine runs on a 23-to-1 air-to-fuel mixture, compared to a more conventional 15-to-1 ratio.[19]

A major drawback of lean-burn engines is that historically they have given off high levels of nitrogen oxides. Both Honda and Mitsubishi are attempting to control this problem. U.S. carmakers, who believe the problem may be intractable, are looking elsewhere for fuel savings. A leading candidate is the two-stroke engine (sometimes called a two-cycle engine), until now used only in motorcycles, lawnmowers, chainsaws, and other small machines. The entire engine cycle—fuel intake, compression, combustion, and exhaust—is accomplished in only two piston strokes, compared to four in conventional automobile engines. This is, in principle, a more elegant arrangement that may translate to fuel savings of about 25 percent.[20] Two-stroke engines are also smaller and lighter than their four-stroke counterparts. An experimental engine in a Ford Escort was 200 pounds lighter than a normal engine, and a small suitcase could fit in the space it saved.[21]

Despite the potential advantages of two-stroke engines, they have been dismissed, until recently, as both dirty and inefficient. An apparent breakthrough came in 1985 with a new model introduced by the Orbital Engine Company of Australia. The key is a microcomputer-controlled fuel injection system, which results in nearly complete combustion, cutting down on the quantity of unburned fuel spewed out the exhaust pipe. These engines, like the Honda and Mitsubishi models just described, tend to run very lean.

Orbital plans to start making automotive engines in its Tecumseh, Michigan, plant in 1993.[22] Both General Motors and Ford have licensed Orbital two-stroke technology, but so far no major automaker has bought the engine outright.[23] The main questions surrounding this type of engine are its reliability over the long haul and its ability to pass emissions standards that are bound to become more stringent.

In January 1992, General Motors unveiled a super-efficient concept car that sports a three-cylinder, two-stroke engine designed for high performance. Dubbed the Ultralite, GM's four-seater gets over 100 miles per gallon at a constant 50 mph, yet accelerates to 60 mph in under eight seconds. The car meets all federal safety and emission requirements. GM claims that it will soon incorporate many features of the Ultralite into production, including its two-stroke engine, low-resistance tires, and the use of carbon fibers in the body.

The development of high-temperature engines is another research avenue that has held promise for years, without yet delivering the big payoff. These engines offer higher thermodynamic efficiencies—simply put, an engine that can bring fuel to higher temperatures can convert more of the fuel's potential energy into usable power. Ceramic materials are one key to high-temperature engine technology, which is being pursued in both diesel and gas turbine engines. These ceramics are both lighter than typical engine components and more heat tolerant.

In 1985, Nissan introduced a ceramic turbocharge system designed to recover waste heat from the exhaust.[24] General Motors has recently tested a ceramic gas turbine engine (operating at 2,500° F) that converts 46 to 48 percent of its fuel to usable power—roughly double the efficiency of a standard gasoline-powered engine.[25] Isuzu, meanwhile, is working on a ceramic diesel engine that, in concert with a turbocharge system, should be 30-percent more efficient than today's diesel engines.[26] Even more advanced ceramic models may boost mileage by 60 percent over that of conventional engines.[27]

There are still problems to be ironed out: traditional ceramics are notoriously brittle and they tend to crack or chip under stress. Ceramics will surely continue to be more widely used in automobiles. However, until high-temperature engines prove themselves on the road, claims of dramatic fuel savings must be regarded as speculative.

Meanwhile, significant savings can be achieved by modifying existing engines. For example, engines with four valves per cylinder, rather than the standard two, can run on 5- to 9-percent less fuel. Most of the savings stem from the use of a smaller engine, and such down-sizing can be done without sacrificing performance.[28] Although these smaller four-valve engines are relatively common in Japanese cars, General Motors is the only U.S. manufacturer making them; they appear on some Oldsmobile and Pontiac models as a $600 option.[29]

A more dramatic breakthrough has come from Clemson University, where researchers have invented a new camshaft that might boost mileage by 20 percent. Camshafts are rotating rods that control the opening and closing of valves in the engine cylinders. Most camshafts are set so that the engine runs best at highway speeds; as a result, fuel is wasted during city driving. The Clemson model, however, is controlled by an on-board computer that can vary the timing of valve operations depending on whether the car is traveling at low or high speeds. The result is more efficient fuel use.[30]

Lightweight Materials

The laws of physics dictate that the heavier a car is, the more energy it takes to accelerate it over a given distance. If a car can be made lighter, all other things being equal, it will consume less gas. The Office of Technology Assessment estimates that a 10-percent weight reduction improves mileage by nearly 7 percent. Looking ahead to the year 2010, the OTA predicts potential weight reductions of 20 to 30 percent in the average U.S. vehicle, translating to efficiency gains of about 12 to 20 percent.[31]

Since the mid-1970s, the average U.S. car has shed roughly 1,000 pounds. Weight can be trimmed in three basic ways. The first is through technological advances (such as lean-burn or two-stroke engines) that eliminate equipment or reduce its size. The second is via vehicle redesign—a switch to a front-wheel drive, for instance, which reduces weight by eliminating the drive shaft and rear axles. Finally, the substitution of light materials for heavy ones can reduce vehicle weight substantially. Fuel savings come to about 10 percent, according to researchers Marc Ledbetter of the American Council for an Energy Efficient Economy and Marc Ross of the University of Michigan.[32]

Hundreds of pounds can be trimmed by substituting other materials for standard-grade steel in a car. Starting around 1983, cars like the GM Fiero and the Honda CRX employed bodies made largely of plastics. Honda developed a new, recyclable, high-strength plastic for use on CRX panels.

General Motors has also made extensive use of plastics, though not always with energy efficiency in mind. For years, the sporty Chevrolet Corvette has had a plastic body. The Chevrolet Lumina van, introduced in 1989, also has a body composed almost entirely of plastics. The

---

THE RECYCLING PROBLEM IN A WORD: PLASTICS

Both Volkswagen and BMW are building plants where cars will be taken apart and reusable materials salvaged. By the year 2000, BMW hopes to recycle every single scrap from every single scrapped car.

"An opposite idea seems to have taken hold at General Motors," claimed a 1990 editorial in the industry journal *Automotive News.* "[General Motors] has spent a lot of money to design materials that won't corrode, but it is only starting to consider the problem that indestructibility will cause."[81] It's a huge problem. Nonrecyclable plastics (sheet-molded composites) comprise the outer skin of the Chevrolet Corvette, the Pontiac Fiero, and Chevrolet Lumina APV mini-van. GM hopes to produce 250,000 mini-vans a year at its Tarrytown, New York, plant. Each of these vans contains about 325 pounds of sheet-molded composites, plus another 112 pounds of interior plastics.

The typical U.S. car may contain 60 different kinds of plastic, virtually ruling out reuse. Altogether, these plastics add up to several hundred pounds—a little over 10 percent of the total vehicle weight—a figure that is steadily rising.[82] With nine million cars junked each year,[83] automotive recyclers are stuck with mountains of material that simply cannot be reused. As a result, landfills overflow and the plastic wastes (called shredder fluff) often have to be carted off to distant landfills or incinerators. These transportation costs cut deep into recyclers' profits. "Basically, the car you are

(continued)

THE RECYCLING PROBLEM
IN A WORD: PLASTICS   *(continued)*

producing has become, due to the inability or difficulty in landfilling the fluff, unrecyclable," explains Robert Waxman, who runs a huge recycling firm in Ontario, Canada. "We're not going to take the vehicle if we're not going to make any money on it."[84]

Ultimately, this could be a huge economic and environmental blow because valuable resources would be lost if car recycling proves unfeasible. The automotive recycling industry is the 16th largest industry in the United States. Each year, more than 10 million automobiles, buses, trucks, and motorcycles are recycled, saving 85 million barrels of oil that would have been consumed in the manufacture of new replacement parts.[85] More than seven million tons of steel, two million tons of cast iron, and one-half million tons of aluminum are recovered annually. The use of scrap iron and steel in place of ore cuts down on air pollution by 86 percent and water pollution by 76 percent, according to the Environmental Protection Agency.[86]

What can be done, short of giving up the many advantages offered by plastics—among them, weight reduction, corrosion resistance, and lower-cost tooling? Chrysler has decided to use only thermoplastics—substances that can be melted and easily reused—on its body panels. GM's new line of Saturn cars also uses recyclable plastics. GM chemists are now working on a technique called pyrolysis to handle even the most recycle-resistant compounds. Plastics are placed in a 1400° F oven and baked until the materials return to their original reusable constituents.

By 1995, laws in many European countries will require that 80 percent of the plastic in scrapped cars be recycled.[87] All plastic parts in small BMW cars are now stamped so that they can be sorted for recycling. Plastic parts are also coded in new VW cars to identify which ones can be reused.

Recyclability, obviously, is not the only consideration in choosing an automotive material, but it is becoming more important. BMW, for example, recently stopped research on a plastic car body. "We're thinking our domestic and soon our U.S. customers might not want to drive such a nonrecyclable car," explains product information manager Christopher Huss.[88]

COMPARATIVE FUEL EFFICIENCIES

In the EPA's *1992 Gas Mileage Guide*, the following models are rated for having city and highway driving fuel efficiencies of at least 30 mpg.

Subcompacts	MPG/City	MPG/Highway
• Daihatsu Charade (manual)	38	42
• Daihatsu Charade (automatic)	30	32
• Dodge/Plymouth Colt (manual)	31	36
• Eagle Summit (manual)	31	36
• Ford Festiva (automatic)	31	33
• Ford Festiva (manual)	35	41
• Geo Metro (automatic)	36	39
• Geo Metro (manual)	46	50
• Geo Metro XFi (manual)	53	58
• Geo Storm (manual)	30	36
• Honda Civic (automatic)	30	37
• Honda Civic (manual)	42	48
• Honda Civic HB VX (manual)	48	55
• Hyundai Excel (manual)	30	36
• Mitsubishi Mirage (manual)	31	36
• Subaru Justy (manual)	33	37
• Subaru Justy (CVT)[†]	33	35
• Subaru Justy 4WD (CVT)	31	31
• Suzuki Swift (automatic)	36	39
• Suzuki Swift (manual)	39	43

Compacts		
• Ford Escort FS (manual)	32	40
• Isuzu Stylus (manual)	31	37
• Lincoln/Mercury Tracer (manual)	30	37
• Volkswagen Jetta (manual)	37	40 (Turbo Diesel)

Small Station Wagons		
• Ford Escort (manual)	30	37
• Lincoln/Mercury Tracer (manual)	30	37

[†]CVT, Continuously Variable Transmission

fuel-efficient Geo Metro uses plastics in its construction, as well as a lightweight aluminum engine.[33]

Concern about the recyclability of plastics has prompted European manufacturers to investigate aluminum, magnesium, and high-grade steel. Audi has teamed up with the Aluminum Company of America (Alcoa) to produce a sedan with an aluminum body.[34] Aluminum comprises one fourth of the weight of Volvo's LCP 2000 prototype. The car's engine block, wheels, and chassis are made out of magnesium, which is one-third lighter than aluminum.

That Streamlined Look

During highway driving, aerodynamic drag becomes the major power drain on a car, consuming more than 60 percent of the energy supplied to the wheels.[35] (The aerodynamic drag exerted on a car is proportional to the square of its speed.) The main way to minimize this drag is to streamline the car—smoothing out the vehicle's overall shape and eliminating any protrusions or outcroppings that retard motion.

The typical U.S. car of today has a drag coefficient of 0.37, which indicates how much resistance the vehicle encounters as it moves through the air. Reducing the drag coefficient by 10 percent would boost fuel economy by roughly 6 percent on the highway and 2 to 3 percent on city streets.[36] But even the sleekest designs will do nothing for a car that's idling in traffic, except perhaps attract attention. The best vehicles on the road today, from an aerodynamic standpoint, have drag coefficients of about 0.28. Driving that figure down requires major design changes, such as covering the wheels with "skirts." Ford has developed an experimental vehicle, the Probe V, with a drag coefficient of 0.137, below that of an F-15 fighter jet.[37] Although roomier everyday cars may never approach such sleekness, the OTA predicts that by the year 2010, it might be possible to reduce the average drag coefficient of new U.S. cars to 0.20—46 percent below the current average.[38]

More Technical Improvements

Automotive engineers aren't content simply to reduce drag. The Toyota Camry and the Mitsubishi Galant use electronic controls that automatically switch gears to keep the engine running as efficiently as possible. The system improves mileage by about 10 percent.[39]

Continuously variable transmissions, or CVTs, which make an almost endless number of gears available, offer even higher efficiencies. The Subaru Justy was the first car to make use of this technology. Fuel economy is 20 percent better than the same car would get with a three-speed automatic transmission and 10 percent better than with a five-speed manual transmission.[40] CVTs are also offered in some Ford Fiestas sold in Europe. So far, the technology is suitable only for small cars, but several companies are trying to develop versions that will work in larger cars as well.

A 10-percent drop in the rolling resistance of tires can improve fuel economy by 3 to 4 percent.[41] With half the rolling resistance of modern radials, tires on GM's prototype electric vehicle, the Impact, show just how much room there is for improvement.[42]

Since less surface comes into contact with the ground, narrower tires generate less friction. But tires can get only so narrow before concerns about comfort and safety arise. The Goodyear Tire and Rubber Company and Lotus Engineering of England have joined forces to address the comfort issue. Together they are developing a "smart tire" that would inflate or deflate depending on road conditions. The tires would maintain a high, fuel-saving pressure on smooth highways and deflate to a lower pressure on pothole-strewn roads to make the ride less bumpy. Tire pressure is regulated by an on-board computer processor linked to silicon sensors embedded in the tire. The companies hope to have smart tires on the market in 1993 or 1994 model cars.[43]

Fuel efficiency suffers during braking and idling because the engine's power is not being used to propel the vehicle forward. In city driving, up to one third of a fuel's potential energy may be wasted in this way.[44] Volkswagen has developed a system called Glider Automatic to tap this energy, which is normally dissipated. While the car is idling or decelerating, excess engine power charges a spinning flywheel. The engine then shuts off during idle periods and the flywheel takes over the job of running fans and other accessories. The engine switches back on automatically once the accelerator is depressed.[45]

A more advanced system being developed at the University of Wisconsin would keep the vehicle engine operating at its most efficient setting at all times, channeling excess output to a flywheel. Energy recovered during braking is also used to charge the flywheel. The flywheel can be drawn on, when needed, to boost the engine's power. This technology may increase fuel economy by 50 percent in stop-and-go driving, according to preliminary lab tests.[46]

A Few Simple Things

Before bothering to install currently expensive and exotic gadgets in our cars, such as smart tires or flywheels, it makes sense to do some simple things first, like keeping tires properly inflated. The Department of Energy (DOE) reckons that 100,000 barrels of oil are wasted nationwide each day owing to underinflated automobile tires. Frank Wicks, an engineering professor at Union College in Schenectady, New York, considers these estimates way too low. His research found that tires tend to be even less inflated than DOE assumed; he calculates that Americans could save 230,000 barrels of oil a day (worth more than $12 million) by not letting their tires go soft. This figure is close to DOE's low-range estimates of potential oil production at the Arctic National Wildlife Refuge—290,000 barrels a day.[47]

The Department of Energy calculates that 40,000 barrels a day could be saved if just 20 percent of the families with two cars decided to drive the more efficient vehicle when given a choice. Driving at the speed limit, 55 mph on most highways, could save an additional 50,000 barrels a day, according to DOE statistics.[48] Fuel consumption goes up 30 percent when the speed increases from 55 to 75 mph.[49] So does the accident rate. According to the GEICO Insurance Company, when Michigan raised its maximum speed limit from 55 mph to 65 mph, fatalities on the affected roads increased by 28 percent, serious injuries by 39 percent, and moderate injuries by 24 percent. Over a 25-month period when the 65 mph limit was in force, there were 31 additional deaths on these Michigan highways, 420 additional serious injuries, and 491 additional moderate injuries. The total dollar cost of these accidents was $98 million.[50]

THE GREAT SAFETY DEBATE

The automobile industry has poured more than $10 million into the Coalition for Vehicle Choice, a group whose sole mission is to lobby against the higher fuel efficiency standards proposed by Senator Rich-ard Bryan.[51] The basic argument is that raising the efficiency of the nation's automobiles will needlessly kill people forced to drive smaller vehicles. Some critics have gone so far as to call Bryan's bill "the National Highway Death Act."[52]

At base, this pitched battle has little to do with protecting drivers and passengers, and a lot to do with protecting the higher profit margins manufacturers realize from selling bigger, more expensive cars. If safety were Detroit's paramount concern, the auto industry would not have spent more than two decades and $20 million fighting against the introduction of air bags[53]—a technology that Jerry Curry, head of the National Highway Traffic Safety Administration (NHTSA), considers the most important step toward making cars safer.[54]

Obviously, safety is not the sole consideration in car design. Nor is efficiency. The reasonable strategy is to make cars that are both efficient and safe, and history shows that it can be done. The fuel economy of new cars in the United States doubled from 1974 to 1990, while the death rate (measured in fatalities per mile) dropped by 40 percent. The Volkswagen Rabbit gets 25-percent better mileage than the VW Beetle it replaced, yet has a 44-percent lower fatality rate. Similarly, modifi-cations of the Honda Civic made in 1981 yielded a 12-percent boost in mileage, along with a 44-percent drop in fatalities.[55]

Clarence Ditlow, head of the Center for Auto Safety, claims that technological improvements, not a move toward smaller cars, are what account for 86 percent of the boost in auto fuel efficiency that has occurred since 1974.[56] For instance, substituting a variable camshaft for a standard one—a move that might improve efficiency by 20 percent—has no effect whatsoever on the size or safety of a car, but it does save energy. Even if smaller cars became a necessity, they wouldn't nec-essarily be less safe than big cars: what matters most is how they are designed. For example, in safety tests conducted by NHTSA in 1985, GM's Astro mini-van, which tipped the scales at a hefty 4,100 pounds, scored dead last in safety. The Astro didn't fare much better in a 1989 ranking by *Consumer Reports* magazine. The compact Ford Escort, on the other hand, has consistently ranked near the top in federal govern-ment safety tests.[57] Even without air bags, the Escort received the high-est possible rating for driver and passenger protection and structural integrity in a 1991 *Consumer Reports* rating.[58] Similarly, the 2,000-

pound VW Rabbit had a lower serious injury rate than the Ford Crown Victoria, which, at 3,900 pounds, weighed nearly twice as much.[59] The issue is not big versus small, but whether manufacturers will decide to make cars with fuel economy standards *and* safety features commensurate with the best available technology.[60]

Joan Claybrook, president of the organization Public Citizen and former NHTSA head, maintains that efficiency improvements need not come at the expense of safety, but she believes that Detroit's "go slow and only if pushed" attitude is imperiling the auto industry. As soon as the next inevitable oil crisis occurs, she says, the public will be interested in fuel economy again. American automakers may then find themselves way behind Japanese and German manufacturers who have made efficiency a high research and development priority for more than a decade. "As the president of Honda has said, 'If you don't build fuel efficiency into your cars, you are going to be out of the automotive business,' " Claybrook notes. "And I think that if the U.S. companies don't compete in fuel efficiency, they're not going to be in the business very long."[61]

CLEARING THE AIR

The Honda Civic VX that appeared on the U.S. market in the fall of 1991 did not show up on California car lots because, technically speaking, it was illegal. The car's lean-burn engine gave off nitrogen oxide emissions at levels below U.S. new-car emission standards, but above the stricter California standards.[62]

This raises an important issue. Ideally, gains in fuel efficiency should not be made at the expense of air quality, and vice versa. But engineering reality may force some compromises. Civic VXs sold in California will use exhaust gas recirculation (EGR) devices that save fuel by capturing energy from the exhaust stream that would otherwise be wasted. But a conventional engine with an EGR device still burns more fuel than a lean-burn engine does, so Civics sold in California will be somewhat less efficient than those sold in the other 49 states. "We haven't found a way to eliminate trade-offs, not yet anyway," explains Toni Harrington, manager of Honda's Washington office.[63] Meanwhile, Honda engineers are working on a new catalytic converter that might solve the pollution problem. The company expects the engine to satisfy federal standards due to become more stringent in 1994. Steve Albu of the California Air Resources Board (CARB) believes the Honda engine might pass the federal test. But it won't be able to meet new California requirements scheduled to take effect in 1996 unless the car runs on a fuel cleaner than today's gasoline.[64]

Tests conducted on an advanced version of the Orbital two-stroke engine indicate emission levels below California's ULEV (ultra-low emissions vehicle) standards.[65] Albu, however, is skeptical about the laboratory results proving true on the road. Orbital engineers think they can get nitrogen oxide emissions below federal standards, Albu says, but he doubts that the engines can meet California's standards for the required 100,000 miles.[66]

Only time will tell whether the Honda and Mitsubishi lean-burn engines and the Orbital two-stroke—machines that are promising from an energy efficiency standpoint—will ultimately pass the clean air test. One or more of these models might have to be abandoned, at least in the United States, on pollution grounds. Still, most efforts to make cars cleaner don't cut into mileage. For example, computerized fuel-injection devices and exhaust gas recovery systems designed to burn gas more completely (and thus more cleanly) also boost fuel efficiency.

By the same token, most efforts to make cars more efficient don't make them more polluting. In general, the more efficient a car, the cleaner it runs. In fact, the 50 most efficient cars sold in the United States emit, on average, only half as many hydrocarbons as the 50 least efficient cars, according to Chris Calwell of the Natural Resources Defense Council.[67]

Catalytic Converters

The catalytic converter, standard equipment on new American cars since 1975, has been a formidable weapon against air pollution, contributing to a 96-percent reduction of the carbon monoxide and hydrocarbons and 76-percent reduction of the nitrogen oxides given off by car engines.[68] But with air quality deteriorating in many metropolitan areas, those reductions are no longer considered good enough. Efforts are now under way to wring additional improvements out of the celebrated pollution control device.

Catalytic converters work effectively only after they are heated to about 700° F. During a typical car trip, 60 percent of the pollutants are given off in the initial minute or two before the car heats up.[69] Not surprisingly, engineers are trying to shorten the time it takes to heat the converter.

W. R. Grace and Company has built a prototype converter that heats up in eight seconds, after receiving a powerful jolt of electricity.[70] The extra battery needed to supply the jolt will add about 40 pounds to the vehicle, but the extra weight, according to CARB's Steve Albu, will not affect fuel economy noticeably. The long-term solution, in his opinion, is an ultra-capacitor—a battery-like storage device that can supply a large electrical current that will heat up the catalytic converter in a second or two. Another possibility is the zeolite trap—a canister that absorbs polluting vapors for a few seconds until the converter reaches its operating temperature.[71] Ford of England has also developed a process to heat the catalytic converter quickly. A fuel-rich mixture from the engine is burned, using a spark plug, just before it enters the catalyst. The catalyst reaches operating temperature in less than ten seconds.[72]

Putting Vapors in Their Place

While reducing the lead content of gasoline over the past two decades, petroleum refiners also added light hydrocarbons that make the gasoline more volatile. This gasoline evaporates more readily, especially during hot summer months. Fuel systems in all U.S. cars have charcoal-filled canisters that trap these hydrocarbon vapors and send them back to the engine for more complete burning. But the highly volatile gasoline used today can saturate these canisters, allowing vapors to escape and contributing significantly to smog.

This problem has not gone unnoticed. The Environmental Protection Agency has imposed limits on the volatility of gasoline sold during the summer. The initial limits, set in 1989, reduced smog-forming emissions nationwide by about 6 percent. Lower limits, in effect since 1992, should reduce emissions by an additional 7 percent.[73]

Another defense against smog—one adopted in the District of Columbia, parts of Maryland and Virginia, California, Massachusetts, and other states—is to require service stations to install special vapor-trapping gas pump nozzles that prevent fumes from escaping during refueling. The gasoline vapors captured by these nozzles are rerouted to the filling station's underground tanks, where they condense back to a liquid. Pollution experts in Washington, D.C., predict that the nozzles will be the area's single biggest smog-fighting measure, cutting regional smog by some 40 percent.[74]

Controlling gasoline vapors, though, may not bring about as many smog benefits as some air pollution experts think. The problem is that EPA regulations have traditionally clamped down on man-made hydrocarbon vapors, while giving less serious attention to the other key ingredient of smog, nitrogen oxides. But ozone or smog can still form in some regions—even if man-made hydrocarbon sources are totally eliminated—when nitrogen oxides react with hydrocarbons naturally given off by trees and other vegetation.

While the optimal smog-fighting strategy is still a matter of scientific and political debate, the government has finally ruled on a related issue that has been locked in stalemate for 15 years. In March 1992, President Bush ordered service stations in most states to install new vapor collectors on gas pump nozzles. Oil companies had been resisting the move, claiming it would be cheaper and more effective to eliminate emissions from the vehicles themselves. But this time around the auto industry won.

Fine Tuning

According to the EPA, about half of all auto emissions come from just 10 percent of the cars on the road today.[75] Getting those dirty cars cleaned up will go a long way toward controlling air pollution nationwide. The trick is finding a way to catch the polluting vehicles in the act.

Donald Stedman, a chemistry professor at the University of Denver, has invented a device that can do just that—set an "emissions trap" that environmental officials can use in the same way highway patrolmen use radar to set speed traps. The pollution-testing unit consists of an infrared sensor that can measure carbon monoxide and hydrocarbon emissions coming out of a car's tailpipe, coupled with a video camera that records license plates. The owners of polluting vehicles can be tracked down and forced to get a tune-up. The tune-up may set them back about $50, but it's a lot cheaper—and far more effective, according to Stedman—than purchasing sophisticated emission control equipment or switching to exotic, so-called clean fuels. (Of course, some dirty cars will no doubt need an engine overhaul costing a few hundred dollars, not just a simple tune-up.)

Stedman and colleagues have tested the emissions trap on 250,000 moving vehicles. Their findings are in basic agreement with the EPA: 10 percent of the vehicles produce half the carbon monoxide while 14 percent account for half the hydrocarbons. A study of 7,000 vehicles in Los Angeles revealed, moreover, that three fourths of the cars with the highest hydrocarbon emissions had been tampered with to increase power.[76] Similarly, Stedman cites an EPA study of 84 vehicles that showed that 46 percent of the carbon monoxide pollution came from just *four* cars. Requiring these four especially dirty vehicles to get tune-ups that bring their emissions down to the average level would reduce total pollution by 43 percent.[77]

According to Stedman, a couple of vans, plus six mobile testing units costing about $50,000 each, could cover a city the size of Denver. Identifying the few bad apples would be much more effective than the standard smog tests administered by auto mechanics. Such tests monitor the emissions of vehicles that are idling, so they are among "the easiest tests in the world to pass," says Gary Bishop, a University of Denver biochemist. "Having a car pass at idle may have nothing to do with how that car performs on the road." On balance, Stedman figures that it's twice as effective, and much cheaper and simpler, to tune up the dirtiest 10 percent of vehicles than it would be to force the entire fleet to shift to new, cleaner blends of gasoline. Besides, he points out, if a car runs dirty because of a mechanical deficiency, no amount of tinkering with its fuel is going to clean it up.[78]

Tune-ups, vapor traps, new catalytic converters, and cleaner-burning engines can all help clamp down on pollution from motor vehicles. But they cannot affect the release of carbon dioxide, a major greenhouse gas—which is why, at some point (and sooner rather than later) people will have to abandon gasoline-burning cars altogether. "It's possible that with new pollution-control technology, we can get emissions in the internal combustion engine down to acceptable levels,'' says William Chameides, an atmospheric chemist at the Georgia Institute of Technology. ''But people continue to drive more and more miles, and the problem seems to be getting worse, not better.''[79] In the long run, he adds, ''we must get away from all forms of combustion'' by switching to emissionless vehicles that run on electricity or some other non-polluting, carbon-free energy source. ''Every other approach is just a stopgap remedy.''[80]

4

Weighing the Alternatives

We're all in the game. We all drive cars, and
we're all hooked on oil. The question is how we
can get unhooked before we drown in the stuff.

ROSS MCDONALD,
Sleeping Beauty

Given the liabilities of our growing dependence on foreign oil, plus the
health and global environmental threats posed by gas-burning vehicles,
it's no surprise that some creative people are seeking alternatives. Louis
Wichinsky, an inventor from Hurleyville, New York, is one such person. He modified his '79 VW Rabbit so that it can run on vegetable
oil that has already been used in deep fryers at local diners and fast-
food establishments. Wichinsky was motivated in part by a desire "to
leave behind a cleaner world, with a little bit better air to breathe."[1]
Vegetable oil produces smaller quantities of polyaromatic hydrocarbons
and nitrogen oxides than standard fuels, but tailgaters can't help notic-
ing an unusual smell. "It's like driving behind a french fry machine,"
says Richard Sapienza, a chemist at the Brookhaven National Laboratory on Long Island who has investigated Wichinsky's system.[2]

One obstacle to the widespread use of vegetable oil as a transportation fuel is its high cost, typically $2.50 to $5.00 a gallon. Wichinsky
avoids this expense by salvaging grease recently retired from the
potato- and chicken-frying trades. Since this approach is not practical
for the population at large, Wichinsky suggests we "grow our own."
But that won't work either, because to make enough fuel for the U.S.
fleet, a good fraction of our country would have to be set aside for the
exclusive cultivation of peanuts, rapeseed, and soybeans.

For now we are left with more mainstream alternatives. What promise do new fuels hold? What are the drawbacks? What are the alternatives to these alternatives?

61

REFORMULATED GAS

On August 14, 1989, the Atlantic Richfield Company (Arco), the eighth-largest U.S. oil company, began selling a cleaner-burning gasoline, called EC-1, in California. Arco juggled the ingredients in gasoline—a complex mixture of liquid hydrocarbons—to produce its improved recipe. It was, in the words of Arco chairman Lodwrick Cook, "the first gasoline reformulated to reduce auto emissions."[3] California air quality officials backed up the company's claim that the EC-1 cut pollutants in old cars by about 20 percent.[4]

In the next two years, eight other oil companies introduced special blends of gasoline designed to combat air pollution. Most of the concoctions involved adding oxygen to the fuel. The extra dose of oxygen makes combustion more complete, thus reducing emissions of carbon monoxide and unburned hydrocarbons. Gasoline's oxygen content can be enhanced by mixing in alcohols, such as methanol or ethanol, or compounds (ethers) made from the two and known as MBTE or EBTE.

In July 1991, Arco announced that it had developed an even cleaner gas called EC-X. With this new fuel, emissions of unburned hydrocarbons are reduced by 28 percent, evaporative hydrocarbons by 36 percent, nitrogen oxides by 26 percent, and carbon monoxide by 25 percent. All told, EC-X would reduce the reactivity of auto exhaust—in other words, its propensity to create ozone smog—by 37 percent.[5]

Arco has not yet put the new gas on the market because it costs about 15 to 20 cents more per gallon to produce. The company probably won't begin selling EC-X until compelled to do so by air quality regulations. In California that means 1996, when new pollution laws will force refiners to make fuels that emit 30 to 40 percent fewer pollutants than today's blends. Under an agreement forged by environmental officials in the District of Columbia and eight Northeastern and mid-Atlantic states, oil companies will have to market increasing amounts of cleaner, reformulated gasoline by 1995.[6] Meanwhile, other oil companies are quietly following Arco's lead, developing their own versions of EC-X. "We have gotten similar data from half a dozen other oil companies," says William Sessa, a spokesman for California's Air Resources Board.[7]

Fuel reformulation makes a great deal of sense. As Sessa points out, "for the foreseeable future, the dominant fuel in this country will be gasoline.''[8] The advantage of gasoline blends like EC-X, compared to such alternative fuels as methanol or natural gas, is that any car can run on them without losing power or requiring mechanical adjustments. A shift to methanol or natural gas would require costly modifications to the millions of cars produced each year, as well as the installation of new pumps and tanks at the nation's 200,000 gas stations. Retooling oil refineries so that they can produce cleaner gas may cost $20 to $40 billion. But that's small change compared to the cost of altering the design and manufacture of cars, plus changing the infrastructure for making and distributing the fuel that these new vehicles will run on. Bernard Picchi, an oil analyst at Salomon Brothers, Inc., figures that these new-fuel expenses could ultimately tally several hundred billion dollars.[9]

The big question, of course, is whether oil companies can go much farther in reducing gasoline emissions. "We have no idea how clean you can make a refined petroleum product," says David Hawkins of the Natural Resources Defense Council. "And I'm not sure the industry has any idea either."[10]

The bottom line is that clean gas is not a long-term solution, despite the environmental advantages it offers now. Since any form of gasoline contains about the same amount of carbon as any other, changing the formula of gasoline would not lessen the greenhouse effect in any way, nor would it help us cut back significantly on oil imports. We should do everything possible to improve gasoline as long as we use it, keeping in mind that we will eventually have to switch to something even better.

METHANOL

In a June 1989 speech, President George Bush promised that "twenty years from now, every American in every city in America will breathe clean air." The solution, as he saw it, was alternative-fuel vehicles, with methanol the leading candidate to replace gasoline.[11]

Methanol, also known as wood alcohol, can be produced from wood, coal, or natural gas. One of methanol's main selling points is that it is a liquid fuel, like gasoline, that can be used in modified gasoline engines. In fact, race cars at the Indy 500 have run on methanol since 1965.[12] Racers favor the fuel because its high octane affords more power and quicker acceleration. Another plus is that unlike most alternatives, methanol already appears to be comparable in price to gasoline. The Office of Technology Assessment (OTA) estimates that consumers would pay about $1.00 to $1.50 at the pump for the equivalent of a gallon of gasoline.[13]

General Motors has agreed to provide the state of California more than 2,000 demonstration vehicles designed to run on mixtures of gasoline and methanol. The first 20 of these vehicles, Chevrolet Corsicas, were delivered in 1989; 200 Chevy Luminas arrived in the following year. Another 2,000 Luminas were to be ready to roll by mid-1992.[14] The Ford Motor Company, meanwhile, is developing methanol-fueled models of the compact Escort, the mid-sized Taurus, and the full-sized Crown Victoria. Chrysler is working on its own methanol car, as are most major Japanese and European manufacturers.

Enthusiasm for methanol should be tempered by a dose of reality, says Mark DeLuchi, a researcher at the University of California at Davis. President Bush's 1989 speech "raised expectations beyond what is supportable." "On the whole," DeLuchi adds, "[methanol vehicles] can be considered only slightly 'cleaner' than comparable gasoline vehicles."[15]

Unfortunately, plenty of factors make methanol *less* appealing than gasoline. For one thing, cars running on pure methanol are hard to start in cool weather—anything much below 50° F. To get around this problem, mixtures such as M85—a blend of 85 percent methanol, 15 percent gas—are normally used in so-called flexible fuel vehicles that run on a combination of the two fuels.

When methanol is burned, it yields only about half the energy that the same amount of gasoline delivers. A methanol-powered car would thus have only half the range of a standard gasoline car, unless, of course, the methanol tank were twice the size of an ordinary gas tank.

Gallon for gallon, methanol is more toxic than gasoline. Inhaling, ingesting, or otherwise contacting the fuel is so hazardous that self-service methanol pumps may not be feasible. The fuel is also highly corrosive, so filling stations would need new storage tanks, and methanol vehicles would have to have stainless steel fuel tanks, plus corrosion-resistant fuel lines, carburetors, and other equipment costing hundreds of extra dollars.

What a switch to methanol vehicles would do to air quality is the central issue and also the most controversial. Most scientists agree that methanol vehicles produce somewhat lower quantities of certain key pollutants, but few experts agree on just how much lower. Several factors complicate the picture. For example, some of the most favorable data for methanol's pollution benefits come from EPA tests of 100-percent methanol cars, but most commercial development is geared toward "hybrid" methanol-gasoline cars relying on a mix of 85 percent methanol or less. The other big question in trying to compute the relative advantages of methanol over gasoline is what exactly to compare methanol to—the average gasoline sold today or the best reformulations available? And what kind of emission standards are being assumed for the "typical" gas-powered car?

Methanol vehicles have traditionally yielded much more formaldehyde—a toxic pollutant, a potent smog-forming chemical, and a proven carcinogen—than gasoline-powered cars do. GM, Ford, and Chrysler are all working on technologies to remove formaldehyde from methanol exhaust, but the problem awaits a definitive solution. The story on other pollutants is mixed: some studies show reduced carbon monoxide and unburned hydrocarbon emissions from methanol, others show the fuel contributing to higher ozone levels than those produced by standard gasoline.

Owing to a host of confounding factors, the U.S. Office of Technology Assessment (OTA) concluded the "M85 use could yield as much as a 40-percent advantage over gasoline or, at the negative extreme, a 20-percent increase in ozone [smog] potential over gasoline." On balance, the agency determined that "M85 has significant but *poorly quantified and highly variable* potential to reduce urban ozone."[16] In other words, methanol's precise impact on smog eludes even the nation's top experts.

Sizing up a particular fuel requires looking at the big picture. For example, the environmental benefits or drawbacks of methanol depend in part on how it is made. Making methanol from coal is a dirty process that is likely to create enough pollution to offset many—if not all—of the air pollution advantages methanol might have as an automotive fuel.[17] If every car in the United States were to run on methanol made from coal, we would have to double coal production nationwide—a move that would have devastating environmental, health, and safety costs.[18]

Methanol's potential influence on global warming is less controversial than this fuel's potential impact on air pollution. Cars powered by methanol produced from natural gas will give off essentially the same amount of greenhouse gases (and thus have about the same impact on global warming) as gasoline-fueled cars. Producing methanol from coal, however, would increase the total output of greenhouse gases by about 50 percent, as compared to gasoline, because of the copious carbon dioxide emissions at the coal-to-methanol plant.[19]

A final drawback is that methanol cannot be regarded as an indigenous fuel. Although the United States possesses vast coal reserves, making methanol from coal would be an unmitigated environmental disaster. If methanol is made from natural gas, it would most likely be made overseas because foreign sources would be considerably cheaper than domestic ones. In addition, the Department of Energy claims that domestic gas production probably won't be able to keep up with projected growth in domestic demand even if methanol production doesn't expand.[20] A shift from gasoline to methanol would thus involve substituting one imported fuel for another. There could be a real security advantage, however: we would be able to import much of the methanol from sources other than those in the Middle East.

ETHANOL

No gas station in Brazil sells just gasoline; normal cars run on a gas-ethanol mixture called gasohol (one part ethanol and nine parts gasoline). Ethanol is grain alcohol, normally made from organic matter, or biomass, such as sugarcane or corn. About 6 percent of the fuel pumped in U.S. service stations in 1989 was gasohol. All told, about 850 million gallons of ethanol are mixed with gasoline each year, satisfying only about 0.5 percent of the nation's automotive energy needs. Over 95 percent of this ethanol is made from corn, consuming about 4 percent of the total crop.[21]

As a transportation fuel, ethanol has serious limitations. A gallon of ethanol currently costs about twice as much as a gallon of gasoline, but has only two thirds of the energy.[22] Gasohol production is heavily subsidized. The federal government kicks in 6 cents for every gallon of gasohol, which translates to a subsidy of 60 cents per gallon of ethanol, or roughly a third of the total production cost.[23] Many states also exempt gasohol from their fuel taxes. Total subsidies in 1988 amounted to $636 million, about 8 cents per gallon.[24] Thanks to these federal and state subsidies, ethanol has been called "a farm support effort" rather than a viable energy source.

Beyond economics, the chief limitation is the enormous quantity of biomass resources that would be needed to power transportation vehicles. Simply put, there is not enough farmland available to produce the corn needed to make significant quantities of automotive fuels. Even if land weren't limited, it's much more sensible overall to use prime agricultural land to grow food for people rather than fuel for cars.

"The entire world corn crop, were it available for conversion to ethanol, would meet only 17 percent of global gasoline demand," explain Nicholas Lenssen and John Young of the Worldwatch Institute. "It takes two acres of corn to run an automobile for a year on ethanol; yet the same area of solar [thermal-electric] troughs could power more than 80 electric vehicles."[25]

The impact of ethanol blends on air quality is being hotly debated. A gloomy report issued in May 1990, cowritten by Thomas Austin, former head of the California Air Resources Board, found that the standard mix of ethanol and gasoline is a mixed blessing, at best. Carbon monoxide emissions would be reduced by 25 percent, but hydrocarbons would rise 50 percent and nitrogen oxides would go up 8 to 15 percent. The net effect would be a 6-percent increase in smog. "Motorists will end up paying more [and getting] dirtier air," Austin claims.[26]

Although his report was not universally embraced, most researchers concede that if there is any antipollution advantage to be had from using gasohol in place of gasoline, it is bound to be slim. "The jury is still out," says CARB spokesman Jerry Martin. "We still are not certain whether there's a benefit or not."[27]

Even if motor vehicle emissions fell modestly with a switch to ethanol, this gain might be offset by pollution in rural areas: the fertilizers used to grow corn, the oil burned to power the tractors used to gather that corn, and emissions from biomass fermentation and from distilleries would all have negative environmental impacts. Taking a broad view of corn-to-ethanol production, numerous studies suggest the approach might be a net energy loser. In other words, it may take more energy to grow and harvest corn and then convert it to ethanol than is later obtained by burning ethanol in car engines.

As for ethanol's contribution to global warming, OTA concludes that

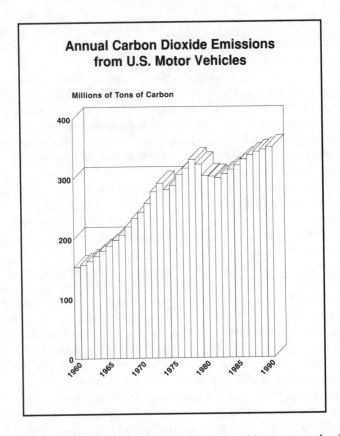

Annual Carbon Dioxide Emissions from U.S. Motor Vehicles

Millions of Tons of Carbon

"it is unlikely that ethanol production and use with current technology and fuel use patterns will create any significant greenhouse benefits."[28] A possible exception, OTA notes, is the production of ethanol from forestry and agricultural wastes, which might help offset greenhouse warming. Researchers at the National Renewable Energy Laboratory in Golden, Colorado, are exploring techniques for converting leftover organic material into ethanol.

The creation of ethanol from solid wastes, rather than corn, also deserves further study. Pilot programs, according to David Lindahl, director of the Alcohols Fuels Program at the Department of Energy, already show great promise in making ethanol from "paper, plastic—virtually everything in a landfill."[29]

COMPRESSED NATURAL GAS

Methane proponents have seen the future, and they call it CNG—short for compressed natural gas. They figure that the owners of 700,000 natural gas vehicles worldwide can't all be wrong. Almost all of these vehicles have modified gasoline or diesel engines that run on natural gas stored in high-pressure tanks. Some 300,000 CNG vehicles roam the streets of Italy, where the fuel has been used since the 1930s. New Zealanders drive more than 100,000 natural gas vehicles; another 30,000 can be found on U.S. thoroughfares.[30] A network of 50 natural gas refueling stations set up after the 1979 oil crisis serves drivers in British Columbia.[31]

As of 1990, all new buses in greater Buenos Aires began running on CNG; by the end of 1993, the entire bus fleet is supposed to switch over to the gas.[32] In 1991, GM placed the first of 1,000 CNG-fueled Sierra pickup trucks on the market in California and Texas. The United Parcel Service recently announced plans to convert 2,700 delivery trucks in Los Angeles to run on natural gas;[33] UPS may eventually adapt half of its 100,000 vehicles for CNG operation.[34] Mexico City officials are drafting a plan to convert all public transportation vehicles—responsible for 30 percent of the region's air pollution—to natural gas.[35]

What's behind this global surge of activity? The appeal of natural gas runs deep, partly because it's cheap. For the equivalent of about 70 cents a gallon, CNG goes for roughly half the current U.S. price of premium gasoline.[36] There is an additional bonus—some might say "subsidy"—because CNG vehicles pay no federal tax comparable to the gasoline tax (currently 14 cents per gallon).

CNG is a comparatively clean fuel. With its use, carbon monoxide emissions are cut by 90 percent and hydrocarbons by 50 percent compared to gasoline.[37] Because natural gas consists almost entirely of methane (without a complicated mix of chemical additives), exhausts from CNG vehicles are almost free of toxic and carcinogenic pollutants such as benzene. And the fuel is stored in sealed, pressurized containers, so no smog-causing unburned hydrocarbons can escape. The main air quality concern is nitrogen oxide emissions, which conceivably could rise with widespread CNG use.

Greenhouse gas emissions from CNG vehicles are expected to be only slightly lower than those from gasoline vehicles. Carbon dioxide emissions are substantially reduced (20 to 25 percent), but methane (the main constituent of natural gas) is a potent greenhouse gas, and no one knows how much of it might leak into the atmosphere. Given these uncertainties, OTA concludes there may be anywhere from a 25-percent decrease in greenhouse emissions to an 11-percent increase.[38] In short, there is no guarantee that switching to CNG vehicles would reduce global warming gases.

Safety appears to be a selling point. There has never been a fire in a natural gas vehicle.[39] Nor have any pressurized tanks exploded upon impact. Extensive experience in Italy, Australia, the Soviet Union, and elsewhere has pretty much dispelled these concerns. "You know what traffic is like in Italy?" asks Joseph Colucci, head of fuel research at General Motors. "If it isn't going to happen in Italy, it isn't going to happen."[40]

Compressed natural gas appears to be better suited for buses and trucks than for cars. Because the fuel holds only about one fourth as much energy on a volume basis as gasoline, a CNG vehicle needs bulky storage tanks to achieve a decent range. While 10 gallons of gasoline weigh only about 70 pounds, the fuel equivalent in CNG, including the pressurized tanks, would weigh about 300 pounds and fill the trunk of a small car.[41] The extra weight and size of compressed-gas storage tanks requires design changes that make CNG vehicles more expensive to build than comparable gasoline-powered models. It now costs between $2000 and $3000 to convert a van to run on CNG.[42]

Another factor that makes the fuel less practical for personal cars is that the United States has only a few hundred CNG pumping stations, and only a few of these are open to the public. The high-pressure gas compressors needed for refueling cost on the order of $250,000 apiece.[43] So CNG makes most economic sense for fleets of buses, trucks, vans, or short-range cars that regularly return to a central location where a natural gas compressor can be installed.

Although CNG can play a useful role in the short run, primarily as a relatively clean fuel for buses and trucks, it is still a fossil fuel, and hence nonrenewable. Despite the current surplus of natural gas, OTA concludes that domestic production will not be able to keep up with steadily rising demand: "Essentially all major U.S. gas supply forecasts project growing gas imports during the 1990s and beyond *without* any movement of gas to vehicular use. Thus, the natural gas necessary to power a large U.S. fleet of gas-fueled vehicles is likely to come from gas imports.''[44] The most likely source of this gas would be Canada.

ELECTRIC VEHICLES

In 1988, Los Angeles city councilman Marvin Braude took a ride on the G-van—a GM electric vehicle prototype that was commercially released on a limited basis two years later. To Braude, the G-van was as much a vehicle of the past as of the future. He had been on the G-van 10 years before, and it had not improved one iota since his last ride. ''There had been absolutely no change, and it just filled me with indignation,'' Braude said. ''Here was a company selling literally billions of dollars of automobiles in the nation's worst smog area. It seemed to me they had an obligation to their customers to spend some real money developing an electric vehicle.''[45]

In May 1988, Braude proposed ''the L.A. Initiative''—an international competition designed to stimulate the mass production of electric vehicles in the region. The competition was supervised by the Los Angeles Department of Water and Power (DWP) and Southern California Edison, which picked a Swedish firm, Clean Air Transport, from the 19 companies that had submitted proposals. DWP and Southern California Edison agreed to invest $7 million in Clean Air Transport, which in turn promised to have 10,000 electric vehicles on sale in greater Los Angeles by 1995.

The car developed by Clean Air Transport, the LA 301, is a hybrid powered by batteries and a small auxiliary gasoline engine. It will have a sticker price of about $25,000, will seat four, and will reach a range of 60 miles on batteries alone (and about 160 miles overall) and a top speed of 75 miles per hour. The LA 301 is powered by a $2000 lead-acid battery pack that takes six to eight hours to recharge and lasts four to five years. Operating costs for the car should be one-third to one-half those for a conventional vehicle, not counting the expense of replacing batteries, according to Jerry Enzenauer, head of DWP's electric vehicle program.[46] Clean Air Transport plans to fit the car with a more advanced battery system that will extend its driving range. (As of June

1992, the company was facing problems raising the $30 million needed to begin manufacturing operations.)

Before Clean Air Transport stepped in, Los Angeles had solicited bids from all over the world, but the only major automaker in the United States, Japan, or Europe to respond was Peugeot. "I think everyone's a bit surprised that a small company from Sweden can become the market leader in electric vehicles," says Clean Air Transport spokesperson, Lars Kyrklund. "Even the large companies are. Maybe they didn't expect this whole market to open up this quickly."[47]

The L.A. Initiative, explains DWP assistant general manager Eldon Cotton, was supposed to be the "spark plug" that would finally energize the field of electric vehicles.[48] "What we expect to happen is that when Clean Air Transport demonstrates that this is successful, other car companies will jump into this market," Enzenauer adds. "[But] they're going to be four years behind."[49]

Meanwhile, circumstances have changed dramatically since Braude first cooked up this initiative. With California's clean air regulations to contend with, the major automakers can indeed no longer afford to ignore electric vehicles. Standards adopted in 1990 by the California Air Resources Board require that 2 percent of the cars sold in the state in 1998 be emission free. And for now, emission-free vehicles pretty much means electric vehicles. By 2003, the number of emission-free vehicles is required to rise to 10 percent of the new cars sold in California, about 200,000 vehicles. These standards, CARB spokesman Bill Sessa claims, are "setting a foundation for a whole new generation of cars."[50]

Twelve Northeastern states and the District of Columbia have expressed their intent to adopt California's regulations, specifying that 1 of every 10 cars sold in 2003 be emission free. These states, combined with California, account for one third of the nation's auto sales and constitute a huge market for electric vehicles. Such demand, says Michael Bradley of Northeast States for Coordinated Air Use Management, "should create economies of scale—and a substantial incentive for auto manufacturers to produce high-quality, low-emission vehicles." The rationale for the imposing new standards in the region is simple, Bradley explains. "If Detroit is going to manufacture very clean cars for sale in California, why not require the same clean cars in the Northeast?"[51]

The message finally seems to be getting through to Detroit. ''Without the environmental issues and the regulations in California, we probably wouldn't be moving the electric vehicle technology out of research,'' explains Roberta Nichols, director of electric vehicle programs at Ford. But carmakers will have to comply with the regulations if they want to sell any cars in California and other states which follow its lead. ''If you don't sell 2 percent in '98 as Zero Emission Vehicles, you can't sell the other 98 percent you want to sell,'' says Joseph Colluci, GM's head of fuel research.[52]

The appeal of electric cars owes much to their role in easing urban air pollution problems: no other vehicles, except for hydrogen cars, hold out the promise of zero tailpipe emissions. Beyond that, electric cars appear to be a decade or so closer to commercial readiness than their hydrogen counterparts.

Even though electric vehicles don't create any exhaust themselves, power plants obviously do. For this reason, the air quality benefits of electric cars will depend on how we produce the electricity that charges them. Assuming the current mix of generating capacity, OTA estimated that driving electric vehicles in place of gasoline ones would cut carbon monoxide and hydrocarbon emissions by 90 percent. Nitrogen oxides would stay roughly the same, depending on which type of power plants are relied on and how stringently they are controlled.[53] The California Council for Environmental and Economic Balance was even more optimistic, predicting 99 percent less carbon monoxide and reactive hydrocarbons and 80 percent less nitrogen oxides, assuming reliance on modern power plants.[54] Both groups concluded, however, that sulfur emissions—the main contributor to acid rain—would *rise* if coal-fired electricity replaces gasoline.

On balance, urbanites would breathe easier with an electric fleet because these vehicles emit no street-level air pollutants. In the Los Angeles area, where cars produce 70 to 80 percent of all air pollution, electric cars would drastically reduce smog, since 80 percent of the city's electricity is generated outside the L.A. basin.[55] The benefits would be especially great if most vehicles were recharged at night, since ozone (or smog) forms only when the sun is shining.

Greenhouse gas emissions would decrease if the U.S. fleet went electric, as long as coal did not become the dominant fuel. Mark DeLuchi of the University of California at Davis computes that carbon dioxide emissions would go down 40 percent if the mix of power plants in the United States remained about what it is today. A switch to solar-powered plants would cut carbon dioxide by 100 percent. The use of nuclear plants would lead to a 90-percent reduction, natural gas-fired plants to a 20-percent reduction, and coal plants to a 30-percent *increase*.[56] Clearly, transferring our allegiance to electric cars can greatly reduce the risk of global warming *if* we make intelligent choices about how the power to run them is generated.

Another draw is that electricity, save for some hydropower imported from Quebec, is entirely domestically produced, and enough excess power is available to fuel large numbers of electric cars. A study by the Electric Power Research Institute (EPRI), the research arm of the nation's utilities, found that 20 million electric cars could be supported without any additional power plants, so long as the cars were recharged at night, when there is a huge surplus of generating capacity.[57]

Other benefits would come from charging cars at off-peak, nighttime hours. First, the most efficient so-called baseload power plants can be used in place of costlier "peak power" facilities. Second, less smog will be created since, as we have noted, smog cannot form at night. Still, these benefits are strictly theoretical unless pricing policies and other incentives or restrictions are adopted to make sure that most people actually do their recharging after the sun goes down.

From an engineering standpoint, electric motors should last longer and cost less to maintain than gasoline engines, but batteries are still not durable and powerful enough to perform as well as gas-powered models, despite 100 years of research. Both Thomas Edison and Henry Ford abandoned electric vehicles because they could not solve the battery problem.

Standard lead-acid batteries, of the sort used in most conventional cars today, are so heavy that they typically restrict an electric vehicle's range to about 100 miles. Adding more batteries to extend the range can be a losing battle—most of the car's energy may be expended toting around batteries rather than people. Accessories such as air conditioning can drain 10 to 25 percent of a battery's power, further cutting the car's range.

Range can be stretched by making electric vehicles lighter, more streamlined and more efficient. Even so, limited range is not necessarily a fatal flaw since the average American driver goes only 15 to 35 miles a day, according to Donald Runkle, GM's vice president for advanced technology.[58] Electric vehicles may perform perfectly well as second cars for families, used for shopping, short commutes, and the like. (The electric may, in fact, become the "first" car, with a longer-range vehicle reserved for vacations.) The average home-to-work commute is only 8.5 miles, according to the Federal Highway Administration,[59] "and it takes place at an average speed of 31 mph," Peter Gray writes in the *Washington Monthly*. "For that trip, you don't exactly need the Batmobile."[60] Electric vehicles also make sense for urban delivery vehicles that go less than 100 miles in a day. Electric motors don't run when the vehicle is stopped, which makes such vehicles more efficient in stop-and-go city driving. Isuzu and CO-OP EV Development Corporation are developing a two-ton electric truck to put into service by 1994. CO-OP's goal is to replace its entire 10,000-truck fleet with electrics.

"Hybrid" vehicles—which include a small internal combustion engine and fuel tank—can extend the range of electric vehicles. The most efficient arrangement would be to run the engine at a constant speed, thereby acting as a generator for the battery. For short trips, the vehicle would run on the battery only. Ultimately, though, hybrids are compromises: unlike purely electric vehicles, they are neither emission free nor gasoline free.

Volkswagen's hybrid prototype, the Chico, has a range of 250 miles and a top speed of 81 miles per hour. This compact city car can seat two adults and two small children. General Motors' electric van prototype, the HX-3, uses a small gasoline generator, fed by a 10-gallon tank, to recharge the battery. Over short stretches, the van (which has a total range of about 300 miles) runs just on electricity.[61] So far, GM has not announced any plans to produce the HX-3.

Another GM prototype, the Impact, is entirely electric. Its ultra-efficient design provides a respectable range without the need for an auxiliary gasoline engine. The prototype was built for GM with the assistance of AeroEnvironment Inc., a Monrovia, California, company that also built GM's record-setting solar race car, the Sunraycer. The Impact, which is expected to cost between $15,000 and $30,000, has a maximum range of about 120 miles and a top speed of 100 mph. It can accelerate from 0 to 60 mph in eight seconds—faster than many sports cars. Its electric motor is about 95-percent efficient, and its regenerative braking system allows the motor to become a generator during deceleration, sending energy back to the batteries. The Impact is exceptionally streamlined—with a drag coefficient of 0.19, compared to about 0.30 for the most efficient gas vehicles on the road today. Its lightweight wheels encounter only half the rolling resistance of conventional tires. The car is propelled by an 870-pound set of 32 lead-acid batteries, which can be recharged in two to eight hours (depending on the extent of battery discharge and the voltage of the power source).[62]

The cost of driving the Impact largely depends on battery longevity. GM estimates the operating cost—including replacing the $1,500 batteries every two years or 20,000 miles—to be about twice that of a standard gasoline car. The company hopes to extend the battery's life so that within a few years operating costs will be competitive.[63] (As an auto fuel, electricity costs about the same as gasoline. It's the need to replace today's generation of lead-acid batteries every couple of years that makes it hard for electric vehicles to compete economically.)

When will GM's celebrated Impact, which was unveiled with great hoopla in 1990, finally make an impact? Eventually, the car will be built at a Lansing, Michigan, plant that used to turn out some 25,000 Buick Reattas per year. But for the moment, GM has not set a production date. Presumably, it is waiting until battery problems are ironed out.[64]

Batteries are clearly the critical, make-or-break factor affecting the performance and economic viability of electric cars. "Pure electric vehicles with half a ton of short-lived, expensive batteries will never be attractive for general use," claims Amory Lovins, an energy efficiency guru at the Rocky Mountain Institute in Snowmass, Colorado.[65]

Replacing lead-acid battery packs every 20,000 miles is like buying a couple of years' worth of gasoline in advance. To ease that financial burden, GM is considering leasing batteries and then recycling them. Recycling will keep toxic chemicals such as lead and cadmium from getting into the environment and will reduce the need to mine more materials.

Another challenge has been finding a way to recharge batteries in less than the eight hours it can now take. According to the OTA, high-current recharging systems that might do the job more quickly require expensive equipment and the use of experimental batteries.[66] A huge

---

BATTERY RECYCLING: BETTER LEAD THAN DEAD?

Car owners currently dump about 20 million dead batteries a year, each containing about 18 pounds of lead.[121] About 60 percent of all the lead that ends up in landfills or incinerators comes from car batteries. Unless precautions are taken, these numbers could grow tremendously as the use of electric vehicles expands.

To keep this problem within bounds, lead-recycling legislation has been proposed in Congress by Esteban Torres, a U.S. congressman from New Mexico. About 85 percent of car batteries are now recycled, according to Jonathan Kimmelman of the Natural Resources Defense Council. In about three dozen states, the law mandates this practice, though there is still no federal statute forcing anyone to recycle auto batteries.[122] In New York, for example, throwing car batteries in with conventional wastes is illegal. Car owners pay a deposit on batteries, which they collect when they turn them in at designated drop-off sites. The lead in the plates is then salvaged and reused.

Considering how ecologically devastating toxic wastes can be, Kimmelman believes recyclability should be a major criterion in determining what kinds of materials should be used for advanced batteries. The ideal battery would be capable of storing enough energy to propel a car hundreds of miles and also provide the bursts of power needed for adequate acceleration. But if this high-performance battery is made out of toxic materials that cannot be used again, it may not be used in the first place.

---

power source would also be needed, so quick recharges probably could not be done at home.

Overnight charging, on the other hand, could be done at home, perhaps using an ordinary electric socket. This approach may not work for many urban dwellers, who do not have garages. At the very least, new electrical outlets would have to be installed for those who park their cars in lots, driveways, and on the street. Battery swapping is another alternative. In this scenario, drivers would pull into a service station and have their battery replaced with a fully charged one, ideally in about the time it takes to fill a gas tank. One drawback is that this system would require an extraordinary degree of standardization so that batteries would be more or less interchangeable. Gas stations would need large inventories, which might be a problem in small towns with relatively few regular customers. The whole project would involve huge capital outlays and perhaps a complex financing scheme.

To come up with a high-performance advanced battery, the Big Three automakers announced plans in January 1991 for a "Manhattan Project–style" research effort that the Department of Energy, EPRI, battery makers, and Southern California Edison will also join.[67] The United States Advanced Battery Consortium will spend $260 million over the next four years in its search for a better battery.[68]

Meanwhile, engineers continue to experiment with numerous alternatives to the lead-acid battery. For example, Chrysler uses a nickel-iron battery in its electric mini-van, the TEVan, which has a range of 110 to 120 miles and can travel up to 70 mph.[69] The battery, about 30 percent lighter than the lead-acid variety, is supposed to last about 100,000 miles.[70] Nickel is expensive. The initial cost of the TEVan's battery is $6,000 to $10,000, three times more than a lead-acid pack would cost, but the hope is that a nickel-iron cell will last the lifetime of the vehicle—which is why Chrysler engineers are banking on it over the long run.[71] Chrysler has teamed up with Westinghouse in an effort to put an electric car with a 200-mile range on the market sometime in the 1990s.[72]

Ford, meanwhile, has developed an ETX II mini-van modeled after its European Escort van, which employs sodium-sulfur batteries—a technology that the company has been working on for 30 years. Ford plans to have 7,200 of these vans (which have a range of about 100 miles) on the road by late 1992.[73]

BMW has come out with its E1 prototype—a compact, four-passenger electric car with a range of 150 miles. The sodium-sulfur battery that powers this car weighs about 400 pounds—one fifth of the total vehicle weight—and can be recharged in six to eight hours. The E1 is a forerunner to electric cars BMW expects to have on the market by 1998, in time to meet California's zero-emission vehicle requirements.

The appeal of sodium-sulfur batteries is that they store four times more energy per pound than lead-acid cells do. This translates directly into increased range. Some laboratory tests suggest these batteries will be long-lived, lasting more than 100,000 miles. But other tests are much less encouraging. The biggest disadvantage is that sodium-sulfur batteries operate at extremely high temperatures—on the order of 700° F— so heavy-duty insulation is needed to keep the heat inside the battery and away from the rest of the car. Another engineering headache is that the battery must be kept near its operating temperature, no matter how long the car sits unused, because the battery deteriorates if its main ingredients freeze and thaw too often. Internal corrosion poses a further problem that may drastically curtail useful battery life.

Although sodium-sulfur cells may eventually prove practical, cooler batteries would clearly make life less complicated. Researchers at Texas A & M University are more inclined toward zinc-bromine systems, which operate at about 100° F. "The materials for these batteries look pretty cheap, but you never know until you build 100,000," says David Swan, assistant director of the Center for Electrochemical Systems and Hydrogen Research. In 1992, the center will have a battery ready that carries about twice the energy per pound as a lead-acid pack. The power density of zinc-bromine cells is comparatively low, however, which hurts acceleration. "This won't be the battery for a high-performance vehicle," Swan says. "It's not real sexy, not real fast. But it looks practical, and practical may win out in the end."[74]

In mid-1991, Nissan announced it had developed an electric car that can be fully recharged in 15 minutes—about eight times faster than its closest rival.[75] A short recharging time would make the car more attractive for long-distance driving. The car, the FEV ("future electric vehicle"), comes equipped with nickel-cadmium batteries that can be quickly recharged and can carry a car about 120 miles on a single charge. The FEV is 216 pounds lighter than the Impact, mainly because its batteries are lighter.[76]

Several automakers have been enticed by the performance record of nickel-cadmium cells. For example, an electric vehicle prototype built by the Tokyo Electric Power Company with this type of battery has a range of 310 miles.[77] Volkswagen uses nickel-cadmium batteries in two of its hybrid vehicles, the Chico and Eco-Golf. Peugeot is also investigating nickel-cadmium-powered electric vehicles.

Two critical problems restrict the use of cadmium, a byproduct of zinc production. The first is availability. "There is simply not enough cadmium around," notes battery expert Jim George, head of George Consulting International. He estimates that the entire world supply could support only 100,000 vehicles a year.[78] Further, cadmium is also a proven carcinogen that has been banned in Sweden and other countries—though this hazard can be minimized by recycling, which has already proven economically feasible in two European plants. In any event, nickel-cadmium batteries probably won't ever be more than an interim solution for just a small segment of the electric vehicle fleet.

The Ovonic Battery Company of Troy, Michigan, is betting on an alternative concept—a nickel–metal hydride battery that uses the same nickel electrode found in nickel-cadmium cells. The metal hydride electrode consists of an alloy blend of titanium, zirconium, nickel, vanadium, and chromium. "All of these metals are commonly available in large quantities," says Michael Fetcenko, the company's vice president of technology. "We can even use scrap metals from other industries. Moreover, all of these metals can be recycled back into batteries."[79] Apparently, the U.S. Advanced Battery Consortium agrees with Fetcenko. In May 1992, it awarded Ovonic an $18.5-million contract to further develop its battery for electric vehicle use. This EV battery should be rechargeable a thousand times and able to power a car 130 miles per charge.

Nickel-metal hydride batteries have more than twice the energy density of lead-acid ones, Fetcenko says. If the GM Impact ran on Ovonic's current battery, it could go 240 miles between charges. A more advanced battery now under development could yield a 300-mile range. Fetcenko claims the battery would last the lifetime of a vehicle. It operates at room temperature and can be recharged in 15 minutes. It is completely sealed and maintenance-free—"idiot-proof," according to Fetcenko.[80]

If he's right—and that's a big if, given the unmet promises that have stalled progress in the field for decades—Ovonic's nickel–metal hydride may prove to be the wonder battery that U.S. automakers have been waiting for. Jim George is not so sure, citing a potential drawback of high cost. For now, he is betting on lead-acid batteries, "which still look the best, even after decades of research on alternatives. That's kind of depressing because it means we have a long way to go."[81]

SOLAR CARS

Solar cars, simply put, are electric cars that derive some fraction of their energy from the sun. In this field, James Worden is a man to follow. Worden started making solar-electric go-carts in the fifth grade, and he's been making more glorified versions ever since. In high school, Worden moved on to solar cars, which he designed and raced— a pastime he has pursued through his undergraduate years at MIT and beyond. After racking up numerous victories—with first place finishes in the American Tour del Sol in May 1991 and the California Clean Air Race two months later—Worden is setting his sights on a more elusive prize, building a practical commuter car that people actually want to buy. "I enjoy racing," he says. "But right now we're concentrating on making this business viable."[82]

The vehicle for his vehicle is the Waltham, Massachusetts–based Solectria Corporation that Worden started in 1989, shortly after earning an undergraduate degree in mechanical engineering from MIT. By the time he was 24, he had already beaten GM and its much-vaunted Impact to the electric vehicle marketplace. His car, the Force, is a Geo Metro converted to run on lead-acid batteries powered by a combination of sunlight and electricity. Its motor is 98-percent efficient. The two-seat version of the Force, which sells for about $25,000, can travel up to 135 miles with a nickel-cadmium "range-extender." The four-seat model can go up to 90 miles.

Solectria put the Force on sale in May 1991 and sold eight that year. "It's better than any solar-electric car available today," Worden maintains—a claim also made by the California Air Resources Board. The company hopes to deliver about 50 vehicles in 1992. Solectria has also built two cars from scratch—the Flash and Lightspeed—that are superior to the Force in range and acceleration. Lightspeed, for instance, can travel 150 miles before needing a recharge. With the same range, the three-wheel Flash weighs only 860 pounds, 400 pounds of which are nickel-cadmium batteries.[83]

Worden maintains that the Force is already practical for commuters—a statement backed up by five years of continuous, on-road experience. In fact, he and Solectria president Anita Rajan drive the Force to work together, seven miles each day, from Arlington to Waltham. It costs only two thirds to three fourths as much to operate and maintain the Force—including the cost of electricity and replacing the batteries every four years—as a 50-mile-per-gallon Geo Metro, he claims.[84] The initial purchase price, however, is nearly three times as high. Worden figures a consumer would break even, due to the Force's lower operating cost, in about 12 years.[85]

The sticker price of the Force should drop when Solectria scales up production. Right now, cars are made about five at a time, but the company has the capacity to manufacture about 20 per month. By 1997, Worden hopes to have an assembly line cranking out 20 Forces (or its more advanced progeny) a week.

His own personal Force has photovoltaics, or solar cells—semiconductor devices that convert sunlight directly into electricity—mounted on the roof. This panel provides the Force with a free bonus: enough power to go eight miles after the car has been in the sun all day. The beauty of a solar car, Worden says, is that "if you're sitting in a traffic jam in the sun, this car isn't using power. It's gaining power. There's no pollution. No noise."[86]

At night, the car's battery pack is recharged by plugging it into an electric socket. Worden looks forward to a time when sunlight will supply all of a car's energy needs. For instance, solar panels at the workplace might charge up cars parked during the day, while panels installed on the garage at home charge storage batteries overnight for the next morning's commute.

On a grander scale, solar electricity generated in the desert or wind-generated electricity captured in the Great Plains might be fed into the power grid and distributed throughout the country. "Those are the only totally pollution-free ways to go," Worden says.[87] But even if the electricity comes entirely from coal-fired power plants, electric cars would still pollute far less than a gasoline car. Switching to these high-efficiency vehicles would reduce carbon dioxide emissions by about 30 percent if recharged from the average mix of fossil, hydro, and nuclear power plants.

Worden's vision is being played out on a small scale in the Swiss village of Liestal, where a solar park-and-ride facility opened in 1989. On sunny days, mini electric vehicles—very popular in Europe—can get a recharge from solar panels installed at the municipal parking lot. Roughly a dozen cars can get charged up at the same time.[88]

"The solar carport," the first solar parking facility in the United States, is scheduled to begin operating in July 1992 at the South Coast Air Quality Management District (AQMD) headquarters in Diamond Bar, California. Initially, five parking spaces will be equipped with plugs carrying electricity produced by a 3,000-square-foot array of solar cells directly to the car batteries. Excess electricity will be fed back into the normal power grid. This small-scale demonstration, it is hoped, will spur builders to erect structures at shopping centers and office parks. "By the year 2000, we'd like at least 10 percent of the electricity for California's electric vehicles to come from the sun," explains Nick Patapoff, project manager from Southern California Edison, the company that is building the AQMD carport. "Fortunately, this can be accomplished using only a small fraction of the space already available at business and shopping center parking lots."[89]

A Swiss company, ESORO AG, is developing an ultralight solar-powered car called the ESORO II. The 1,300-pound car could run entirely on solar energy, the company maintains. A stationary 50-square-foot photovoltaic array can provide enough energy for over 6,000 miles of travel a year, more than enough for a small city car.[90]

Although one-of-a-kind solar race cars have demonstrated that solar vehicles can go long distances—across the entire Australian continent (1,867 miles) in the case of Sunraycer—using nothing but sunlight falling on the vehicle's surface, this approach is impractical for everyday cars. In general, it makes better sense to place most of the solar panels on rooftops or other structures that have steady and direct access to sunlight, rather than on the cars themselves. With this arrangement, cars can be recharged wherever and whenever they are parked. A practical car simply doesn't have enough area for solar cells to power it more than a few miles per day, unless batteries are dramatically improved. Still, a small array of solar cells installed on the car could, according to a Jet Propulsion Lab study, extend and maybe even double the battery's life. In fact, stretching out the battery's life may ultimately matter more than extending the vehicle's range.

"It's really important that electric vehicle lead-acid batteries not sit all day in a discharge state," explains William Yerkes, founder of Arco Solar, the world's largest manufacturer of photovoltaic cells, which was recently purchased by Siemens of Germany. "A small amount of photovoltaics on the roof can start recharging the battery the minute you stop, if there's any sunlight at all.''[91] Installing a small photovoltaic panel on the car might cost about $1,000, he estimates, but that would be $1,000 well spent since the solar cell would last as long as the car and thus increase the longevity of several generations of batteries.[92]

In 1991, approximately 10,000 solar panels were installed on the roofs of conventional gas-powered automobiles in Europe. There they powered electronic accessories, ventilated car interiors on hot days, and charged batteries while the cars were sitting idle.[93] In the same year, Mazda also introduced solar-powered ventilators that reduce the buildup of hot air in parked cars, reducing the need for a blast of air conditioning when the driver returns.[94] Eventually, solar cells will do more for a car than simply run window ventilation units. "We will in due course find solar panels installed on perfectly nifty electric cars in American cities," Yerkes maintains. "The real question is will they be designed by American engineers in Detroit or imported?"[95]

HYDROGEN DREAMS

"Yes, my friends," Jules Verne wrote in 1874. "I believe that water will one day be employed as fuel, that hydrogen and oxygen which constitute it, used singly or together, will furnish an inexhaustible source of heat and light, of an intensity of which coal is not capable.''[96] At the time of Verne's musings, the United States was gradually embracing coal as its primary energy source. The nation then moved from coal to oil and natural gas—a shift toward fuels that had proportionately more hydrogen and less carbon. Given this progression, hydrogen enthusiasts argue that it's only a matter of time before pure hydrogen becomes the fuel of choice, just as Verne once prophesied.

Simple extrapolation should not be confused with destiny, however. Peter Hoffman, editor of *The Hydrogen Letter,* has heard grandiose predictions about this potentially clean and abundant energy source for more than two decades. "They didn't happen," he says.[97] But now he sees grounds for optimism:

• About 20 prototype Mercedes-Benz cars and vans now run on hydrogen fuel. These test vehicles, which have an average range of about 124 miles,[98] have collectively logged over half a million miles.

In 1997, hydrogen-powered Mercedes buses may begin transporting passengers in Hamburg.[99]

- BMW is currently testing two sedans that can go about 190 miles on a tankful of liquid hydrogen.[100] The company plans to have a fleet of 100 hydrogen vehicles on the road in the 1990s.
- Mazda's hydrogen-powered prototype, the HR-X, was unveiled at the Tokyo Motor Show in October 1991. Mazda expects to be able to mass-produce hydrogen cars by the end of the decade.[101]
- In June 1991, a converted Ford Fiesta powered by an electric battery and hydrogen fuel cell made its public debut in Harrisburg, Pennsylvania. The car, called Lasercel-1, was designed by Roger Billings, president of the Missouri-based Energy Innovations, Inc. Lasercel-1 has a reported range of 300 miles. It is the first motor vehicle to run on a fuel cell (which electrochemically combines oxygen from the air with hydrogen to produce electricity and water vapor), except for some early prototypes abandoned two or three decades ago.[102] The car and fuel cell represent the culmination of five years of research by Billings, sponsored partly by a $60,000 grant from the Pennsylvania Energy Office.
- A 500-kilowatt plant going up in West Germany will use solar-generated electricity to create hydrogen. West Germany and Saudi Arabia are erecting a similar 350-kilowatt facility near Riyadh.
- The European Community is spending $4.2 million to study the feasibility of making hydrogen from surplus hydroelectric power in Quebec. Tankers would transport the hydrogen across the Atlantic.

Hydrogen can also be used to heat buildings, another major use of fossil fuels today. And though hydrogen is the most abundant element in the universe, it cannot—unlike crude oil, natural gas, or coal—be pumped out of the ground or excavated from the Earth. Hydrogen simply does not occur in significant amounts on the Earth except in combination with other elements. Today, most hydrogen is derived from natural gas, but this supply is, of course, ultimately limited. Running cars on hydrogen derived from coal, a messy procedure, would approximately double greenhouse gas emissions compared to those stemming from gasoline use.[103] In the long run, probably the best way to "make" hydrogen is to pass an electric current through water—a process called electrolysis that is commonly demonstrated in junior high school science labs. Ideally, the electricity will be produced from clean, inexhaustible sources.

Hydrogen may at least partly solve a problem that has slowed the spread of renewable energy technologies for years—storing intermittent power from the sun or wind. Electricity generated by, say, windmills or photovoltaic arrays can be used to produce hydrogen that can in turn be stored in tanks or, on a larger scale, in depleted underground oil or gas wells. Later the hydrogen can be piped all over the country or continent. For long distances (greater than several hundred miles), transmitting hydrogen through pipelines is considerably less expensive than sending electricity through a wire. Long-distance transmission of hydrogen using pipelines is well established; Germany already has a 120-mile hydrogen pipeline in operation.[104]

Hydrogen is about as pristine as fuel can get. Burning it in modified internal combustion engines produces water vapor and minute quantities of hydrocarbons (from the crankcase) and nitrogen oxides. Vehicles powered by fuel cells would run even cleaner: the only significant byproduct would be water vapor.

Mention the word *hydrogen,* and many people immediately conjure up images of the Hindenburg—the dirigible that caught fire and burned in New Jersey in 1937. (There were 62 survivors and 35 fatalities; 27 of the deaths resulted from jumping from the airship.) Fortunately, OTA concludes, hydrogen is "not a particularly dangerous fuel."[105] If it leaks or spills, hydrogen disperses and evaporates much faster than gasoline, which minimizes the explosion hazard. Also in its favor: hydrogen is nontoxic and noncarcinogenic. The main thing holding back this pollution-free fuel is its high cost, claims John Appleby, an electrochemist who heads the Center for Electrochemical Studies and Hydrogen Research at Texas A & M University. Even liquid hydrogen derived from natural gas—the cheapest source right now, and the one that fuels NASA rockets and the space shuttle—costs 4.4 times more than gasoline at 1990 U.S. prices. Hydrogen produced from solar energy and electrolysis, Appleby says, is even more expensive.[106]

Princeton University physicists Joan Ogden and Robert Williams believe that breakthroughs in photovoltaic cells are changing the outlook. Thin, amorphous silicon cells offer one attractive long-term prospect for delivering low-cost electricity. By the year 2000, Ogden and Williams calculate, solar-generated hydrogen could sell for between $1.68 and $2.35 for the equivalent of a gallon of gasoline—less than what most Europeans now pay.[107]

Skeptics claim the costs will run much higher. Although hydrogen will not necessarily be cheaper than the alternatives, Ogden says, "in the long run, it's probably going to be in the same general ballpark. That means we don't have to be driven solely by economics, narrowly defined. In other words, if environmental costs are included in the price of fossil fuels, hydrogen will prove to be equal, if not cheaper."[108]

Even so, hydrogen-powered cars face practical difficulties. The biggest hurdle is finding a good way to store the fuel in the vehicle—a problem comparable to finding suitable batteries for electric cars. The easy answer would be storing pressurized hydrogen gas, but the tanks required are heavy and bulky. To get a decent cruising range, a car's trunk would have to be filled with gas tanks. Mercedes-Benz is placing its bets on metal hydrides, which appear to be the most promising storage option for gaseous hydrogen at the moment. Hydrides consist of powdered metal mixtures—including iron, nickel, titanium, vanadium, and manganese—that absorb hydrogen like a sponge soaks up water. When the hydride tanks are heated, hydrogen is released to the engine. Heat from exhaust gases can be used to "liberate" hydrogen from storage.

Unfortunately, metal hydride systems are heavy. A typical car unit might weigh about 800 pounds, only 1 to 2 percent of which is hydrogen. This weight restricts the range of hydride cars to about 100 miles. The Michigan-based Ovonic Battery Company claims to have developed an "amorphous" nickel hydride that can hold up to 7 percent hydrogen by weight. If confirmed, this development could greatly expand the potential range of hydrogen vehicles.[109]

To refuel hydrogen vehicles with metal hydride storage, hydrogen gas is fed into the storage tank through a hose. With Mercedes models, a water hose removes the heat generated when hydrogen is absorbed by the powdered metals. These refueling stops take only 10 to 15 minutes, but the process is slow compared to a gasoline fill-up. "It's the same problem with electric vehicles," Ovonic's Michael Fetcenko says.[110] Still, refueling hydride beds is simple enough, in principle, so that it could be done at home if hydrogen ends up being distributed by pipes, as natural gas is now.

Refueling headaches may be offset by another benefit: hydride systems offer a particularly safe way to store hydrogen because they aren't susceptible to major leaks. In a test conducted by U.S. army engineers, a hydride tank was fired upon by armor-piercing bullets. The barrage yielded only a pilot-light-sized flame that burned calmly for days. "The same test on a gasoline tank produced the kind of dramatic fireball that is usually only seen in Hollywood movie car-crash scenes," David Chandler reported in the *Boston Globe*.[111]

Another option is storing hydrogen as a liquid. Hydrogen doesn't liquefy until temperatures drop to $-423°$ F ($-253°$ C), which greatly complicates storing and distributing the fuel. But this is the approach used in BMW test vehicles. "It isn't simple to store liquid hydrogen at minus 250 degrees C in a car," admits Wolfgang Strobl, a hydrogen researcher at BMW. "On the other hand, nobody could imagine 20 years ago that even inexpensive cars would be equipped with computers."[112]

Liquid hydrogen storage systems are not much heavier than gasoline tanks. But the systems are five to six times bulkier, which will severely cut into vehicle space.[113] Liquid, or cryogenic, hydrogen steadily evaporates at a rate of about 2 percent each day, compared to 1 percent of gasoline lost in an entire month.[114] This "boil-off" creates a potential safety hazard for cars parked in confined spaces (where hydrogen gas could accumulate), as well as an economic loss.

All told, the technical difficulties of handling a liquid that must be kept at $-423°$ F (and is dangerous to contact) may make it impractical for the general public. "Who handles cryogenic hydrogen?" asks Philip Ross of the Lawrence Berkeley Laboratory. "NASA."[115] But BMW is developing a robotic pump that could take care of refueling. Under this scheme, a driver pulls into a service station, parks, and opens the fuel tank lid from inside. A robot does the rest.

An alternative to the cryogenic approach is to store hydrogen in the form of liquid ammonia. Ammonia, made by combining hydrogen and nitrogen, can be stored at room temperature. Hydrogen can be retrieved simply by heating the ammonia. William Avery of the Johns Hopkins Applied Physics Laboratory estimates that ammonia would cost half as much to make and store as liquid hydrogen, mainly because it does not require expensive refrigeration. Another plus is that a large ammonia industry already exists—over 100 million tons are produced worldwide

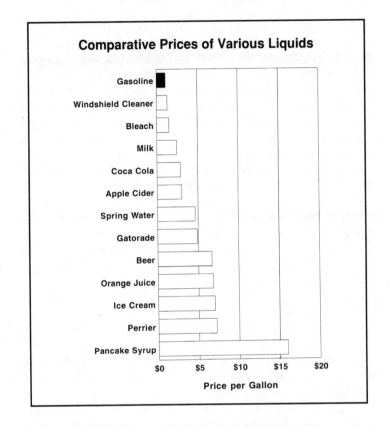

each year. Ammonia's smell and toxicity, though, are liabilities that will probably rule this liquid out as a day-to-day automotive fuel. But ammonia could still be an important fuel during an energy crisis, according to Philip Ross.[116]

No matter how hydrogen is ultimately stored, only fuel-efficient vehicles will be able to approach the range of today's conventional vehicles. Fuel cells offer the most dramatic improvements. They can convert up to 60 percent of hydrogen's fuel value into useful energy, which makes such a hydrogen-fueled engine about three times as efficient as a gasoline one.

The higher efficiencies made possible by fuel cells can compensate for the higher cost of hydrogen itself, so that hydrogen at the equivalent of $4.50 a gallon could compete with gasoline at $1.50 a gallon. In fact, inventor Roger Billings estimates, the costs of operating the Lasercel-1 are less than those for running a conventional car on gasoline at $1.12 a gallon. However, these and other claims relating to the Lasercel-1 have not yet been substantiated by independent testing. "People are wondering just how much the fuel cell is putting out, or whether the car is running mostly on batteries," one hydrogen expert confessed. "We hope Billings is right about the performance and cost figures, but no one really knows."

The consensus is that hydrogen technology won't be practical for another decade or two. Right now, fuel cells are quite expensive because they are used only for select applications like powering spacecraft. But if Billings is correct, hydrogen vehicles are much closer to commercial readiness than is generally acknowledged. Appleby of Texas A & M is another believer who doesn't consider current fuel cell costs an insurmountable obstacle: "If you went to a machine shop and asked them to make an internal combustion engine from scratch, it would cost about $100,000." Mass production, as he points out, has reduced that cost nearly a hundredfold. Similarly, he says, "there's no reason why hydrogen fuel cells shouldn't be economically viable, if you get them into mass production." The cells shouldn't cost more than internal combustion engines because they are made of plastics worth only about a dollar a pound.[117]

Large-scale projects that would drive up demand for fuel cells—subsidized, at least in part, by the federal government—could help drive down costs. But projects of this nature and magnitude have yet to materialize. "There is a terrible tendency in the United States to take the short-term view," notes Appleby.[118] Taking the long-term view, for a change, could lead the nation down a brave new road.

THE RECKONING

At the moment, only two demonstrated approaches—electric and hydrogen-powered vehicles—offer the hope of emission-free transportation without pouring additional greenhouse gases into the atmosphere. But neither hydrogen nor electricity can be considered nonpolluting unless they are derived from such clean energy sources as the sun or the wind.

It's possible that neither hydrogen nor electric vehicles will, despite their environmental merits, ever match gasoline models in certain measures of performance or cost. But the end of an era doesn't have to mean the end of the road. The "crisis" before us is largely cultural and perceptual; we may simply have to change our image of what a car looks like and does.

Just as the giant American cars of the 1960s are quickly becoming dinosaurs, so too may our current fleet of gas-powered cars become relics of a bygone era. "The car of the future"—a term that has traditionally meant bigger, better, or faster—may in fact deliver less rather than more. This modest car may not be able to travel hundreds of miles in a single bound. Instead, it is likely to be a lightweight (yet structurally sound), pollution-free vehicle eminently suited for the great majority of trips taken today—that is, jaunts on the order of tens of miles instead of hundreds. To the dismay of auto buffs, cars may be relegated to a basic transportation role. Rather than taking people places in style, they may just get them there.

Many questions remain unanswered. It's too early to tell, for example, which combination of hydrogen and electricity will work best. Perhaps electric vehicles will be confined, by and large, to city driving, while hydrogen becomes the fuel choice for longer-range applications or heavy-duty vehicles. It could be the other way around. Hydrogen and electricity may be combined on the same vehicle, as in the hybrid Lasercel-1. More specific questions regarding the best battery type or the best method of on-board hydrogen storage also await bankable solutions. But these uncertainties, and the extensive development work still needed, don't change the basic fact that only two vehicle types are capable of transporting us about without undermining national security or further degrading the environment.

Rather than settling for the first available alternative fuel, why not set our sights high, even if it means paying a little more to drive around than we are accustomed to? After all, what's the point in substituting a new fuel for gasoline which shares most, if not all, of its predecessor's drawbacks? Besides, as Joan Ogden of the Center for Energy and Environmental Studies at Princeton points out: "If you look at the costs of owning and operating a car, fuel accounts for only 10 to 20 percent of the total. The debate tends to focus almost exclusively on fuel prices, even though they are not that important to the consumer in the long run. And as cars become more efficient, fuel costs will become even less important."[119]

Even if hydrogen ends up costing somewhat more than gasoline, consumers might accept the increase if they knew they were paying for cleaner air and a more stable climate. After extensive research on consumer behavior, Daniel Sperling—a professor of civil engineering and environmental studies at the University of California at Davis—found that people may be "willing to adjust their behavior if there are clear messages from the government explaining why this option is needed."[120]

A similar economic and environmental case can be made for solar-electric vehicles—some of which are already cheaper to operate than standard gasoline models, though the initial purchase price is still much higher. On balance, electric vehicles may prove more efficient than hydrogen cars because electricity is needed to create hydrogen (via electrolysis), which is later converted back to electricity in fuel cells. Yet, no matter what mix of hydrogen and electricity we ultimately choose, it will take decades, at least, to complete the switch to a renewable energy-based transportation system.

In the meantime, it's important to do everything possible to improve fuel economy and reduce pollution. So-called clean gasoline—used in concert with efficient, well-tuned cars—can surely help. If needed, methanol and ethanol-derived additives can be used to stretch supplies of gasoline and make it burn cleaner. But, again, why spend hundreds of billions of dollars converting to a transportation system based on ethanol, methanol, or CNG—fuels that are not sustainable over the long haul? By the time we have paid for the sweeping infrastructure changes needed, we would soon have to make yet another wrenching (and perhaps bankrupting) switch to renewable-fuel vehicles.

Although the precise course is still unclear, we now know at least roughly what our long-term destination is, or rather our means to that end—electric or hydrogen vehicles. So why not get it right the first time, thus avoiding a costly and unnecessary intermediary step? As the noted scholar Evel Knievel once said, "You can't jump a canyon in two leaps."

The Road Not Taken

Right now, primarily what we've got are some
bus systems and a road system, but we don't
have a transportation system.

NORTON YOUNGLOVE,
South Coast Air Quality Management District

We enjoy the most advanced mass transit
system in the world—the private automobile,
which gets you from where you are to where
you want to go. And when distances are longer,
you drive to the airport.

JOHN BRADLEY,
management consultant, New York City

Imagine a city without traffic jams or smog. One with elevators and walkways powered by solar electricity, but no cars. One where 6,000 residents live together in energy-efficient dwellings, spaced closely enough so that everything people need is within comfortable walking distance. The idea is to stem the inexorable creep of fringe development so that the urban area can be surrounded by miles of beautiful landscape rather than an endless string of gas stations, car washes, and hamburger outlets.

More than two decades ago, Paolo Soleri, visionary architect and philosopher, started building such a community in the Arizona desert, 65 miles north of Phoenix. Soleri considers this project, called Arcosanti, an antidote to urban sprawl and pollution. Denser than New York City or Delhi, India, the complex as planned would occupy only 2 percent of the land that would be devoted to a typical suburban community of the same population.[1]

In the early 1970s, students and pioneers in alternative lifestyles descended on the desert en masse to help make Soleri's dream a reality. Today, with a skeleton work crew, only 50 full-time residents, and the city less than 5 percent complete, the 72-year-old Soleri has had to scale down his conception dramatically.² It exists primarily as an off-beat tourist attraction, and the odds are that the city as originally conceived will never be finished.

Despite its potential environmental merits, Arcosanti is not now considered fashionable or practical. On the other hand, as Arcosanti wanes, people continue to flock to Southern California by the millions, making roads there among the nation's most crowded and the air some of the least breathable. One might argue that that particular slice of life is not working out so well either.

The ineluctable truth is that we have got to hit upon new means of getting from here to there besides noisy machines that convert fossil fuels into dangerous pollutants. Assuming, optimistically, that we manage to mass-produce noise-free, pollution-free, solar-powered cars, we will still need to find ways to bypass the enveloping quagmire of urban gridlock. That will mean less driving and greater reliance on mass transit, bicycling, and walking. Creating a balanced, effective transportation system will require a fundamental transition perhaps as dramatic as the one from horse to motorcar.

It is not realistic to propose eliminating cars, which are clearly destined to figure centrally in the nation's transportation future. The idea, instead, is to create a host of attractive alternatives, so that a person needing a newspaper or a gallon of milk—or a convenient way to get to work—won't automatically hop into a car. As things stand right now, according to Rutgers University urban planner John Pucher, "for the vast majority of Americans, the alternative to the automobile is immobility."³

This arrangement is socially unfair as well as environmentally unfriendly: many of the people who most need the services an automobile can provide—elderly and disabled people who cannot make their way by bike or foot—are often unable, or ineligible, to drive. Poor people who cannot afford cars often have no way of getting to jobs in the suburbs.

We need real choices in urban and suburban transportation, not the usual debate over which car to take to the shopping center. "Just as an ecological system is healthiest when it displays great diversity and differentiation, so too is a transportation system most healthy and robust when diverse modal options are available to those moving people or goods," says Michael Repogle of the Institute for Transportation and

Development Policy in Washington, D.C. ''A transportation system dependent on only one or two modes of transport is far more susceptible to disruption and system failures.''[4]

This fine argument notwithstanding, most people will still choose to drive a car unless given good reason to do otherwise. If we are stuck with cars and stuck with roads, where do we go from here?

MORE ROADS, MORE TRAFFIC

Building more roads, or widening existing roadways, has been the traditional response to traffic problems. History shows, however, that this approach leads only to increased traffic and lower air quality. Congestion forces people to alter their travel routes and to avoid, if possible, driving at peak travel times. New roads may initially alleviate congestion, but soon encourage people to shift from other routes, or from other modes of transport, until the new roads are as badly congested as the old ones were.

Residents of Berkeley and Emeryville, California, opposed the widening of a local segment of Interstate 80 for this reason. California's Department of Transportation (Caltrans), the state agency that supported the project, admitted that the additional lanes would spur suburban development, which in turn would generate more traffic, eventually bringing speeds on the highway back down to the current snail's pace.[5] The project has been tied up in controversy for three years.

On the other side of the country, testifying before Maine's board of environmental protection, transportation consultant Thomas Adler argued that enlarging a 30-mile stretch of the Maine Turnpike from four to six lanes would simply add more cars and trucks to rush-hour traffic and strain already overburdened secondary roads. Citing previous highway construction projects, including the widening of Interstate 89 near Burlington, Vermont, Adler said, ''one of the immediate effects is a substantial increase in peak-hour traffic.''[6]

Although highway congestion is a major headache for everyone concerned, it serves at least one useful function: fear of gridlock helps regulate rush-hour traffic. For example, when contemplating a drive to northern New England during holiday weekends, Adler says, ''everyone considers congestion [in deciding] whether to leave Boston at

© 1989 USA Today. Reprinted with permission.

3 [P.M.] or 8.'' On the basis of that testimony, E. Christopher Livesay, chairman of the state's environmental board, concluded that the current four-lane Maine Turnpike constituted ''something of a benign and almost beneficial bottleneck.''[7]

Australian researchers Peter Newman, Jeffrey Kenworthy, and T. J. Lyons discovered that road-building projects designed to make traffic free flowing can save fuel and reduce emissions for individual vehicles, but from the standpoint of an entire city, and an entire city's cars, they do just the opposite. Their analysis of 32 cities around the world revealed that ''cities with the most constrained traffic flow have the lowest per capita gasoline use,'' and, consequently, the lowest vehicular emissions.[8] Apparently, where traffic flows freely, so does pollution.

While logic unequivocally dictates against further road construction, citizen action often speaks even more forcefully. New York's Westway project—a major artery that would parallel the Hudson River in Manhattan—was canceled by court order after a drawn-out legal debate. The court sided with environmentalists, who claimed that construction would damage the habitat of striped bass in the Hudson.[9] The 17-mile Century Freeway project in Los Angeles was delayed for 10 years by lawsuits before construction was finally allowed to begin at a cost of $100 million per mile.[10] More than 6,000 homes were destroyed to clear a path for the new road. It's the same old story; experts concede that the new freeway will be jammed from the day it opens in 1993.[11]

Shortages of money (in many cases, the final arbiter of these disputes) and the unavailability of land all but rule out major new roads in this country, especially when nobody seems to have the funds needed to keep the roads we already have in good repair. The U.S. network of interstate highways, initiated in 1956, "is a middle-aged system that's beginning to show symptoms of age," says Stephen Lockwood of the Federal Highway Administration (FHWA). More than 25 percent of the interstates are now, or soon will be, in poor shape.[12]

A 1991 Department of Transportation report appraising 1.2 million miles of U.S. highways and major arteries rated 643,000 miles of pavement in "poor" or "low fair" condition. Bridges are in the most dire shape, with 226,000 of the country's 577,000 bridges classified as either "structurally deficient" or "functionally obsolete."[13]

Traffic Abatement

With road-building or -widening projects often prohibitively expensive, city planners are scrambling to find new ways to get traffic moving. Experience gained during the 1984 Olympic Games in Los Angeles shows that traffic management techniques can make a difference. A combination of measures kept vehicles on the freeways moving along at 55 miles an hour, despite an 11-percent boost in the number of vehicles on the road. This seemingly amazing feat was accomplished by altering work schedules, limiting hours when delivery trucks were allowed to use the freeways, and making additional parking spaces and bus service available at freeway entrances.[14]

Technology is also being enlisted in the war against traffic. For example, some highways in Chicago, Los Angeles, Minneapolis, and other metropolitan regions have electronic sensors embedded in the pavement to provide nonstop monitoring of traffic volume and speeds. When highways become too clogged, stoplights placed on the entrance ramps delay the advance of incoming vehicles.

Since stalled or damaged vehicles cause half of the bumper-to-bumper traffic crunches, Chicago's highway authority employs a mobile crane that can remove 60-ton obstructions from the roads. (So far the giant instrument, known as Mad Max, has hoisted everything from a fish-tailed truck to a corn-fed hog.) Television cameras installed on Interstate 66 and Interstate 395 in Virginia provide instant knowledge of breakdowns to traffic officials, who then alert tow-truck operators.[15]

In a small room filled with computers, transportation officials in Los Angeles oversee traffic problems on the region's freeways. Reams of data on pileups, jam-ups, tie-ups, accidents, curiosity factors, and abandoned vehicles are fed into computers in this traffic control room, considered among the most technologically advanced in the country. A small fraction of this information is relayed back to motorists via the radio or electronic signs installed along the highways.

In the basement of City Hall, just three blocks away, a separate computer system operated by the Los Angeles Department of Transportation monitors conditions on the secondary streets. ATSAC, the Automated Traffic Surveillance and Control system, started up several weeks before the 1984 Olympic Games began. At the time, 396 detectors were installed in a four-square-mile area with 118 intersections. The system, since expanded to encompass 800 intersections, is eventually expected to include 4,000.

Of course we can't unclog congested thoroughfares simply by looking at them. Nevertheless, detailed monitoring of vehicular flow patterns does afford traffic engineers valuable lessons, and mathematicians are theorizing about the dynamic interactions occurring on the nation's roadways. *New York Times* writer James Gleick, author of the bestselling *Chaos*, explains:

"Herds of cars, like schools of fish, produce strangely complex behavior with patterns that are largely invisible to the individual participants or the victims. Computers are just beginning to make it possible to understand the peculiar patterns of congested flow—

bunching and clustering on dense roadways, rolling 'shock waves' that can instantly shut down the flow, the ghostly tie-up that lingers long after the cause has been removed.''[16]

Models have shown, for instance, that highways function optimally at 30 to 40 miles per hour. Although individual trips take longer at these reduced speeds, vehicles can bunch together more tightly, increasing the total number of cars, trucks, and buses that the road can handle. Fuel efficiency also rises if speeds can be kept within that range with stops and idling held to a minimum.[17]

Models also indicate a straightforward way to enhance the flow on side streets simply by adjusting the time it takes for a traffic signal to go from green to red and back to green again at a controlled intersection. In many cases, traffic will move more smoothly by trimming a one-minute cycle to 45 seconds. "Unfortunately, a lot of the way traffic engineers do things is by custom rather than by logic," notes Gordon Newell, a transportation theorist at the University of California at Berkeley.[18]

At least some traffic managers are gradually beginning to take advantage of insights gleaned from recent research. For example, when congestion in central Manhattan reaches a critical threshold, computers initiate a coordinated response in an array of traffic lights to discourage more motorists from piling up in the city's core. ATSAC computers in Los Angeles automatically select (and switch) the timing of traffic signals at any of the hundreds of intersections under the system's control. For instance, when traffic at a stoplight starts backing up in one direction, the green light is then set to run for a longer period until the problem is alleviated. Closed-circuit television cameras have been installed at the busiest intersections, enabling operators to observe unusual incidents and see how well the system is performing.

A 1987 evaluation of ATSAC noted the following benefits: a 13-percent decrease in travel time, a 35-percent decrease in the number of stops, a 15-percent increase in average speed, a 12-percent decrease in fuel consumption, and a 10-percent decrease in vehicle emissions. The system's $5.6 million construction cost was recovered—in terms of net savings to motorists (reduced fuel and maintenance costs, and saved time)—within the first eight months of operation. Savings accrued in one week cover annual operating expenses.[19]

High-Tech Tolls

America's roads and highways, carrying far greater loads than they were designed for decades ago, are crumbling beneath us. With public funds dwindling, pay-as-you-go toll roads are one way to cover maintenance costs, particularly on crucial bridges and tunnels. The Bush administration, in fact, has encouraged more states to consider establishing toll roads rather than relying on federal funding. The biggest drawback of this approach is that traditional toll booths, located on the nation's busiest thoroughfares, create bottlenecks and their inevitable companion, air pollution.

Advanced toll-collection systems—recently introduced in New Orleans, San Diego, Detroit, Philadelphia, Dallas, New York City, and New Hampshire, with others being tested or planned in New York, New Jersey, Pennsylvania, Denver, and Orlando—offer some hope for the harried commuter. These systems typically employ a credit card–sized device that is attached to the windshield. Scanning machines that resemble the bar-code scanners used in grocery stores read the code for each passing vehicle, and drivers are billed for toll charges.

Driving at speeds of 25 miles per hour or more, cars pass through such automatic toll facilities in less than a second, as compared to about 12 seconds at staffed booths (not counting the time spent in line waiting to reach the booth). The time savings mean fewer idling engines and fewer vehicular emissions. Air pollution was a principal reason for creating an automatic collection system for a bus lane in New York's Lincoln Tunnel.[20] Conversely, alarm over increased emissions caused by traffic jams forced officials to close conventional stop-and-go toll booths on a Staten Island bridge.[21]

Smart Cars, Smart Highways, Average People

Futurama, a General Motors exhibit at the 1939 New York World's Fair, presented a visionary look forward at American life in 1960. About 28,000 visitors a day toured this brave new world, explained to them by an unseen voice emanating from their roving chairs. Futurama's centerpiece was the 1960 Express Motorway—a seven-lane, one-direction highway that whisked along tightly packed chains of cars at speeds up to 100 miles per hour. Traffic was monitored by a control tower that beamed instructions via radio. "Safe distance between cars is maintained by automatic radio control,"[22] the mysterious chair-voice proclaimed. "Is this motorway actually the roadway of 1960? Perhaps. We only know that the world moves on and on, and that the highways of a nation are what set the pace for advancing civilization."[23]

A few decades later, 1960 came and went, and the realization of GM's dream—now referred to as "smart highways"—was still at least a generation away. Nevertheless, some progress has been made.

The first and simplest step toward bringing Futurama closer to the present is providing up-to-the-minute information to drivers to help them avoid the worst traffic deadlocks and find the best alternative routes. "We're not going to expand our highways system significantly, so we've got to learn to use it better," explains Jerry Baxter, Caltrans regional director in Los Angeles. "We are confident that if drivers have complete information, they will make wise commute decisions."[24]

With this idea in mind, in May 1991 a company called SmartRoute Systems began offering Boston subscribers the last word on traffic conditions on various thoroughfares. Commuters can hear about the most promising routes by telephoning the service from their home before they start their engines or by dialing from cellular car phones. "In a way we're selling behavior modification—getting people to change their habits by calling for traffic information," explains company head John Liebesny.[25]

TravelPilot—a navigational unit manufactured by ETAK, a Menlo Park, California, company—is being used in a $1.8-million demonstration project called Pathfinder, sponsored by Caltrans, the U.S. Department of Transportation, and General Motors. The program, which went on-line in the fall of 1990, feeds traffic data—gathered by sensors on a 12-mile stretch of the Santa Monica Freeway and five parallel arteries—from a central computer to the navigational systems of 25 specially equipped Oldsmobile Delta 88s. The information is displayed on the car's computer screen or conveyed in digitized voice messages. The program's major objective, according to Caltrans, is to determine whether it actually helps drivers avoid frustrating traffic snarls.

A larger $8-million project called TravTek was scheduled to begin in Orlando, Florida, in 1992. In this scheme, 100 cars equipped with computerized displays receive instantaneous traffic updates and detour instructions from a central traffic command post. TravTek, unlike the more limited Pathfinder, will cover the entire Orlando metropolitan area.

Even more ambitious projects are under way in Europe, many of them sponsored by Prometheus, an eight-year, $800-million effort launched in 1986 by 12 major European carmakers, more than 70 universities and research institutes, and more than 100 electronics companies. In West Berlin, for example, route guidance information on nearly 2,000 miles of roads is provided to the drivers of some 700 cars. In London, about 2,000 drivers obtain a competitive edge with the help of a similar high-tech system called Trafficmaster.[26]

The next step involves going beyond simply providing information to drivers. The idea is to speed up traffic by eliminating the stop-and-go patterns typical on congested roadways. Highway lanes of the next century, according to proponents of IVHS ("intelligent vehicle highway systems"), will transport regularly spaced lines of vehicles that move in synchrony, like cars on a high-speed train. Before entering freeways, drivers (soon to become passengers) will punch in their destinations on their on-board computers, a process just like programming a microwave oven or VCR. They can then sit back and relax while their autos pilot along on autopilot.

Volkswagen researchers in Wolfsburg, West Germany, have already sent cars down an experimental stretch of automated roadway. Computerized navigational systems, making use of radar and sonar signals, prevent collisions between vehicles and keep cars in their respective lanes. For example, radar devices installed in one vehicle measure the distance to the vehicle ahead and then maintain a constant speed and safe interval behind it. All the functions normally handled by human operators—steering, acceleration, braking (and perhaps, someday, swearing)—are controlled automatically. Because electronic systems can react faster than people, radar-equipped cars can be packed very close together.

An experimental program called PATH (Program for Advanced Technology for the Highway), like the Volkswagen effort, is being road-tested on special freeway lanes in San Diego. Two cars speed by, the second crowding the first in what appears to be the most flagrant case of tailgating on record. But the second driver never even touches the gas pedal or the brakes; a radar system holds his car just behind the bumper of the leader. Automated steering is guided by a wire embedded in the road.

A 4-car pack was tested in 1991 to determine how swiftly, closely, and safely these caravans can run on remote control highways. The next goal will be to test a fleet of 15 cars electronically locked in tight formation. A demonstration of a 15-car "platoon," if successful, will still be a modest step toward a fully automated highway crammed with vehicles darting on and off, streaming along at dizzying speeds. Some experts predict that another 25 to 50 years will pass before that goal— essentially the vision depicted in Futurama more than a half-century ago—will be realized.

While traffic control measures might reduce congestion by 10 to 15 percent, smart highways could increase the flow of traffic three-, four- or fivefold, according to Adib Kanafani, director of the University of California's Institute of Transportation Studies.[27] Another advantage of traveling in closely bunched platoons is that each vehicle has approximately 40 percent less wind resistance to overcome, which makes fuel savings of 10 to 20 percent possible.[28]

If smart vehicle and smart highway technology can be perfected and put into widespread use, will drivers be able to assimilate the deluge of information transmitted to them? Will drivers voluntarily relinquish control of the gas pedal and brakes, becoming mere pawns in a remote-control system? Will people sit passively in a stream of cars spaced only a few feet apart, going perhaps 80 miles per hour, without panicking? "We don't know," Kanafani says. "We're doing research to find out."[29]

Other questions arise over the dissemination of information. Obviously, drivers of the specially outfitted Olds 88s who learn of a major bottleneck on the Santa Monica Freeway can pull off at an earlier exit and avoid the mess. That might work fine for the 25 cars in the Pathfinder experiment, but what if every car on the freeway is privy to this information? How long would the alternative route remain the alternative route if every car on the freeway pulled onto it?

Traffic agencies will have to answer similar questions as our highways become more "intelligent." To further the flow of traffic, officials may have to hold back on the flow of information. "Telling the traffic truth, the whole truth, and nothing but the truth could prove a recipe for gridlock," technology writer Michael Schrage says. Stephen Ritchie, a civil engineer at the University of California at Irvine, agrees: "From a theoretical point of view, there may be times [when it's] better to withhold information."[30]

If that turns out to be the case, drivers will be forced to play a guessing game about as impossible to win as the blindfolded game they play today. For all the millions or billions of dollars spent, how much better off will we be?

Advocates maintain that automated highways will be much safer than our current mayhem on wheels. They point out that over 90 percent of accidents today are caused by human error. However, computerized systems pose the potential for disasters on a scale seldom witnessed before on our roads. When accidents do occur, they are more likely to resemble airplane crashes than run-of-the-mill fender-benders. "If something goes wrong, you could have 200 cars in a crash," and you could sue at least three parties—the other drivers, the automaker or electronics manufacturer, and the highway department—claims Kan Chen of the IVHS program at the University of Michigan.[31]

The liability issue is an important consideration; operators of automated highway systems would be held to much more stringent standards than those usually expected of drivers. James Womack, an automobile industry expert from MIT, says, "The presumption is that it's quite okay for 50,000 people a year to be killed by cars driven by humans, but the number of people that can be killed by cars driven by computers is vanishingly small."[32]

But perhaps the least inviting aspect of smart systems is that like new highway construction they might lead us in exactly the wrong direction. For example, if high technology increases highway capacity, more people will probably elect to drive. Eventually even the most intelligent road will be able to offer its passengers only a slow crawl. "These systems are sexy and attract a lot of money and attention, but in some ways they get us deeper into the soup by perpetuating a one-man, one-car syndrome" and by ignoring such alternative approaches as car pools and mass transit, says Ronnie Lipschutz, a political scientist at the University of California at Santa Cruz. "The smart car is technology that doesn't address the fundamental societal problems of traffic, congestion, and driving patterns."[33]

Encouraging the public to shell out hundreds, even thousands of dollars for the latest navigational aids is a misguided strategy that "ignores the social and environmental costs of an astronomical growth in the number of autos on our highways," argues Lipschutz and Linda Nash, his colleague at the Pacific Institute, a Berkeley-based environ-

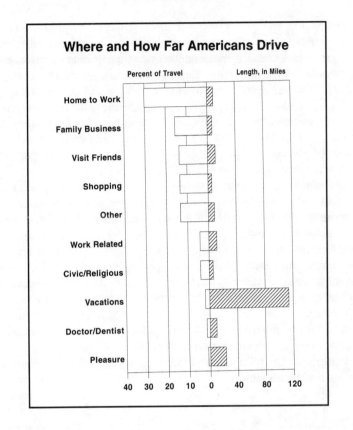

Where and How Far Americans Drive

mental think tank. "All that smart cars will really do is make it possible to put off, once again, the politically difficult decision to invest in urgently needed regional transit systems."[34]

DETERRENTS TO SOLO DRIVING

Congestion nightmares and insalubrious air are byproducts of U.S. policies that have consistently promoted private automobiles at the expense of alternative forms of transport. "We've made a massive commitment to autos, especially those with only one or two people in them," says Richard Kiley, chairman of the New York Metropolitan Transit Authority until early 1991. "Now we're paying the price."[35]

Rather than trying to cram ever more vehicles onto existing roadways, it makes sense first to try cramming ever more passengers into existing vehicles and then to find ways to get people to drive less. Ideally, we will create transportation options convenient, economical, and comfortable enough that would-be drivers will eagerly abandon their cars. Realistically, though, disincentives that make traveling alone in a car (particularly during peak traffic periods) a less attractive proposition may also be needed. As long as solo commuting offers some practical advantages—including the only privacy some people ever get—most drivers will rather fight than switch.

Unfortunately, no single measure can solve all our transportation problems. Car pools offer obvious benefits, but work only when two or more people are going from the same general starting point to the same general destination at the same general time. In many regions, mass transit systems seem ill-equipped to service the disjointed, sprawling communities that auto-induced mobility helped to create. Urban planning, though essential, can't undo the chaotic maze of homes, commercial buildings, and roads already set in concrete foundations.

The best we can hope for is a combination of steps that can ease to some extent the related problems of air pollution, congestion, and urban sprawl. Long-range planning can make future residential and commercial developments follow reason rather than the fitful meanderings of gasoline-powered vehicles.

Double or Nothing

Ride sharing became popular during the Arab oil crises of the 1970s, when gasoline prices began skyrocketing and lines at filling stations extended around the block. As gas prices started to decline, however, so did enthusiasm for this sociable form of commuting. From 1977 to 1990, the average number of people riding in a vehicle went down from 1.9 to 1.5, according to a Department of Transportation survey.[36] Whereas 33 percent of all U.S. commuters who drove to work in 1980 traveled in car pools, only 22 percent did so in 1990.[37] Today, out of the roughly 93 million working Americans who commute by car, more than 70 million drive to work alone.[38]

"The reasons are many and maybe predictable," explains Calvin Sims in the *New York Times*.

Some commuters drive alone because they want to be able to leave work early or stay late and not be bothered by someone else's schedule. Some want their own cars on hand so that they can run errands at lunch, or depart immediately in case of family emergencies. Some want to listen to *their* favorite radio stations. Some want to drive as fast, or as slow, as they please. And some, if not most, find the notion of carpooling to be, at bottom, positively alien to their unfettered get-in-the-car-and-go American individualism.''[39]

Steadily deteriorating road conditions are again forcing officials to consider the benefits of doubling up. The arithmetic is elementary: if every car carried two persons rather than one, traffic and pollution would be cut in half. Van pools can make an even bigger dent. Every full van, according to the American Public Transit Association, removes 13 cars from the road.

Los Angeles traffic managers hope to eliminate 1.5 million car trips daily through ride sharing. The South Coast Air Quality Management District (AQMD) has instituted perhaps the most ambitious such program to date. Under the plan known as Reg 15, AQMD employees are rewarded with bonuses of up to $85 per month for taking car pools, van pools, or mass transit. Carpoolers can also receive free parking bonuses. The effort has raised the average occupancy in AQMD employee vehicles from 1.2 to 1.75 persons per car.[40]

Starting in 1991, all businesses in the region with more than 50 employees were required to implement ride-sharing measures that will eventually boost occupancy to 1.5 persons per car. One California hospital decided to open an express lane for carpoolers in its cafeteria, as an added incentive. "We don't care how they make it work, as long as it works," says AQMD spokesman Tom Eichorn.[41] Failure to comply by the deadline (which varies depending on the size of the company) can earn offending companies fines of up to $25,000 per day or possible imprisonment of company officers.[42]

In Santa Monica, city employees can take unmarked police cars home at night if they carpool to work; those who walk to the job can obtain free running shoes. Chiat/Day Advertising in Venice offers tickets to L.A. Dodgers or Kings games as incentives for carpooling. Workers at Capitol Records in Hollywood can receive free CDs, tapes, sweatshirts, and movie passes if they share rides. Capitol also subsidizes the cost of mass transit passes. As a result, the average occupancy of employee cars has gone up from 1.02 to 1.25.[43]

Hughes Aircraft, the Los Angeles basin's biggest employer, spends $500,000 a year on what is possibly the world's largest ride-sharing program. Yet in 1989, 10 years after the program started, only 19 percent of the employees were riding in car pools, even though the company provided a fleet of 302 vans for them to share and offers rides home in case of emergency. A poll revealing that 60 percent of the employees would not even consider giving up the comfort and freedom afforded by private automobiles should scarcely be surprising, with gas at little more than $1.00 per gallon.[44]

City authorities throughout the country can encourage ride sharing without relying on employer practices by establishing high-occupancy vehicle (HOV) highway lanes restricted to buses, vans, or cars carrying three or more passengers. Today about 1 percent of all major U.S. highways have such lanes. Commuters who make use of a 10-mile HOV stretch in Houston shave 20 to 30 minutes off their trip, while saving fuel in the process.[45] In Santa Clara County, California, commuting times have been cut in half for HOV lane users and cut by 10 percent or more for riders in adjacent lanes. Drivers who follow the 12-mile HOV lanes from Springfield, Virginia, to Washington, D.C., on Interstate 95 routinely cut about 15 minutes off the one-way trip— an average of more than one minute saved per mile.[46]

Although traditional car pools can in theory reduce traffic delays by 50 to 75 percent, they suffer from many limitations, according to Robert Behnke, an Oregon-based transportation consultant. "It requires too much planning. And if something happens to your ride, you have no alternative." Behnke has an idea, called parataxi, to get around these deficiencies. Suppose you're working in a downtown office and have space in your car for a few passengers for the return ride. You tap into a computer network, leaving word of your workplace, destination, and departure time. The computer then hooks you up with a couple of other riders (among thousands enrolled in the system) whose starting point, end point, and departure time most closely match yours. For your trouble, you're rewarded with a parking bonus, plus access to the speedy HOV lanes on the return trip. Behnke's plan is being tested by Caltrans at six sites in California.[47]

Any system that offers rewards or shortcuts is bound to attract unscrupulous types trying to exploit the system. HOV lanes, accordingly, are ripe targets for abuse. Highway Patrol officers on the San Francisco Bay Bridge, for example, have witnessed every variety of deception; commuters have transported papier-maché dummies and even bogus caskets to secure passage on the diamond-marked express lanes.[48]

Although HOV lanes work reasonably well on highways leading to urban centers, they are less effective in handling the bulk of commuters traveling from suburb to suburb. In intersuburban travel, the number of possible routes is essentially limitless, making it hard to find two commuters heading exactly the same way and harder still to justify setting aside a special lane for them. This brings up another drawback of HOVs—the lane almost invariably ends as soon as the driver pulls off the freeway, leaving little ride-sharing incentive for travelers who spend the bulk of their time on arterial routes.

An extensive network of HOV lanes might convince more motorists to double, triple, or quadruple up, but lanes have been discontinued in some places owing to vehement citizen backlash. Apparently, some motorists believe they should not be discriminated against just for exercising their inalienable right to drive a car in the same way John Wayne rode a horse—alone.

Congestion Pricing

An attack on the pocketbook often hits harder than impassioned moral (or logical) pleas. That's the basic idea behind so-called variable pricing strategies—charging people for driving during the most congested periods, in the same way that electricity and telephone users pay more for services rendered during peak hours.

The goal is to encourage motorists to eliminate inessential travel or to drive at off-peak times. The potential for shifting travel times appears considerable: one study found that drivers making non-work-related trips outnumbered commuters during morning rush hour on L.A. freeways. During the evening rush hour, commuters were outnumbered nearly three to one.[49]

"At the very time when most people want and need mobility—during the morning and evening peak periods—the system actually carries fewer of them than it does at various off-peak times," say Michael Cameron, author of a 1991 study for the Environmenta fense Fund and the Regional Institute for Southern California. During off-peak hours, when freeway traffic actually flows freely, about 30 cars per lane may pass a given spot in a minute, compared to only 20 during congested periods. To alleviate this traffic crunch, Cameron proposes a "congestion pricing" scheme that would make people pay more for rush-hour trips, and include increased parking fees, a "smog tax" for private vehicles, and expanded mini-van services.[50]

Here's how a variable pricing system might work. Drivers who hit the expressway at 8 A.M. would be slapped with a stiff fee, while those traveling at quieter hours would pay little or nothing. Discounts could be given to drivers of multi-passenger vehicles. Fees could be determined by electronic monitoring devices so that bottlenecks caused by stop-and-go toll booths would not offset gains in traffic flow.

A system like this is already being tried in Hong Kong. Drivers are issued monthly bills for highway transit, based on tallies made by electronic sensors. Those traveling during rush hour are assessed at a higher rate. Since 1975, motorists entering Singapore's central business district at peak periods must display a sticker that costs $30 a month, though cars with four or more occupants can enter at no charge.[51]

No jurist has yet argued that solo driving is protected under the Bill of Rights. Even so, the concept of variable pricing may be harder to sell in the United States, where the idea of paying extra for a commodity that has traditionally been free goes against the grain. Federal Highway Administration head Thomas Larson claims, "If it were put to a vote now in any governmental body I know of, congestion pricing probably would not fly."[52] Perhaps it won't fly very far, but the new 1991 transportation act authorizes up to five congestion-pricing pilot programs, 80 percent of which will be paid for by the federal government.

Parking

"T⌐   ⌐rking is the single greatest determinant as to whether
               ⌐, assuming they have an alternative," says Andrew
               ⌐yst at the Boston-based Conservation Law Founda-
               ⌐ng spaces become too expensive or impossible to
               ⌐seriously about taking public transportation, car-
               ⌐king.

Free parking is available to about 90 percent of the Americans who drive to work,[54] which goes a long way toward explaining why nearly 90 percent of all Americans drive to work. This habit is encouraged by the federal tax code. Under federal law, employers can give their workers unlimited compensation for parking, while tax-free compensation for mass transit is held to only $21 a month. If the mass transit subsidy adds up to a penny over $21 a month, the worker must pay taxes on the entire amount. "The Treasury rakes in $50 million to $60 million a year this way, much of it from lower income people," writes Neal Pierce in the *National Journal*. "But what about taxing employer-provided free parking? Get serious. This is America. Free parking is 100 percent tax-free."[55]

Since parking can easily be the biggest expense in driving to work, the subsidy handsomely rewards those driving alone. The average value of an employer-provided parking space comes to about $700 a year.[56] In New York City, where parking may cost more than $350 a month, the annual sum could run to $4,200 and up.[57] All told, John Pucher estimates, $50 billion worth of parking spaces are provided to U.S. workers each year free of charge.[58]

Transportation planners in Sacramento determined that it costs a company between $10,000 and $15,000 to build and maintain a parking space over 20 years—more than it would cost to supply employees with free transit passes. But few companies have opted to abandon parking and go the transit route. On the contrary, explains Jessica Mathews, vice president of the World Resources Institute, standard business practice is actually hostile to mass transportation. The extravagant parking subsidy "nullifies" the money spent each year to promote public transit, she says. "Nothing can compete economically or psychologically with free parking."[59]

National Energy Strategy legislation pending in mid-1992 in Congress would at least partly redress this problem. The legislation passed by the House of Representatives would raise the tax-free limit on employer-provided transit assistance to $60 per month. At the same time, the measure would cap at $160 the amount of monthly tax-free benefits that employers could provide their workers. (Both caps would be adjusted for inflation.)

Meanwhile, Martin Wachs, former head of UCLA's Urban Planning Program, ridicules the notion of spending millions or more on technically dubious automated highway systems before doing simpler things like eliminating free parking. "If companies want to subsidize their help, give them cash instead," Wachs says. "Whoever wants to blow it all on a parking space can do so. Those who want to pocket some of it will car pool. Traffic would drop one-third. It would cost the public nothing. That's why no one is pushing this—it doesn't create construction jobs."[60]

Patterns, however firmly entrenched, can be reversed. A U.S. Department of Transportation study, for example, shows that at least 20 percent fewer employees drive to work alone when they pay to park than when their employer provides free parking.[61] A study of commuters to the Los Angeles Civic Center found that only 40 percent of federal employees (who pay to park) drive to work alone, while 72 percent of county employees (who park free) drive alone. When Commuter Computer, a nonprofit ride-sharing agency in Southern California, ended free parking for agency employees who drove to work alone, the number of solo drivers dropped from 42 percent to 8 percent, while carpooling rose from 17 percent of all employees to 58 percent. Similarly, when a company based in the Warner Center in Los Angeles ended parking subsidies for solo drivers, the number of single-occupancy cars was cut roughly in half, from 90 to 46 percent.[62]

Parking caps, which limit the number of spaces allowed within a city, represent an entirely different strategy to encourage transit use. In 1972, the city of Portland, Oregon, began restricting the amount of parking allowed downtown. Although employment has since doubled in the central business district, the number of cars entering the city has remained constant. Mass transit has accommodated the influx of additional workers.[63] Had it not been for the region's new light rail system, the city would have had to build 40 five-story parking structures to handle that much job growth.[64] Automobile traffic in downtown Copenhagen has been similarly reduced by a ban on street parking. Some of the space previously devoted to cars has since been converted to public squares or bicycle parking facilities.[65]

On July 30, 1990, the city of Cambridge, Massachusetts, imposed a parking freeze to help curb air pollution. "People still have a right to go anywhere in Cambridge, but they don't have a right to bring 5,000 pounds of metal with them," explains Sonia Hamel of the Central Transportation Planning Staff.[66] A citizen's group has drafted a plan to

MANKOFF

"Amazing, three failed marriages, scores of disastrous relationships, many financial reversals, and countless physical ailments, but through it all I've always had good luck parking."

raise $12.5 million a year from increases in parking meter rates—money that would be used to pay for 10 express buses, 50 vans, and other mass transit improvements.

Driving Bans

Parking bans limit the number of cars that can park in an area, but have no effect on the number that drive through. One way to ward off problems caused by an overabundance of vehicles is to keep them out of urban centers altogether. Auto-free zones—as a way to reduce air pollution, boost tourism, and enhance the quality of life—are becoming increasingly popular in Europe. The experience in the United States has been more limited; car-restricted zones are generally confined to small tourist or shopping districts and have little impact on a city's overall transportation patterns.

By contrast, Gothenburg, Sweden, divided its city center into five pie-shaped sectors in 1970 as a way to limit through traffic and encourage public transportation. Emergency vehicles, mass transit vehicles, bicycles, and mopeds can pass freely from one zone to the next, but automobiles can't. Reduced auto traffic in downtown Gothenburg has led to improved transit service and a lower accident rate. This so-called traffic cell approach, which originated in Bremen, West Germany, is also used in Groningen, Holland, and Besançon, France.[67]

In 1977, Buenos Aires restricted private vehicles from entering the downtown district from 10 A.M. to 7 P.M. on weekdays. Buses and taxis are allowed on a few streets. The ban was implemented to combat the congestion and air pollution caused by the one million people who flood central Buenos Aires ("good airs" in Spanish) each working day. Initially police barricades were used to enforce the measure; now small signs explaining the policy are sufficient.[68]

Partial or total car bans have been established in most large Italian cities—including Rome, Florence, Naples, Bologna, and Genoa—as well as in many smaller ones. From 7:30 A.M. to 7:30 P.M., only buses, taxis, delivery vehicles, and cars belonging to area residents may enter the central districts of Rome and Florence. Similar bans are already in effect in Athens, Amsterdam, Barcelona, Budapest, Mexico City, and Munich.[69] Within a decade, Bordeaux, France, intends to exile motor vehicles from half of the city's streets, reserving these thoroughfares for pedestrians and cyclists.[70] As John Pucher points out, "There is hardly a city in Europe without at least one pedestrian zone, and many cities have extensive districts in which automobile traffic is prohibited."[71]

No-Drive Days

Late in 1991, Rome, Milan, Naples, Turin, and seven other Italian cities declared war on pollution by limiting the number of cars on the road. Under the plan, cars with odd-numbered license plates are banned from driving on one day, and cars with even-numbered plates are banned on the next. Many motorists, bridling at any restrictions on their right to drive, have ignored the odd-even rule. On a single day in December, Roman police officers wrote 12,983 citations, fining mavericks for driving on the wrong day or for tampering with their plates. With rigid enforcement, however, Italy's environment minister, Giorgio Ruffolo, believes the alternate-day ban can reduce pollution by 20 to 30 percent.[72]

Mexico City—a metropolis of 20 million generally credited with having the world's most unsavory air—instituted a one-day-a-week driving ban two years earlier, in November 1989. "People thought we were crazy," said Ramon Ojeda, a government environmental official who helped devise the plan. But thanks to the ban, pollution has dropped by about 10 percent, according to both government and independent estimates.[73]

Some motorists tried to ignore the aggressive ad campaign staged by the Mexico City government to publicize the "No Driving Today" policy, as well as the $150 fine for violating it. One well-to-do businessman, for instance, assumed he simply had to bribe an occasional policeman if perchance he were stopped on a day he should have left his car at home. On the inaugural day on the program, however, he was hit up by four traffic cops in an eight-mile stretch of road. "After the fourth 'bite,' I was persuaded to park the car and walk to the bus stop," the businessman said.[74]

Although residents initially griped about the program, 80 percent now want it to continue.[75] The success of the Mexico City driving ban has encouraged two of the country's other biggest cities, Monterrey and Guadalajara, to start programs of their own. "Who knows?" Ojeda said. "Maybe Los Angeles will be next."[76]

A controversial contingency plan has, in fact, been drafted to help the Los Angeles basin meet the standards of the new Clean Air Act. Starting in the year 2000, "no-drive" days will be imposed as a last resort to lower ozone and carbon monoxide levels. If the plan is implemented, every motorist will have to leave his or her car at home one day a week, the day of rest depending on the license-plate number.[77]

Innovative Work Schedules

Staggering work hours, as Los Angeles did during the 1984 Summer Olympics, can help distribute peak traffic over the entire day. By starting the regular workday or school day an hour or two earlier, or by ending it earlier, the worst traffic crunches can be alleviated. Although many Americans grew up believing the workday starts at 9:00 A.M., there's no reason why business hours can't change. "When eight million people need to be somewhere in the same 30-minute period, somebody's got to say, 'Hey, I'll work different hours,' " notes Sergeant John Amott of the L.A. Police Department.[78]

Some weeks after the start of the 1991 war against Iraq, the Virginia Department of Transportation noted a 21-percent drop in rush-hour traffic on the beltway surrounding Washington. Commuters who had come to expect a grueling 45-minute-plus ordeal found themselves making their trip in a comparatively pain-free 15 minutes. Part of the reason was that Pentagon workers were coming and going at all hours of the day and night due to the extraordinary circumstances, unintentionally easing the peak-hour traffic crunch.[79]

Four-day work weeks are another traffic reduction strategy. In a move that deftly reduced commuting by 20 percent, Southern California's Air Quality Management District put its employees on a four-day schedule. (Consider, though, that people who are not driving to work may well be driving somewhere else.) Three-day weekends are also a routine affair for the 1,600 employees at the Los Angeles County Department of Public Works headquarters in Alhambra. The workers follow a four-day, ten-hour-a-day schedule, Monday through Thursday. On Fridays the entire building is shut down. Officials believe the measure will not only cut smog and traffic, but will also save $1.7 million a year in operating costs.[80]

Telecommuting

Another strategy goes even further toward alleviating traffic problems. The idea is to encourage people to conduct their affairs from offices tucked away in their own homes. Some experts insist that the proliferation of personal computers, modems, FAX machines, voice mail, video conferences, and other communications systems will soon enable millions of Americans to "commute" to work electronically, without adding another car to already saturated roadways. Employers can reduce overhead while employees save time and money. And employees can have far more choice about where they live.

Donna Cunningham, for example, is a media relations manager for AT & T Bell Labs in Short Hills, New Jersey. Like her colleagues, she gets up weekday mornings early—around five o'clock. She sips some coffee, reads the paper, and then heads to work. Unlike her colleagues, battling traffic hundreds of miles away in New Jersey, she simply descends one flight of stairs to her home-based office in Burlington, Vermont.[81]

For decades, futurists like Alvin Toffler have claimed that telecommuting was the wave of the future. That dream has yet to pan out. In fact, a study by the Eno Foundation revealed that fewer people are working at home these days than did so a decade ago.[82] However, in a step toward reversing that trend, 50 of the AQMD's 1,100 employees now telecommute from home. Thirty-five employees for Pacific Bell and Southern California Edison work out of a telecommuting center in Riverside, California. The city of Los Angeles, meanwhile, is planning to open three similar "satellite centers" for municipal employees living outside the city.[83]

Whether telecommunications technology will make a dent in U.S. travel time overall remains to be seen. As Fred Reid notes in *Sustainable Communities,* "we forget that there has been a large expansion of telephone, cable, and microwave services since the 60s, and that TV in the 50s represented a great expansion. And there's the original telephone! Travel increased throughout in spite of these developments."[84]

Optimistic that change is possible, Los Angeles officials hope to eliminate three million work trips a day through work-at-home programs and telecommuting.[85] The Center for Futures Research predicts that five million Americans hold computer-related jobs that could be done at home by 1993.[86] And a Southern California Association of Governments study found that if one out of eight workers chose to work either at home or at a nearby "satellite" work station linked electronically to a central office, vehicle delays on the region's freeways could be reduced by nearly one third.[87]

MASS TRANSIT

John Pucher of Rutgers University, who has spent years working and traveling in Europe, was initially baffled by the striking differences in transit use between people living on that continent and in the U States. Americans use public transportation quite sparin just about everywhere. Western Europeans, who t much, use mass transit 2 to 10 times more frequent. icans go to Europe, even those "who otherwise w

dead on mass transit actually enjoy riding the Paris Metro or the London 'Tubes' or the Amsterdam streetcars. And when Europeans come
to the United States, they don't hesitate to rent autos to discover America—they don't have much choice anyway.''[88]

The discrepancy, Pucher concluded, is not cultural so much as political. Policies established decades ago have made it dirt cheap, simple,
and almost necessary to get around by car in the United States. Sales
taxes on new autos, for instance, can run anywhere from 5 to 35 times
higher in Europe than in this country. Gas taxes are 3 to 8 times higher
in Europe. The high gasoline taxes there are meant to discourage driving, and proceeds from these taxes subsidize rail and transit systems.

In the United States, as we have seen, federal transportation spending
primarily means spending to promote auto and truck use. Money collected from the federal gas tax, now 14 cents a gallon, is fed into the
Highway Trust Fund, 12.5 cents of which is devoted to highways, 1.5
cents to mass transit.[89]

Obtaining a driver's license is easier and cheaper in the United States
than in Europe, and so is parking. European governments deliberately
make parking more expensive and less available, while encouraging
employers to provide transit passes to employees. In Paris, the *carte
d'orange* makes transit use almost free. In Eastern Europe, where owning and operating a car is an expensive bureaucratic hassle, mass transit
costs next to nothing—about 5 cents a ride.[90] To drive in Stockholm,
motorists must pay $45 a month. However, they can use the same
permit to ride on mass transit at no additional charge.[91]

It's not surprising, in view of these differences, that Americans take
82 percent of all their trips in private automobiles and only 2.5 percent
on subways, buses, street cars, light rail systems, trains, planes, and
taxis combined. That has not always been the case, however. Earlier
in this century, transit systems thrived throughout the country's largest
cities. The mass transit peak occurred during World War II, when trol-
leys and buses carried more than 25 billion passengers annually.[92] Public transportation ridership in the United States is now down to 9 billion
trips a year.[93]

Why the precipitous drop? As discussed in Chapter 1, 90 percent of
the nation's trolley system was dismantled by the late 1950s, an effort
that paved the way for untrammeled car use. The mass migration to

the suburbs, which accelerated in the 1950s, and the attendant rise in automobile ownership cut into public transit's traditional ridership. Then, too, the suburban population settled in a disorganized fashion that public transport was ill-equipped to serve. Until the late 1960s, federal subsidies for transit systems were virtually nonexistent. In 1965, for example, federal grants for urban mass transit came to only $51 million, compared to the $4.1 billion spent on highway construction.[94] This pronounced and prolonged disparity forced mass transit into a hole out of which it has not yet climbed.

Mass transit in the United States was essentially a private business, expected to turn a profit, until it became a publicly owned, subsidized enterprise in the late 1970s. Urban transit systems are continually criticized for being unprofitable, but, as John Pucher explains, "all countries subsidize public transit to some extent; it is not profitable anywhere."[95]

Before worrying about breaking even, we should start bringing the sums spent on public transportation in this country up to par with subsidies promoting auto use—road construction being just the most obvious example. "Outside the United States, transit is considered an essential public service and as such is not expected to pay its own way," writes auto historian James Flink. "Accordingly, the most important standard for evaluating transit in Europe is the quality of service, not its cost effectiveness."[96]

Public transportation endured further assaults during the 1980s: federal highway funding increased 85 percent,[97] while spending on transit systems was cut in half (inflation factored in).[98] Despite the steady barrage, mass transit is alive, and indeed vital, in many parts of the country. Of the two million commuter trips to and from downtown Chicago, 80 percent are on mass transit, according to the American Public Transit Association (APTA). About two thirds of the people entering lower Manhattan at any given time do so by way of public transportation.[99] Approximately one third of the United States' transit rides are in the Big Apple, and the city's subway system carries 3.7 million people a day over 720 miles of tracks.[100]

"The T," Boston's subway system, carries about half of all commuters heading downtown. Cars on one of its branches, the Green Line, run on tracks first laid in 1897. The T has stimulated economic growth in Boston over the past century and may be the key to its economic future. Mayor Ray Flynn recently proposed adding a new subway line that would hook up the city's centers for biomedical research—a field expected to account for half of Boston's job growth in the coming decade.[101] "The challenge now is to make sure we can get people to these places of employment if we are to expand our economy, which is what we are trying to do," says Flynn.[102]

Public transportation offers clear-cut environmental advantages— cleaner air, lower energy use, and reduced congestion on our city streets. Per passenger mile traveled, taking a bus instead of driving alone to work cuts nitrogen-oxide emissions by 25 percent, carbon monoxide by 80 percent, and hydrocarbon emissions by 90 percent.[103] Abandoning the solo commute by car for rail transport reduces pollution even more: nitrogen oxide emissions fall by 77 percent and carbon monoxide and hydrocarbons by well over 99 percent. The switch to mass transit alternatives also brings substantial fuel savings. Per passenger mile traveled, a transit train with 22 persons per car consumes 43 percent less energy than an automobile with a single driver; a transit bus with 11 riders on board takes 45 percent less energy.[104] As for congestion, one subway rail line can carry 35 times more people than a highway lane carrying single-occupant cars; surface trains carry 25 times more; buses or light rail trains 15 times more.

Another benefit, often overlooked, is that public transportation systems attempt to deliver exactly what they advertise: transportation for the public. These systems provide essential services for people who can't afford cars, disabled people who can't drive, others who are either too young or too old to drive, as well as those who would simply rather not.

Mass transit is often cited as *the* solution—or, at least, a critical part of the solution—to many bedeviling transportation problems. It won't be, though, unless systems are designed that people truly want to ride. Motorists won't abandon their cars without a compelling alternative. So long as they are convinced that driving is the cheapest, most practical way to go, that is what they will continue to do.

New York Times writer Matthew Wald summed up the commuting dilemma with this scenario: suppose a person has to go from home in Haworth, New Jersey, to a job in Newark, 20 miles away, arriving no later than 9 A.M. Here are three options:

[1.] The bus to eternity: Take 7:17 a.m. bus across the Hudson River to Port Authority terminal in Manhattan, arriving at 8:11. Then take 8:20 a.m. bus back across the river to New Jersey, arriving in Newark at 8:55 if all goes well. Minimum transit time—1 hour, 38 minutes.

[2.] Railroad three-step: Drive car to station in neighboring Oradell, take New Jersey Transit train to Hoboken, then the PATH tube to Newark. Transit time—not much over an hour.

[3.] By car: Insert lucky coffee mug in coffee-mug caddy. Buckle up. Blast off. Time on road maybe 40 minutes, depending on traffic.[105]

Given the reality of late trains and buses, the headache of transfers between several different modes of transport, and the time spent waiting in between, it's no wonder that most people don't bother. Still, Deborah Sheiman of the Natural Resources Defense Council insists that taking mass transit doesn't have to be a sacrifice. Where the systems perform well, riding on public transportation can be a luxury. People lucky enough to leave their cars in the garage and avoid gruesome traffic tie-ups, she says, "don't look at that as giving up something."[106] They may very well be gaining something—such as time on a train to read the newspaper or take a nap.

Light Rail

San Jose officials set out to make their $500-million, 21-mile rail network more convenient than driving. To do so, they put transit stops close to commercial centers and office complexes and placed the parking lots farther away. Each day 23,000 passengers now ride the system, which began operating in late 1987, exceeding initial estimates of 20,000 riders. Most of these passengers would otherwise be driving cars, claims Rich Golda, superintendent of operations for the Santa Clara County Light Rail.[107]

New light rail systems—technologically updated versions of the trolley cars that once roamed the land—are appearing in many U.S. cities. The main advantage of light rail vehicles, which normally consist of one or two cars, is that they are substantially cheaper and quicker to build than "heavy rail" or "rapid rail" systems featuring subways and above-ground trains.

Besides San Jose, other cities that christened new light rail systems in the 1980s include San Diego, Buffalo, Portland, and Sacramento. The story has an O. Henry twist: modern trolley cars have been resurrected as the antidote to mounting pollution and congestion in urban centers caused by automobiles—the same vehicles that did in trolley systems a half century ago.

Of course, the usual disclaimers apply. "Light rail should not be considered a panacea," cautions James Mills, chairman of the San Diego Metropolitan Transit Development Board and the former state senator who first proposed building San Diego's light rail system.

> "Travel patterns are so diverse in large cities that a diversity of technologies may best serve the many demands put on transit systems. . . . But in the right corridors, [light rail] can be the right answer to the needs of a lot of Americans. It can make their lives more pleasant. It can make the cities where they live more vital and interesting places. And it can contribute to the quality of air they breathe."[108]

The San Diego experience appears to bear that out. The light rail line that connects the city's downtown to the Mexican border opened in 1981—the first major new U.S. trolley system since 1950. From the day it began running the rail system attracted more people than expected—11,000 riders daily, compared to the predicted 9,800. Ridership has grown 12.2 percent a year, luring drivers from cars, so that by 1988 over 22,000 passengers were using the service each day. Fares cover 85 percent of the year-round operating costs and over 100 percent of those costs during summer months.

The biggest increase in ridership is among commuters heading to and from work. "These are people who, we were warned, would never get out of their cars to ride transit," Mills notes. But "if San Diegans are given a pleasant alternative to their cars, a large number of them will take advantage of it to get to work. Our surveys show that one-third of the people who ride our system each day come to it in their cars and park at the lots at our stations."[109]

In a novel twist, Sacramento took money earmarked for a 4.5-mile stretch of interstate highway—some of which was built but never opened—and instead laid down an 18.3-mile, $176-million light rail system that began rolling in March 1987. Portland, Oregon's light rail, called MAX, has similar origins. In the late 1970s, local officials decided to abandon a planned segment of interstate highway, the Mount Hood Freeway, and use most of the money set aside for it on mass transit instead. The resulting 15.4-mile light rail line, which runs from downtown Portland to suburban Gresham, opened for business in September 1986. A waterfront park now stands where the freeway was supposed to go.

MAX figures heavily in the region's strategy for "balanced transportation investments," explains G. B. Arrington, an official from Tri-Met, the region's transit agency. "Rather than widening major radial highway corridors to accommodate growth, the region chose to invest in transit. Today, transit carries the equivalent of two new lanes on every arterial [road] entering downtown Portland."[110]

The city's strategy has paid off handsomely. MAX's operating cost per passenger is about half that of the city's bus system. Light rail has spurred great interest in Portland; 200,000 passengers rode during the first two and a half days of free service.[111] Moreover, weekday ridership is twice as high as originally expected. Forty-three percent of commuters to downtown Portland arrive by bus or train—a higher rate of transit ridership than those of most U.S. cities of comparable size.[112] Private development has also exceeded early estimates: by 1989, investments in businesses lining the MAX route totalled more than three times the $214 million cost of the rail project.[113] City officials attribute the region's improved air quality to the transit system's success. In the early 1970s, Portland suffered from unhealthy air one day out of every three; by 1989, the number of unhealthy days dropped to zero.[114]

Los Angeles's new Blue Line, an $877-million light rail system that opened in July 1990, is the first rail project to serve the city since the Big Red Car trolleys (defunct since 1961) spanned 1,100 miles and connected dozens of towns in the metropolitan area, including Pasadena, Long Beach, Santa Monica, and Riverside. The new Blue Line stretches 22 miles, linking downtown Los Angeles with Long Beach. It is the first leg of the Metrorail—a planned 150-mile network connecting the downtown city with its suburbs. At an estimated $5 billion, Metrorail would rank among the world's costliest mass transit systems.

California suddenly seems bullish on trains. As a result of a recent referendum, more than $18 billion derived from additional new gas taxes will be funneled in part into new rail systems.[115] In addition, state residents authorized another $5 billion in rail bond issues.[116] But the $877-million question remains: Will enough people ride the new Blue Line to make it worthwhile? When rides were free during the first month of operations, a daily average of over 37,000 people took the light rail. However, only 11,000 people made the trip on August 1, 1990—the first day they had to pay to ride. Officials weren't too worried about the rapid fall-off since they had originally forecast only 5,000 to 7,000 paying customers a day.[117] But how many hardcore commuters will continue to make the trip—day in, day out—long after the novelty has worn off? Ken Small, an economics professor at the University of California at Irvine, says that "we'll see more rail projects built [in Southern California], but that's not the same as saying there will be more use."[118] A case in point: Shirley and Michael Coulter, two New Yorkers who moved to L.A. just as the Blue Line began running, were delighted to find a rail system in the car-crazed metropolis. "I think it's great," Shirley Coulter said. "And we'll ride it—at least until we get a car."[119]

That's the rub. If the Blue Line doesn't attract enough steady riders and the rest of the Metrorail project proves too expensive to build, officials may be forced to scale down their ambitious plans in future decades. This prospect underscores the fact that some cities contemplating rail transit systems may lack the minimum population density needed to make a system viable. Some have gotten the message. Dallas, for example, voted down a proposed 93-mile rail system in 1988; it has only 3,000 people per square mile, compared to 60,000 per square mile in New York City.[120]

Recent history also shows that even in theoretically hospitable environments, rail transit systems do not always live up to their early promise. A government study of U.S. rapid rail systems completed in the 1980s found that costs ran 44 percent over budget, while ridership was 64 percent below predicted levels.[121] Public transport officials have found it tough to win over drivers spoiled by free parking and dollar-a-gallon gasoline.

Miami's Metrorail—a combined heavy and light rail system that started down the tracks in 1986—is an oft-cited example. Critics call it "Metrofail" and "the Train to Nowhere." About 50,000 people ride Miami's trains each day—well below initial estimates. One reason for the passenger shortfall is that many Miamians have to take several modes of transit to reach their destinations. A commuter may have to drive or take a bus to a Metrorail station, hop on the elevated (heavy rail) trains for a few stops, and from there take Metromover, an elevated light rail system connecting points in central Miami. Another problem is that in an attempt to save money by using existing rights of way, Miami built a rail system that leaves some of its population out in the cold.

A Miami official, however, defended Metrorail by saying, "This is a service, not a business."[122] Nelson Alba, a spokesperson for the Dade County transit agency, maintains that ridership has grown steadily each year. "Metrorail is popular among many riders because, so far as I know, it's the only transit system in the country to provide day-care centers at station parking lots." The Metromover, which runs on rubber wheels, offers a smooth, quiet ride. The only drawback, Alba notes, is the dead pigeons that litter the tracks; "It's so quiet, they don't hear the cars coming."[123]

Morgantown, West Virginia's People Mover—an automated system of small, gondola-style cars that ride on tracks—was built in the 1970s near the University of West Virginia campus. The rider-responsive system can take people directly to their destination, bypassing other stops along the way. No other mass transit system in the world is run entirely by computers, and no other system offers nonstop service from starting point to destination. But the 33-mile system, built with U.S. Department of Transportation funds and projected to cost $19 million,[124] ended up costing $138 million.[125] Skeptics argue that the only thing this demonstration project demonstrated is the bankrupting potential of high-tech solutions to low-tech public transport problems. On the plus side, the People Mover did show transit planners one way to make fixed-rail travel more flexible.

Buses

Rigidity still typifies conventional rail transport since trains can't run where tracks were not laid. Citing this inherent limitation and the unjustifiable expense of installing trains in low-density areas, former U.S. transportation secretary James Burnley came to favor buses, which "can be rerouted overnight to meet changing transportation patterns."[126]

Easily the cheapest mode of public transport, buses are also far more flexible than trains. However, with changing demographic and commuting patterns, bus routes and schedules also need continual updating. As an observer in Boston once noted, "these buses go from where people no longer live to where they used to work."[127]

One drawback is that buses pollute more than trains. Another is that buses can get trapped in the same traffic jams that cars do, though HOV lanes or special express lanes can give buses a jump on the competition. Washington, Los Angeles, San Francisco, and many other U.S. cities have exclusive busways leading into and out of central residential and commercial districts.

Los Angeles has the country's largest bus system, transporting 1.5 million riders a day and coming closer to achieving full capacity than in any other system in the United States.[128] Elsewhere throughout the country, city governments are hoping that innovative programs will attract new riders. In an attempt to alleviate congestion in Denver's most crowded district, a 12-block stretch of bustling 16th Street has been converted into a busway closed to cars. Buses are always free and during crowded periods they run every 70 seconds. "It's more like a moving sidewalk," explains Dick Bauman of the city's transit agency.[129] Waiving fares certainly encourages people to use buses. Portland, Washington's City Center bus lines, which cover 300 square blocks, are free to riders. Seattle also provides free bus service in its central business district, and more than 350,000 riders use it each month.[130]

The Dallas Area Rapid Transit (DART) provides, arguably, the most imaginative service. On routes not heavily traveled enough to warrant regular bus service, passengers can dial a number; a van is then dispatched to pick them up and take them, and other passengers, to their desired destinations, or at least to a regular bus line that is going there. When enough people start using the vans to reach the same destination, a new bus line is introduced to service the route. The program, called Dart-About, is now carrying about 8,500 passengers a month at a cost to them of $1.75 per ride (25 cents for students and senior citizens), which adds up to 10 to 15 percent of total operating costs.[131] (Even if dial-a-bus or dial-a-van services like Dart-About are not always economical for suburban areas, they do provide essential transportation services for the elderly and handicapped.)

A number of cities are starting to provide inner-city residents with transportation to previously inaccessible jobs opening up in suburbia. Suburban Job-Link, for example, helps 600 workers from Chicago's West Side commute by bus, van, or car pool to jobs in northwestern suburbs. Accessible Services in Philadelphia coordinates bus and van services that enable 150 inner-city residents to get to blue-collar jobs in outlying towns. In Baltimore, the Greater BWI Commuter Transportation Center is devoted to solving the commuting problems of 10,000 Baltimore residents who work at the international airport.[132]

Roanoke, Virginia, has tried a different tactic—a sort of cosmetic surgery—to encourage more people to take the bus. Ridership in the city increased by 12 percent after an attractive new bus station opened up in an historic section of the city. The new station, Campbell Court, "does away with the stigma that bus stations are dirty, rundown places in undesirable parts of town," says Stephen Mancuso, general manager of the city's transit system. The $4.4-million station was built with federal, state, and local funds, but private businesses now cover the bus system's $2 million a year operating costs.[133]

Buses, regarded as the lowest form of transport for the poorest of poor, undeniably suffer from an image problem. On the TV show "Cheers," bartender Sam Malone once contemplated selling his treasured Corvette. He was quickly talked out of the idea when bar manager Rebecca Howe said, "I'm sure the women will just swoon when they see your new bus pass."

"Buses don't have sex appeal because no one ever tried to make them sexy," says Chris Leinberger, an expert on urban and suburban growth patterns.[134] Light rail systems rate somewhat higher in this regard. "While no one gets excited about the initiation of new bus service, light rail arouses interest," claims John Post, the assistant general manager of Tri-Met in Portland, Oregon.[135] Rail systems can also accommodate more would-be drivers than buses do. A single rail line in southern New Jersey, for example, carries more passengers than an entire network of 28 bus routes in the greater Camden area.[136]

All mass transit systems, rail and bus included, still face an uphill battle trying to entice people to leave their cars behind. It's not simply a matter of image; it's a matter of getting people where they need to go. Nobody has yet figured out how to get people to and from widely dispersed homes and workplaces without cars. And while mass transit works best where population densities are high, nationwide trends continue to run the opposite way: each year since World War II, the United States population has spread itself thinner and thinner.

The paradox is summed up by Jeffrey Zupan, planning director for the New Jersey Transit Authority. People are moving out of urban cores and resettling in suburban areas that are tailored to the automobile and inimical to pedestrian travel and public transit, he says. "So in the very places where transit has worked best, there are fewer people for it to work for. And because there are fewer people, there are fewer rides, and transit isn't going to work as well."[137] Farther from the madding crowd, more people tend to drive cars, which increases the need for transit while decreasing its potential effectiveness.

ANTIDOTES TO SPRAWL

Planners in Southern California have reluctantly concluded that no combination of highway construction, mass transit, ride sharing, and staggered work hours will rid the region of all traffic and smog problems. Not until people live closer to where they work and shop will they drive fewer miles and send fewer pollutants flying out their tailpipes.

Just how feasible is this? Cities built of brick and concrete, sidewalks of concrete, and streets paved with asphalt can't be ripped up and rearranged like so many Lego blocks. Or can they? Through zoning changes, comprehensive land use and transportation planning, and innovative design strategies, officials are at least beginning to revamp our cities and suburbs to make them more livable and workable.

Transportation has run aground in so many of the nation's cities in part because transit and urban development have been poorly coordinated. Land-use regulation is traditionally the responsibility of local governments, while transportation is handled by regional, state, and federal authorities. Even within the same agency, people designing roads and transit systems often have little contact with planners trying to deal with the impact of those construction projects. Planners, in turn, may approve mega-developments without bothering to check whether existing transportation facilities can handle the additional growth.

"Land use is assigned to the planning department, and transportation is assigned to engineering," explains Elizabeth Deakin, an urban planner at the University of California at Berkeley. Many policy specialists have had little training in transportation systems, she says, while engineers tend to be unskilled, and sometimes uninterested, in land-use policy. As a result, development projects inconsistent with available or projected transportation capacity get approved anyway.[138]

While many U.S. cities have been late in embracing such interdisciplinary planning, regional authorities in Portland, Oregon, began integrating land-use planning and transportation in the early 1970s. "In 1970, our downtown, like most of those across the country, was dying," explains G. B. Arrington of Tri-Met.

> Political leaders were determined to turn things around. They took the long-term view and saw transit as a key part of a strategy to achieve downtown growth without the negatives of more cars and more freeway lanes. In Portland, transit is not just for moving people, it's a central part of our strategy to guide growth and protect our quality of life.[139]

Their efforts were rewarded—a revitalized, thriving downtown has emerged, centered around the new transit mall and MAX, the new light rail line. In another move to limit sprawl, the city created an "urban growth boundary"—an imaginary line surrounding the city beyond which new developments are prohibited.

Construction of a light rail system in San Jose, California, prompted officials to take a more careful look at regional planning overall. "Initially, there was no master plan for growth," explains Rich Golda, superintendent for rail operations in Santa Clara County. "The city and county are now trying to establish high-density pockets of residential units around transit stops, so that more people will find light rail convenient. This approach, hopefully, will be an improvement over the haphazard growth that has occurred in the past."[140]

Like his colleagues in Portland and San Jose, Michael Repogle, a transportation planner for Montgomery County, Maryland, is steering his region away from traditional, auto-based developments. "If you build out in the old auto-centered way at the current rate, congestion would choke off economic growth,'' he says.[141] Instead of permitting more sprawl and the paralyzing traffic it brings, the county plans to concentrate housing units along expanded transit corridors. The basic idea is to eliminate single-purpose zoning codes, which isolate residential areas from large shopping plazas and separate both from office parks—an arrangement that forces suburbanites to take a car for virtually every trip imaginable, whether they are going to work or just picking up coffee and a donut.

A study by John Holtzclaw of the Sierra Club found that doubling residential population density reduces per capita auto mileage by 25 to 30 percent.[142] Residents of northeast San Francisco drove only one fourth as much as residents of suburban Danville-San Ramon, which had a population density 26 times lower; San Francisco inhabitants of multi-family dwellings used ''40 times less land, 15 times less roadway, 50 times less lumber, and much less water and fuel'' than their suburban counterparts.[143] Yet people continue to abandon cities for the suburbs.

Holtzclaw endorses a three-point strategy to make communities less auto dependent. First, zoning laws should be changed to allow higher-density, mixed-use development in town centers and along transit routes. Second, zoning ordinances are needed to check further sprawl by forbidding housing construction outside settled areas. Third, parking space in new buildings should be restricted or eliminated.

What would our cities look like if measures like these were adopted? Although population densities would increase in some areas, the finished product need not be cramped, alienating neighborhoods locked in a state of perpetual twilight by towering skyscrapers. An EPA study found that even in compact residential developments consisting of single-family homes mixed in with two- to six-story apartments, 30 percent of the land could be left open for parks. In most spread out suburbs, by contrast, only 9 percent is left undeveloped.[144]

An analysis of 30 international cities by Australian transport researchers Peter Newman and Jeffrey Kenworthy led to an important rule of thumb: ''Generally speaking, the denser an area, the more mixed is the land use because the sheer numbers of people can support a rich diversity of small businesses, shops, and other activities.''[145] Holtzclaw's assessment of the Bay Area ended on the same note; he estimates that the residents of northeast San Francisco ''have nearly 200 times as many restaurants, markets, and other services within walking distance as the residents of suburban Danville–San Ramon do.'' The San Francisco residents also had access to 200 times more transit vehicles.[146]

Given that so many jobs these days are in white-collar service industries, zoning ordinances that segregate homes from the workplace are often outmoded. In a previous era, the rationale for cordoning off work activities was to minimize the eyesores and nuisances residents had to endure. Marcia Lowe, a transportation researcher at the Worldwatch Institute, argues that today ''workplaces are not the smokestack factories and slaughterhouses of the industrial era.'' Most people these days consider road congestion a far bigger nuisance than the prospect of living in close proximity to businesses, claims Robert Cevero of the University of California at Berkeley.[147]

Toronto is one formerly auto-dominated city that has since turned the corner. Officials have employed zoning changes and other measures to encourage developers to build in areas accessible to mass transit. Since 1954, half of the residential buildings erected in Toronto have been within walking distance of a rapid rail stop. Ninety percent of all new office space lies near a transit station. These measures have prompted 77 percent of the city's downtown employees to take public transportation to work.[148] ''Even if all of Toronto's public transport trips were switched to automobiles, Toronto would *still* use less than two-thirds the amount of gasoline per capita that Detroit does,'' Lowe says. ''The reason is that Toronto's layout fosters fewer and shorter trips.''[149]

In Davis, California, a university town of 40,000, aggressive building restrictions have reined in urban sprawl. The town also limits the size of its shopping plazas to eight acres—substituting smaller neighborhood shopping centers (located within a mile of most residents) for giant regional commercial centers that create nightmares for traffic managers.

The South Coast Air Quality Management District and other government agencies in the Los Angeles region have proposed zoning shifts designed to shorten commuter trips by bringing people and jobs closer together. The problem fueling the traffic crunch is simple: there are not enough jobs for people living in a city's outskirts, and there aren't enough people living in the city center to fill all the available jobs. The AQMD plan, therefore, is to move 200,000 jobs that would otherwise be located in urban Los Angeles to outlying regions. Meanwhile, 76,000 housing units that would normally go up on the periphery will instead be placed closer to urban job centers.[150]

Regional officials are also considering imposing penalties on developers whose projects increase the mismatch between where people live and where they work. For example, developers who build an office park far from residential neighborhoods would have to pay the government a fee. Money collected in this way would be used to create jobs in job-deficient areas and housing in housing-deficient areas, thus establishing a more reasonable balance.[151]

Back to the Future

"The problem with current suburbs is not that they are ugly," says architect Andres Duany. "The problem is they don't work." To his way of thinking, small towns designed for people rather than cars work better. "Most of the needs of daily life can be met within a three-to-four-acre area and generally within a five-minute walk of a person's home." The idea of towns "designed for people rather than cars" is not as revolutionary as it sounds, since Duany might have been referring to just about any U.S. town of 50,000 or less before the turn of the century.[152]

The Miami-based architectural team of Duany and Elizabeth Plater-Zyberk (also his wife) has designed new towns in the old-style mold in Alabama, California, Indiana, Maryland, Massachusetts, New Hampshire, New York, Texas, and other states. Residents of these new communities (or enclaves within existing communities) don't live on isolated cul-de-sacs. Instead, their homes, shops, and offices are interspersed around a central hub. People live closer together than in most suburbs, without the luxury of huge yards. On the plus side, they can get to most places they need to go by foot or bike. When that's not practical, they can hop on a bus or train. Suburbs offer few alternatives to auto dependency, Duany says. "Traditional towns provide a choice. Yes, you can drive, but you can also walk."[153]

Seaside, Florida, is the most celebrated example of a new planned community, designed by Duany and Plater-Zyberk in what is now called the neo-traditional style. The town has been a resounding popular success, as reflected in property values that have soared 500 percent in eight years.[154] "Seaside addresses the larger issue of how to create a place where people can live differently from the way they do in the usual suburb or resort area," wrote Philip Langdon in the *Atlantic*. "How can a new community foster a friendly, stimulating atmosphere? How can it make its streets and public areas inviting enough that people will want to spend time in them? How can it achieve a pleasing visual order and treat the natural environment intelligently while also conveniently supplying its inhabitants' daily needs?"[155]

The streets of Seaside are narrow, only 18 feet wide, and on-street parking is allowed so as to limit through traffic. A network of footpaths eases pedestrian travel. "Someone can get a meal or mail a package or buy something by walking or biking only a short way," Langdon says.[156] Could a concept that appears to work very well in the Florida panhandle resort village be applied to major metropolitan areas? Critics have called Duany and Plater-Zyberk's vision a nostalgic anachronism unsuited to modern life. "Like all utopian solutions, it has limits," says Sergio Rodriguez, Miami's assistant city manager and director of planning. "Life is much more complicated. You don't always work where you live; you work where you can get a job."[157]

Clearly, there are limits—we can't undo decades of suburbanization overnight; nor can we transform our cities just by waving a handbook of revised zoning codes. But in just the past few years, Duany and Plater-Zyberk have done their part by designing more than 30 liveable residential developments—either new towns or renovated sections of older cities. In addition, the pair has prepared a package of zoning regulations that just about any city can use to modify existing codes. "Suburbs have all the components that make towns," Duany says about planning regulations for the typical suburb. "But they're not assembled properly; they're assembled in separate pods. We could be laying out towns by the hundreds every year." Zoning codes for the traditional town he and Plater-Zyberk promote can fit onto a single page; in contrast, codes for chaotic-looking suburbs often fill a two-inch stack of paper. "Everything is specified to the Nth degree, even parking lots," Duany says. "That's because the planning codes really care an awful lot about cars and parking. There is nothing in them about what it feels like to be in those places and what the pedestrian life is like."[158] Plater-Zyberk is starting to believe that traditional-style towns may once again become the standard. "Almost everywhere we speak, [people are] saying, 'Finally!' It's as if everybody knows what the right way to live is."[159]

Meanwhile, Peter Calthorpe is building on similar principles in northern California. Sacramento County recently asked the San Francisco-based architect to draft zoning codes that would put mass transit and pedestrians at the center of all new developments in the county. Calthorpe's designs revolve around "pedestrian pockets"—compact clusters or pockets of development, linked by transit systems, with most essential facilities within walking distance of home. The goal is to lay out future communities densely populated enough to make public transit economical. Sutter Bay, a mammoth development 10 miles north of Sacramento that Calthorpe is designing, will ultimately house 175,000 people. Sacramento officials have agreed to extend the light rail line to connect this planned settlement (if and when it gets built) with the state capital.

Construction has already begun on another Calthorpe project, Laguna West, which has been called a "suburb with a downtown of its own." Homes for 8,000 people will surround a town center with stores, schools, daycare facilities, parks, and a transit station. Offices will be located alongside homes.[160]

Calthorpe sees light rail, rather than the freeway, as the main instrument for shaping development patterns. Rail systems are the key to linking pedestrian pockets with existing residential, commercial, educational, and recreational centers, as well as to other pedestrian pockets. He believes people are happy to rely on mass transit when it's convenient to do so. Supporting evidence comes from a study of San Francisco's rapid transit system, BART, which showed that 40 percent of the people living and working within a five-minute walk of the station took the train to work.[161]

Unleashing Human Power

"Single-function land-use zoning at a scale and density that eliminates the pedestrian has been the norm for so long that Americans have forgotten that walking can be part of their daily lives," notes Calthorpe. "Certainly the present suburban environment is not walkable."[162]

Wide boulevards resembling drag strips and freeways that chop up neighborhoods into isolated islands make it unthinkable to walk in large stretches of urban America. However, if the surroundings were more congenial, that could change. The first thing you have to do, says Calthorpe, is "give [people] an environment they might want to walk around in."[163]

Walking can be a liberating experience, especially when compared to stewing in relentless traffic, wedged behind a steering wheel. "Now it happens that the form of mobility which is the most free, walking, is also the most invigorating and inspiring, the least burdensome or disruptive, and the most social," Kenneth Schneider wrote in *Autokind vs. Mankind*. "Human legs also happen to be at the human scale and coincide perfectly with the natural geometry of the living environment. Hence, we will put man on his feet again, permit him to loiter, and present him with real live faces as he goes."[164]

"If we cannot walk around town, where will the mind go?" asks psychologist James Hillman. "Simply said: we may be *driving* ourselves crazy by not attending to the fundamental human need of walking."[165]

Walking certainly takes less space than driving. "One parked vehicle requires the area of about 20 walkers," Schneider adds. "One moving at 30 miles per hour requires the space of more than 60 walkers. That's partly why cars in today's traffic wait mostly for cars, little for pedestrians, while pedestrians do virtually all of their waiting for cars and rarely, but momentarily, for each other."[166]

Zoning practices that shorten travel distances can make walking and bicycling the preferred ways of getting around. Where mass transit is available to handle longer trips, the need for a car can be reduced or eliminated altogether. So far, Europe and other parts of the world are way ahead of the United States on this front. (Or you might say they are way *behind* us since they never went quite so overboard with cars in the first place.) Western Europeans walk some 2 to 4 times more often than Americans and bicycle 6 to 40 times more often. The greater reliance on bicycles in Europe "is not simply a matter of topography and population density," says John Pucher. "A few regions of the United States are as flat and as densely populated as the Netherlands, and thus as potentially conducive to bicycling. Yet nowhere in the

United States does bicycling ever approach the level of importance it holds for the Dutch.''[167]

Safety, or lack thereof, is a big part of the story. ''In the United States, pedestrians and bicyclists are forced to risk their lives every time they make the decision not to use an automobile and instead walk or bicycle,'' Pucher adds. Eight thousand pedestrians and bicyclists are killed each year by autos. One problem is that bikeways are few and far between. And most of those that exist are not separated from traffic, which makes them extremely hazardous.

Of course biking can be made safer. Governments in Western Europe—among them, the Netherlands, Denmark, Belgium, and Germany—have financed the construction and maintenance of networks of bikeways, each with rights of way separate from roads. ''They either give bicycle traffic priority over autos or at least treat it equally,'' says Pucher.

The Netherlands—with over 9,000 miles of bike paths, more than any other country in the world—is widely heralded as the bicycle capital of Europe.[168] As in many European and Asian countries, special parking spaces are set aside for bikes, and train passengers are allowed to bring their bikes aboard. Thanks to such policies, about one third of the trips made in the Netherlands are on bicycles.[169]

Denmark ranks second in Europe after the Netherlands, with 20 percent of all trips there taken on bikes.[170] In a move to reduce pollution and congestion, Copenhagen started the City-Bike program in 1991, which allows residents and visitors to borrow bikes free of charge after putting down a modest refundable deposit. (Bikes can be obtained from coin-operated racks located throughout the city; when bikes are returned to the rack, riders get their money back.)

Bicycle riding doubled in Erlangen, West Germany, after 100 miles of bike paths were built. Fifteen percent of all commuters in Japan use bikes; some cities even have bicycle parking garages. Kasukabe, for example, has a 12-story lot that hoists bikes with a crane, 1,500 at a time. Biking is so prevalent in China that traffic monitors in the city of Tinajin counted more than 50,000 bicycles passing through a single intersection in one hour.[171]

Bicycles are, as a matter of fact, the most widely used form of transport in the world, as well as the most energy efficient. The 800-million-plus bikes on this planet outnumber passenger cars by roughly two to one.[172] In the United States, however, bicycling seldom gets treated seriously as a transportation option. At the U.S. Department of Commerce, "inquiries on bicycle trade are referred to its Division of Toys and Games," writes Marcia Lowe. "And the World Bank, the main source of urban transit investment in the developing world, published a 1985 study on the Chinese transport sector that does not even mention the word bicycle, although the overwhelming majority of trips in China's cities are made by bike."[173] Indeed, many Chinese cities have five- and six-lane bicycle avenues.

Bicycling is booming in the United States as a leisure activity—Americans now own 103 million bikes, more than ever. Yet, only 2 to 3 million of these get used for commuting. Bicyclists thus account for just a small percentage of commuters in America.[174] Pedaling to work seems highly practical, though, since more than half of all commuting trips are less than five miles. Cyclists can travel this distance at least as fast as cars or mass transit, in part because they can slip past traffic snarls.[175]

Twenty-eight percent of the Manhattan office workers surveyed in a 1990 Department of Transportation study said they would bicycle to work if there were safe bicycle lanes, bike parking spaces, and change-and-shower facilities at their workplace. Half of the employees living within 10 miles of the workplace said they would commute by bicycle if the above conditions were met.[176]

Air quality will inevitably improve if biking to work catches on. Not only could cycling substitute for smog-producing cars, says Lowe, it "could do away with the most polluting of automobile drives—short trips, when engines don't heat up enough to fire efficiently."[177]

Six members of Transportation Alternatives—a New York City–based group promoting auto-free transport options—were arrested in October 1990 for blocking cars from the Queensboro Bridge while protesting a ban on the use of bike lanes during weekday afternoons. The group, "the Queensboro Six," was acquitted in a criminal court on March 14, 1991, when Judge Laura Safer Espinoza ruled that "the death and illness of New Yorkers from air pollution and vehicles are far greater harms than that created by disorderly conduct."[178]

There are other encouraging signs. The number of U.S. bike commuters quadrupled from 1975 to 1985, according to Lowe. This growth has been fostered by places like Palo Alto, California, which spent $1 million on new bike paths, bike racks, and bike lockers. Forty miles of bikeways have been built, including a two-mile avenue through the heart of town open only to bicyclists and pedestrians. Palo Alto has enacted innovative measures, including regulations that force large office buildings to provide bike parking and shower facilities to employees. One firm, the Alza Corporation, gives commuters a dollar for every day they bike to work.

Ten percent of the parking spaces in Gainesville, Florida, are reserved for bicycles.[179] In the Phoenix suburb of Glendale, unclaimed stolen bikes are lent to city employees who promise to give up driving three days a week and bicycle to work instead. "It was great to have a bike," said Jim Corbett, a Phoenix employee who participated in the program, "until it was stolen."[180]

David Wilson, an MIT professor of mechanical engineering, rides to work every day, eight miles each way, on the "recumbent," sit-down-style bike that he invented—that is, unless the snow is very deep. Then, he says, "I switch to a ten-speed." When Wilson first arrived in the United States in the 1950s from the United Kingdom, he was regarded as "a freak"—the only adult in town who rode a bike. "How is it acceptable for people to wait 10 to 40 minutes at a bus stop in a wind chill factor of 60 below zero, when it is not acceptable to ride a bicycle?" he asks. "My motor starts every morning without any digging with the key, and so does my heater. In a minute, I'm generating a kilowatt of energy."[181] Wilson endures repeated insults as he pursues his passion. Once he was struck by a car and left for dead on the side of the road. Another time, he was lassoed by kids in a passing van. "If I didn't love biking so much, I wouldn't put up with it," he admits.[182]

Of course bikes, recumbent or upright, are not for everyone—that's why roller blades were invented. Chuck Denman, a strategic analyst at McDonnell Douglas Space Systems, used to drive to and from work and then go to the gym to work out for two hours. Denman found that by the time he finished his routine he had no free time left in the evenings, so he quit the gym and bought some roller blades instead. Now he skates from his home in Long Beach to his office in Huntington Beach, nine miles in each direction. He enjoys gliding his way to work rather than driving a gas-powered "box." "Life is full of enough boxes," he says. "I come to work in a box, a cubicle in a building. I go home to another box and watch TV in another box. For me, expressing my freedom is breaking out of those boxes."[183]

IS THERE LIFE AFTER CARS?

Charlie Komanoff—a respected energy economist who is also president of Transportation Alternatives—believes the time has come to move beyond endless treatises on the evils of the automobile. "There have to be lifestyle changes," he says. "I'm tired of environmentalists who drive cars." Komanoff (an avid cyclist), along with his organization, Transportation Alternatives, has taken on the ambitious task of converting New York City to a "more human scale" by de-emphasizing the automobile and promoting greater reliance on cycling, walking, and transit.[184] Many involved in the project would probably agree that the ultimate goal of auto-free cities may never happen and perhaps shouldn't. Instead, carelessness should be regarded as a target to get us pointed in the right direction.

The decision not to own a car—for those who are not carless owing to poverty or an inability or ineligibility to drive—can profoundly influence a person's life, going beyond what is commonly meant by "lifestyle changes." People who don't own cars have to think carefully about where they live and work, making sure they can reach the places they need to go without the benefit of "wheels."

For special occasions, of course, people who don't own cars can rent them or take taxis. Car-sharing arrangements have also proved practical in the few places they have been tried. The STAR (Short-Term Auto Rental) project started in 1984 in a San Francisco apartment and condominium development is one. A fleet of cars of different sizes and makes are kept in the garage of the housing complex, available on a 24-hour basis. Users are billed monthly, depending on how often they take out a vehicle. The goal is to make it unnecessary for a family to purchase a second car, or for the occasional user to purchase a first car, while reducing the overall costs of personal transportation.[185]

The environmental benefits of this approach—assuming everyone drives no more or less than they would have otherwise—would be modest. A parent who might need a good-sized van to tote the kids around, could take a more fuel-efficient subcompact for a brief junket to the shopping center. Car sharing would reduce the total number of vehicles needed in a neighborhood or a housing complex, thereby cutting down somewhat on the resources devoted to manufacturing and to end-of-the-road disposal problems. The biggest benefit, however, would come from driving less. If people had to pay every time they drove a car—even if that still costs less than owning a car—they might think twice about it and maybe decide to walk or bike.

Of course, not everyone can get by comfortably without a car. People who live far from population centers need a car to get most places, and a parent can't carry home a week's worth of groceries for a family on a bicycle. Most people who, at least in principle, don't desperately *need* a car would still prefer to have one. Mass transit—frequently touted as "the answer"—can in some cases ease pollution and congestion problems while lowering total energy demand, but it has proved neither economical nor energy efficient in sparsely populated regions. Redesigning our cities so that public transportation will work better is a worthwhile goal, but easier said than done; reconfiguring such cities as Manhattan, Phoenix, or Baltimore—where designs are reinforced by habit as well as concrete foundations—will prove much harder than starting from scratch.

Americans face, by any reckoning, a tough road ahead. In a speech to college graduates made years ago, Woody Allen spelled out some of the difficult choices with which future decision makers would have to grapple. "More than any other time in history, mankind now faces a crossroads," Allen said. "One path leads to despair and utter hopelessness. The other, to total extinction. Let us pray we have the wisdom to choose correctly."[186]

So what's to be done? The challenge, obviously, is to find a third path.

6

Overhauling the Transportation Engine

For every complex and difficult problem, there
is an answer that is simple, easy, and wrong.

H. L. MENCKEN

The future is not what it used to be.

THOMAS DEEN,
executive director of
the Transportation Research Board

Following ancient tradition, American Indian leaders look far into the
future—planning not only for their own generation, or for their children's generation, but for seven generations ahead. "Each generation
makes sure that the seventh generation will be here," Oren Lyons, chief
of the Onondaga Nation, explains from his home in upstate New York.
"We're accountable to them. They're the ones who'll ask, 'Why did
you do this?' " What's happened, Lyons says, is that in today's industrial society technology has overtaken common sense. "You can
take a chainsaw and in ten minutes kill a tree that's four hundred years
old."

The problem goes beyond the familiar cry of technology run amok.
At the heart of the environmental crisis, according to Lyons, is not the
inadequate control of our machinery, but rather a poor understanding
of time. "People don't operate on the time frame of a mountain or a
river," he adds. "They operate on the time frame of a human being."
Without a proper appreciation of time or a true long-term perspective,
"you can get your people and your generation in a whole lot of
trouble."[1]

In *New World, New Mind,* Robert Ornstein, a brain researcher, and
Paul Ehrlich, the Stanford biologist who wrote *The Population Bomb,*
go even farther. These two scientists say we are "losing control of our
future" because "civilization is threatened by changes taking place
over years and decades, but changes over a few years or decades are

too *slow* for [the human nervous system] to perceive readily . . . At the same time, the changes are much too *rapid* to allow biological or cultural evolutionary processes to adapt people to them. *We are out of joint with the times,* our times.''[2]

Certainly most political leaders are out of sync. Except maybe in wartime, few politicians think about what the world will be like for the next generation. ''If you talk to a congressman about something that will surface more than two years from now, a glaze comes over his eyes,'' social commentator Norman Cousins said in 1986. ''The mainframe of American society is not constructed to look at or deal with long-term issues.''[3]

Transportation and energy policies have suffered notoriously from this myopia. It is painfully clear that our investment in transportation has too often been an investment in roads—bigger, broader, and more extensive—at the expense of down-to-earth but far-reaching land-use improvements.

To be fair, many U.S. roadways desperately need repairs, and federal and state governments have done more in the realm of transportation than just sponsor highway construction. Tailpipe emission restrictions, state-administered inspection and maintenance programs, CAFE (Corporate Average Fuel Efficiency) standards, gas-guzzler fees, traffic-management programs, and reduced speed limits were all designed to cope with the side effects of a growing motor vehicle population. However, a patchwork quilt of regulations governing fuel efficiency, emissions, and so forth cannot possibly produce a fine-tuned transportation system. Nor will this piecemeal approach to policy making protect the environment or reduce the country's dependence on imported oil.

AN ACT OF CONGRESS

In late 1991, the 102nd Congress took an important first step toward more rational transportation planning by passing the Intermodal Surface Transportation Efficiency Act of 1991. The new law, in many ways the brainchild of Senator Daniel Patrick Moynihan of New York, authorized $151 billion for highway and public transit over the following six years. Of this, $32 billion was set aside for mass transit—twice the previous annual spending and twice the amount recommended by Pres-

Tom Toles for the Buffalo News Leader, © 1989. Reprinted with permission.

ident Bush. And for the first time the same ratio of federal to state funding will apply to both highway and transit projects. Under the agreement, the federal government will pick up 80 percent of the tab for most transportation projects, with states paying the rest.

The new law allocated $119 billion for highways, including $38 billion for a new 155,000-mile National Highway System (NHS) comprised of the existing 44,000-mile interstate system, plus more than 100,000 miles of other roadways already on the map. The act broke new ground, giving states and local governments more leeway in spending federal funds. For starters, states may transfer up to half of their NHS funds to mass transit or other transportation projects. States that aren't meeting federal clean air standards may shift all of their NHS funds to other projects. (In 1989, 39 states were violating either the carbon monoxide or ozone air quality standard.)

The bill created a new $24-billion Surface Transportation Program with funds that state and local governments can spend on wide-ranging projects, including bike lanes, mass transit, or even pedestrian walkways. A total of $3 billion was earmarked for scenic and historic preservation, bicycle and pedestrian facilities, landscaping, and other transportation "enhancement" projects. The law also got "green planning" off the ground: from now on, local metropolitan planning organizations must take energy use, clean air, and other environmental factors into account in their decisions. Finally, this landmark bill requires air bags in all new cars by 1998 and in all light trucks and vans by 1999.

This forward-looking law contrasts sharply with the Bush administration's national energy strategy, which emphasizes increased domestic oil production at environmentally sensitive offshore sites and in the Arctic National Wildlife Refuge. Besides imploring car owners to keep their tires inflated, the administration has done little to promote the prudent energy use that would make drilling in the Alaskan reserve and other wilderness areas unnecessary. "The lifestyle of the nation isn't going to change that quickly," explained U.S. energy secretary James Watkins. "Let's get on with finding out what's up there."[4]

Although it marks a sharp (and welcome) departure from past highway bills, the new law alone can't solve our transportation problems. Deeper changes must come. If we gaze into the future—if not seven human generations ahead, at least seven generations of cars ahead— the need to make three profound technological and social transitions becomes evident. These transitions involve a new mixture of energy sources, new transportation technology and vehicles, and new patterns of residential and commercial land development.

STEP ONE: PHASING OUT OIL USE

To enhance national and economic security, keep global warming within bounds, and fight air and water pollution, one of the nation's highest energy priorities must be reducing oil consumption, especially in transportation, where it makes up 97 percent of all the energy used. Americans simply have to build and buy more fuel-efficient vehicles, reduce wasteful and unnecessary driving, and—over the long term— find substitutes for oil.

"Might I suggest our classic Persian Gulf '89? ... Or would Monsieur prefer a selection from our limited domestic reserve?"

Getting Fuel Prices Right

Most energy analysts agree that the single largest obstacle to boosting motor vehicle efficiency and reducing oil consumption is rock-bottom petroleum prices. Gasoline prices in the United States (in "real," un-inflated dollars) are near their all-time low. U.S. gasoline prices average only one half to one quarter those of our trading partners, while U.S. per capita gasoline use ranges far above that of other industrialized countries.

The federal tax on motor fuels should be raised by at least 10 cents per gallon per year for the next decade. This increase of a dime a year would begin to reflect the many societal risks that gasoline use entails. It would encourage Americans to buy more fuel efficient vehicles and spur changes in travel habits, greater use of public transportation, and, ultimately, the development of nonpolluting vehicles. (Such a tax would also begin to bring U.S. fuel prices in line with those of other industrialized countries, whose motor vehicle fleets tend to be much more efficient than ours.)

Are such tax increases fair? A common objection to higher fuel taxes is that they hurt low-income families who spend proportionately more of their income on energy. But a new analysis by MIT economist James Poterba suggests that in this case the biggest tax burden won't fall on the poor. Poterba found that the poorest Americans, in fact, spend proportionately less on gasoline than any other income group except for the richest 10 percent. Some low-income households may even benefit from a tax hike because federal entitlements—such as food stamps or social security payments—are tied to the consumer price index. A boost in the gas tax would drive up the consumer price index, leading to more generous benefits.[5]

The brunt of a gasoline tax, obviously, has to fall somewhere. Otherwise, it wouldn't have any impact on driving habits, fuel economy, alternative fuels development and use, or mass transit ridership. However, such a tax can't be allowed to harm those who can least afford to pay. Fortunately, there are some simple ways, at least in principle, to take the sting out of higher gas taxes. Payroll taxes for low- and middle-income people could be cut to offset the added burden. Those so poor that they pay no taxes could be reimbursed by a "negative tax" (refund) for any potential losses. For example, social security benefits for retirees could be increased to make up the difference. On balance, the tax hike could be made progressive, while still nudging consumers to do the right thing.

Improving New-Vehicle Fuel Efficiency

A bill introduced in the 102nd Congress by Senator Richard Bryan would require U.S. automakers to improve their CAFE ("Corporate Average Fuel Efficiency") ratings by 20 percent over their 1988 level by the 1996 model year and by 40 percent five years farther down the road. It's a sensible idea given the ample technical opportunities for boosting fuel economy. In fact, the average fuel efficiency of new cars in the U.S. fleet virtually doubled from 1974 to 1985, owing largely to the first CAFE law, whose requirements took effect in 1978, and to higher fuel prices. This law and the more recent proposal push the auto industry in the right direction and set useful intermediate goals.

Although higher efficiency standards for new cars (like those proposed by Senator Bryan) deserve support, we can't pin our hopes for a transportation revolution on them. Taken on their own, these stan-

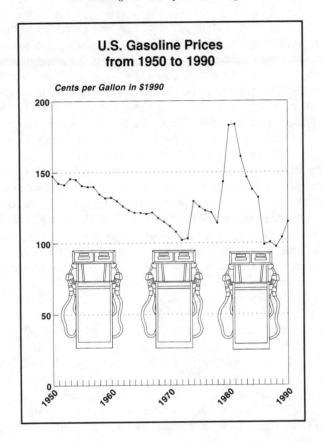

**U.S. Gasoline Prices
from 1950 to 1990**

Cents per Gallon in $1990

dards are not likely to bring overall motor vehicle fuel consumption (or carbon dioxide emissions) down below present levels. Again, the central problem is today's low gasoline prices. If fuel remains this cheap, consumers will have little incentive to buy more fuel efficient cars. Indeed, Detroit manufacturers have put more efficient cars on the market but still can't meet the current CAFE standards because most consumers aren't buying these high-mpg models. In fact, domestic automakers have never once achieved the 27.5 mpg average required by law as of 1985.[6] The Department of Transportation weakened the CAFE standard for model years 1986 through 1989 so that domestic automakers did not have to pay fines that they otherwise would have had to pay during this period. CAFE standards simply don't push people to drive more efficiently, take the subway or bus, carpool, combine errands, or use non-fossil-fuel-powered vehicles. "If you want that to happen, you've got to put a tax on gas," says James Womack, research director of the International Motor Vehicle Program at MIT. "Manufacturers are told to make more fuel efficient cars, but with the real price of gasoline going down, those cars make absolutely no sense to consumers. If this stuff is so cheap, why not use it?"[7]

The problem extends beyond national borders. Foreign manufacturers are picking up on the expressed desires of the American consumer. New imported vehicles are becoming less efficient in response to American preferences for big, powerful cars. The 1991 average of 29.7 mpg for imports is 8 percent below the all-time peak of 32.4 mpg achieved in 1983. Reinforcing this trend is the "voluntary" quota on the number of vehicles imported from Japan. With a limit of 2.3 million imported cars per year in effect since 1985, the Japanese have been pushing larger, more luxurious cars, which tend to be more profitable though less efficient. (In March 1992, Japanese automakers cut this self-imposed ceiling an additional 28 percent, to 1.65 million per year.)[8]

In October 1991, the Congressional Office of Technology Assessment (OTA) estimated that even with the tighter CAFE standards proposed by Bryan, total U.S. oil use would *rise* 10 percent above today's level by the year 2010. Total consumption, of course, would be lower with the CAFE standards than without them. But as a means of reducing oil use, higher new-car efficiencies tend to encourage driving by making it cheaper—a "rebound effect" that could cut anticipated fuel savings by as much as 30 percent.

Paying for Insurance at the Pump

Higher fuel prices might be more palatable if we took a different approach to paying for automotive insurance.[9] What would happen if, as some analysts suggest, motorists paid for part of their auto insurance through a fee imposed on gasoline? First, high-mileage drivers would pay proportionately more each year—only fair since they face increased risks of accidents. Second, there would be no more uninsured drivers on the road. Third, fees collected at the pump would be distributed to insurance companies to meet customer claims, so this plan could be implemented fairly simply. (Extra insurance would be needed to cover those with poor driving records or cars that are expensive to replace.) Insurance at the pump would cost between 50 cents and a dollar per gallon of fuel, but the premiums that motorists now pay to their insurance companies would fall almost commensurately. As for fairness, buying insurance this way would be just, because low-income people drive less than high-income people. Under the plan, the price of gas would rise to about $2 a gallon—enough to dampen the urge to drive, but not to immobilize the country.

Fees and Rebates

Another way to increase new-vehicle fuel efficiency is to slap fees on gas guzzlers and offer rebates on "gas sippers." Actually, there is a "gas-guzzler" tax already in place; buyers of inefficient new cars paid well over $100 million in federal taxes in 1989.[10] But the second half of this package, a "feebate" system, does not yet exist on the federal level. Under such a system, new gas-gulping vehicles would continue to be taxed according to their mpg ratings.[11] The revenues would create a fund for financing the purchase of more efficient vehicles. Presumably, such flexible self-financing would prompt consumers to purchase the more efficient vehicles that might be mandated under a CAFE program.

In April 1992, the Maryland legislature adopted a feebate scheme that when fully implemented would raise the sales tax on gas guzzlers up to one percentage point (from 5 to 6 percent) while reducing the sales tax on gas sippers by an equal amount (from 5 to 4 percent). The law was challenged by the National Highway Traffic Safety Administration on technical grounds, but supporters believe that with some minor adjustments, objections can be met and the proposal put into effect.

Scrapping Older Cars

Programs to scrap older, less efficient and more polluting cars would also cut fuel use and auto emissions. According to the Department of Energy, retiring 2 million or so clunkers from the road could save 150 to 230 million gallons of fuel per year. In fact, eliminating these gas-guzzling, dirty cars (while raising fuel taxes, setting insurance reform in motion, and inaugurating feebates) would improve vehicle efficiency and cut fuel consumption more effectively than any other approach.

The benefits of scrapping aging cars were assessed in a 1991 study sponsored by major oil companies.[12] Researchers compared the advantages of retiring 10 million over-the-hill cars with a hypothetical CAFE requirement that would increase new-car fuel efficiency by one mpg per year through 1996.[13] The two programs, they estimated, would save about the same amount of fuel. In the first, financed by either a gas-guzzler tax or a two-cent-per-gallon gasoline tax, motorists would be paid $700 to scrap their pre-1979 cars. According to Bernard Campbell of the Massachusetts-based consulting firm DRI, this scheme would cut both carbon monoxide and hydrocarbon emissions by 15 percent (compared to less than 1 percent under the CAFE program). Scrapping the fleet's most flagrant violators would also cost less and create more jobs than tightening CAFE standards would. Clearly, getting high-polluting vehicles off the road is an important complement to any effort to raise efficiency and reduce emissions.

In a four-month pilot program administered in 1990 by the Union Oil Company of California (Unocal), car owners were paid $700 to junk their pre-1971 models. All told, more than 8,000 aging cars were removed from the road, preventing the release of 13 million pounds of pollutants each year, according to Unocal estimates. On March 18, 1992, the Bush administration unveiled its "cash for clunkers" program. Under the plan, companies required to reduce emissions from factories, oil refineries, or other large stationary sources can instead achieve a comparable reduction by paying for the elimination of dirty cars.

Avoiding the Wrong Alternative Fuels

However compelling the case for reducing oil consumption may be, the U.S. transportation system would collapse if the oil spigot were simply turned off tomorrow. Both sweeping efficiency improvements *and* alternative fuels must be introduced gradually. That said, among the various substitutes for oil that have been proposed—methanol, ethanol, compressed natural gas (CNG), electricity, and hydrogen—each has drawbacks and each faces barriers to widespread use.

Carbon-based fuel alternatives—CNG, methanol, and ethanol—are particularly fraught with problems. The inescapable fact is that both methanol (most cheaply made from natural gas) and CNG are fossil fuels, so supplies are finite, and their greenhouse gas contributions are expected to be about the same as those of oil-based fuels.[14] The clean-air benefits of methanol (wood alcohol)—relative to those of switching to cleaner conventional vehicles burning reformulated gasoline—are not known for certain, but most likely won't amount to much. Running vehicles on CNG would help clean the air of some pollutants, but, again, supplies of natural gas are too limited to support an entire transportation future. In 1989, gasohol accounted for about 4 percent of U.S. motor fuel sales,[15] but a switch to this fuel, despite its popularity, wouldn't make the air we breathe much cleaner, nor would it yield any significant greenhouse benefits.

The production of ethanol (grain alcohol) entails vast amounts of land. If made from corn, as it is in the United States, ethanol would require about 1 acre of cropland to produce the amount of energy annually that 198 gallons of gasoline contain. Making the equivalent of the 133 billion gallons of gasoline and diesel fuel consumed in 1990 would require about 670 million acres of cropland—well over twice the total amount available in the United States! This rules out ethanol as anything other than a minor source of transportation fuel, perhaps for running agricultural vehicles.

STEP TWO: PHASING IN CLEAN VEHICLES

Vehicles equipped with either electric batteries or hydrogen fuel cells are the only alternatives to the gasoline-powered car that have the potential to drastically reduce air pollution and greenhouse gas emissions while cutting oil imports. Getting these clean machines on the road should be a high priority in all countries. But how? A hint of the answer can be found by looking westward.

Electric vehicles (EVs) will soon appear in droves in California. The Los Angeles Department of Water and Power and Southern California Edison are subsidizing the introduction of 10,000 EVs to be on the road by 1995. Still, commercial prospects remain uncertain. One of the manufacturers of these vehicles, Clean Air Transport of Sweden, hopes to offer more than 30,000 EVs for sale to the public by 1995. These hybrid vehicles (expected to sell for $25,000 each) would be able to run about 60 miles on battery power alone. During longer trips, a small gasoline engine would provide additional range. Unfortunately, as of June 1992, Clean Air was finding it hard to raise manufacturing capital.

Regulatory changes will help usher in these zero emission vehicles (ZEVs). Clean-air regulations adopted by the California Air Resources Board on September 28, 1990, will spur radical changes in the technology used to power vehicles, first in the United States and eventually worldwide. Under the new regulations, zero-emission vehicles must be introduced starting in 1998. That year, 2 percent of all new vehicles sold in California—about 40,000 electric vehicles—must meet this acid test. By 2001, the percentage increases to 5 percent (100,000 vehicles), and by 2003, 10 percent of all new vehicles (about 200,000) would have to be electric. In April 1992, Japan's MITI announced plans to produce 100,000 electric vehicles annually by the year 2000.[16]

Hydrogen-powered cars may also debut in response to California's zero-emission regulations. Mazda Corporation has already unveiled a prototype hydrogen car with a rotary engine.[17] A hydrogen distribution network and better hydrogen storage are both needed before hydrogen cars can be introduced in significant numbers, and any emissions of nitrogen oxides or volatile organic compounds must be eliminated, too. Still, if these problems can be solved, hydrogen cars with rotary engines could be on the road by the year 2000, or even before, says Mazda's Takaharu Kobayakawa.

California's timely leadership has quickly shown the way for other states, and eventually, perhaps, the federal government will follow suit. In October 1991, most of the Northeastern states announced their intent to adopt California's new emission requirements. These states, along with California and three other states considering similar legislation, represent well over a third of all U.S. light-duty vehicle registrations in 1990. If market shares in these states stay about the same over the next decade, more than 100,000 new EVs will be on the road in 1998 and more than 1.8 million by 2003.

Legislation introduced in the 102nd Congress would hasten the introduction of electric vehicles nationwide, including those powered by hydrogen fuel cells. Under a new commercial demonstration program, the federal government would subsidize the initial higher vehicle prices for EV purchasers. At the same time, it would use its purchasing power to create markets for EVs while sponsoring further research on EV technology as well as the development of infrastructure technology (charging equipment, hydrogen compressors for fuel-cell cars, and so forth).

Electric and hydrogen vehicles are the vehicles of choice as the nation makes the switch to renewable energy. However, as long as batteries, fuel cells, and other hydrogen technologies remain expensive and gasoline stays cheap, electric cars and trucks will cost more than conventional vehicles to own and operate. But over time, operating costs for these emissionless vehicles could drop below those of gas-powered cars, and manufacturing costs will certainly drop as production scales upward.

Instead of waiting for this effect to kick in, state and local governments can get electric hydrogen vehicles on the road earlier by making policy changes that enhance the economic competitiveness of these vehicles. For starters, states should allow these cars to use HOV lanes and temporarily waive fees (such as annual registration fees) and tariffs (including sales, personal property, and fuel taxes) that apply to gas or diesel-powered vehicles. They should also provide investment tax credits for manufacturers and users of EVs. Some kind of feebate arrangement, like those designed to promote fuel-efficient cars, could be used to encourage the individual consumer to purchase an electric or hydrogen-powered vehicle rather than the old gas-guzzling standby.

Hydrogen vehicles, whether powered by internal combustion engines or fuel cells, can't operate in a vacuum, so the widespread lack of hydrogen pipelines, compressors, and other relevant equipment needed for refueling poses real problems. Still, carefully designed demonstration programs could begin to address these barriers and help get such vehicles on the road.[18] Hydrogen cars, trucks, and buses could be introduced first in heavily polluted regions such as southern California. Initially, centrally fueled fleets could be tested using hydrogen generated at refueling stations through electrolysis. The electricity would come from conventional power plants at first. Gradually, hydrogen produced using renewable energy sources—such as photovoltaic cells or wind turbines—could be phased in as the economics and performance of these technologies improve and as society learns to bill itself for more of the now-hidden costs of driving vehicles powered by fossil fuels.

Once hydrogen vehicles prove themselves, they could be introduced in fleets and for private use in other parts of the country. Eventually, pipelines could be built from regions with high renewable-energy potential—that is, with high levels of sunlight or wind—to distribute hydrogen to the more populous states. Once established as a transportation fuel, hydrogen could start replacing fossil fuels as a way to heat homes and buildings and to generate electricity in all regions of the country. When this happens, the United States will be well on its way to a sustainable energy economy.

STEP THREE: SHIFTING TO A TRANSPORTATION SYSTEM WE CAN LIVE WITH

Each day, the United States spends nearly $100 million building new streets and roads, or fixing and widening existing ones, despite overwhelming evidence that construction provides only temporary relief from congestion and delays. In many parts of the country, rush-hour and even weekend congestion is testing the mettle of drivers, killing time, lowering worker productivity, adding to air pollution, causing accidents, and wasting fuel. A continued commitment to a system that isn't working anymore shatters lives along with nerves: as noted earlier, the highway death toll now stands at 47,000 annually (1989), and another 1.7 Americans are maimed or disabled on the nation's highways every year.

A certain level of congestion in vibrant cities is inevitable: most people—social animals at heart—want to go where the action is. But congestion is largely a function of how a city is laid out and how far from their jobs most commuters live. For these reasons, no two cities face exactly the same traffic bottlenecks, though the problems often stem from the same basic causes. Employment, housing, and commercial patterns, highway configuration, the availability of public transportation, and commuting patterns all figure into regional congestion. They also tell us where to look for ways to break it up.

Our transportation history teaches us what kind of expectations are realistic. Over the next few years, the options are fairly limited: we must rely primarily on "technological fixes" to forestall area-wide gridlock. That means improving traffic management and pressing for alternatives to solo commuting to work. Over the longer term, the key is expanding the use of public transport systems in the high-density metropolitan areas where they make economic sense. At the same time, we must change land-use and zoning practices so that many of the estimated five or six social, recreational, and errand-related trips we each take every week can be combined, shortened, or made without a car.

Bringing about these changes means restructuring economic incentives that have made car ownership and driving all but birthrights in this country. Cars dominate our transportation system today largely because their use is so heavily subsidized. Ending these subsidies could cool America's fascination with the automobile and open up new transportation avenues.

Technological Fixes for Traffic: Getting into the Flow

Various technological and traffic management measures can be implemented relatively quickly. The Institute of Transportation Engineers (ITE) has evaluated many such tools for reducing congestion: HOV lanes, improved traffic signals, motorist information systems, reversible express lanes, ramp metering, parking management programs, and others.[19] In terms of overall effectiveness, cost, and ease of implementation, no single solution comes out on top in every region. Indeed, as ITE suggests, it's up to state and local transportation officials to survey regional needs and constraints to determine which combination of measures will break up local congestion. Meanwhile, technological fixes can be adopted locally to provide breathing room while housing patterns, land use, and transportation planning are reoriented.

Reducing the number of vehicles on the road, especially during traffic peaks, has to become a major transportation goal in this country if people want to get where they are going on time and in a mental state approximating sanity. Setting aside freeway lanes for high-occupancy vehicles and encouraging big companies to form car and van pools for their workers could help untangle traffic. This shift can be implemented through tax incentives or regulations—as in California, where the law now forces companies to increase the capacity factor of employee vehicles or pay stiff fines.

Integrating Land Use and Transportation Planning

Commuting accounts for only a third of all miles driven. Most other trips—roughly a third for family and personal business and a third for social and recreational reasons[20]—are far less predictable than commuting trips, so mobilizing mass transit and van pools is only a partial solution to congestion.

The need for many of our car trips stems partly from customary zoning and development practices. Because stores and other commercial developments are not allowed in suburban residential areas, meeting even the most routine daily needs—buying a quart of milk or picking up laundered shirts—generally requires a car. Even where shops do exist near residential areas, ditches, busy roads, and other barriers to pedestrian travel often make walking inconvenient. Then, too, the mobility that cars afford has allowed people to buy affordable housing far from city centers and workplaces—a pattern reinforced by commercial zoning laws.

Our land-use and development patterns must change, even though they are literally set in stone. Bucking decades of suburbanization, planners and developers will have to interest mainstream Americans in the kind of high-density urban developments where walking, bicycling, and public transportation are both possible and enjoyable. (Residential densities above seven housing units per acre are needed for cost-effective bus service. For cost-effective light rail service, density must exceed nine housing units per acre.)[21] The rewards are rich: according to California planner and engineer John Holtzclaw, doubling a residential population's density reduces per capita auto mileage by 25 to 30 percent.[22] By allowing mixed residential and commercial development, we could cut the number of daily auto trips per household for personal business by up to 25 percent.[23] Americans need only look to Europe's most beautiful and sophisticated cities to see that a high standard of living and a reduced need for cars can go hand in hand.

We cannot hope to solve congestion problems until regional transit planning is coupled with land-use reform. In the short run, buses and van pools offer a fast and flexible response. In dense urban cores, people will use vans and buses if highway and urban lanes are dedicated exclusively to them and if parking for solo commuters is made scarce. Over the longer term, light and heavy rail are attractive options, especially if zoning regulations are changed so that they favor higher-density mixed development. If parking and transfers at outlying stations are convenient, more suburbanites will board mass transit to get into and out of town.

Since federal support for public transport totalled only about $3 billion in 1990, compared with $15 billion for highway construction, the new transportation legislation passed in late 1991 stands as a major victory for rational transportation planning: it doubled the annual federal commitment to public transit and allowed states to decide whether to spend federal funds on highways or mass transit. That is a start, but we must now go beyond a debate over cars versus mass transit and concentrate instead on the more basic task of converting our cities into places where getting around can be a pleasure rather than a chore.

Paying the Full Toll

Our country's overdependence on vehicles today is not an inexplicable fact of life. Nor is it the product of some peculiarly American love affair with the automobile. Rather, it is the predictable result of numerous federal and state policies that have distorted the true cost of driving, subsidized road construction and parking, underfunded mass transit, discouraged rational transportation planning, and encouraged low-density development, thus stifling most people's interest in walking, bicycling, or public transit.[24] A sampling of these policies reveals the extent to which incentives have been rigged to favor the car and suggests how we might go about restructuring them:

Subsidies to Road Construction and Maintenance. Highway and road projects are funded by local, state, and federal governments. In 1989, governments on all three levels spent a total of roughly $33 billion building, improving, and rehabilitating highways, streets, and roads.[25] An additional $20 billion was spent on maintenance, $6.4 billion on police and safety services, $5.4 billion on administration, and

$6.3 billion on interest and debt retirement.[26] Yet only about $44 billion of the total $74 billion raised for roads and related services was collected through road user–related taxes and tolls. Some $29 billion came from property taxes, general funds, and other sources.[27] In other words, drivers paid only 60 percent of the costs of road construction and maintenance. The remainder—which averages out to about 22 cents per gallon of motor vehicle fuel used—is basically a subsidy that encourages driving. If fuel prices rise to the point where drivers are actually paying as they go for *all* the costs that make their driving possible, some people will choose to stay rather than go, while others will modify their driving habits.

Subsidized Highway Services. Apart from a $.22-per-gallon subsidy for highway construction and maintenance, state and local governments give motorists a panoply of highway services supported by property taxes and other sources unrelated to driving. Government agencies pick up most of the tab for highway patrols, traffic management, parking enforcement, emergency responses to traffic accidents (by firefighters, paramedics, and police), investigations of vehicle accidents and auto theft, and routine street maintenance. Since almost everybody pays for these services, whether they drive or not, auto and truck driving is cheaper than it would be if only users paid.

How much do these subsidized services cost? Civil engineer Stanley Hart has estimated what it costs Pasadena, California to provide motorcycle patrols, auto-theft units, and parking enforcement, to help after road accidents, and to pay for traffic and road engineering;[28] he also chalked up the total collected from motor vehicle user fees. For fiscal year 1982 1983, Hart found, Pasadena's auto-related expenditures added up to nearly $16 million. Of this, users paid only 25 percent. It would take a fuel tax of $0.21 per gallon, Hart calculated, to cover these costs, and a comparable tax to cover similar costs covered by the county.

Extrapolating these findings to the entire United States, Hart estimated the costs of highway services to be $60 billion (in 1986 dollars) annually, or almost 50 cents per gallon (1989 dollars) of gasoline and diesel fuel used. If fuel prices gradually rose to cover the highway services people have been taking for granted, some extraneous driving would no doubt end with the free ride.

Subsidized Parking for Commuters. Roughly 93 million of the 110 million Americans who work commute by car,[29] and at least 9 out of 10 of them park free.[30] Various analyses confirm what intuition suggests about this telling statistic: the availability of free or subsidized parking for commuters strongly encourages solo commuting.[31] According to one estimate, ending employer-paid parking would reduce the number of lone commuters by 18 to 81 percent, depending on local circumstances, and cut the number of cars driven to work by 15 to 28 percent.[32]

Free parking is a nearly universal fringe benefit, largely because the federal tax code makes it a bargain for employers to provide it. In the Washington, D.C., area, for instance, an employer can provide a parking space as a fringe benefit for an employee for roughly $8 per day—about $2000 per year. To provide that same employee with an extra

$2000 in take-home (after taxes) salary to pay for his or her own parking, an employer would have to spend about $4,400 per year. From the employer's standpoint, the decision of whether to offer "free" parking or the equivalent salary increase is easy.

As the U.S. tax code now stands, employers can deduct as a business expense every penny spent providing workers with parking spaces.[33] If, instead, they decide to give their employees a public-transit subsidy, employers can deduct only $21 per employee per month. Under this system, drivers receive a subsidy and public transport users get penalized.

The problems spawned by subsidized commuter parking could be fairly easily surmounted.[34] One strategy would be to require employers who provide free parking to also offer all their workers the option of taking a tax-free travel allowance of equal market value. Workers would then be free to pay for the parking or, instead, to form car pools, take public transit, or find other ways to get to work and pocket the difference. As parking subsidies are offset or removed, other commuting options would become available. Van pools set up and supported by employers, preferential parking for carpoolers, and guaranteed rides home to workers in emergencies would also ease erstwhile drivers' car-separation anxieties.

Economic Reform. The simplest and most effective way to offset the many subsidies that motorists now enjoy would be to increase motor vehicle fuel taxes, as just discussed. By adding, say, 10 cents to the gallon each year for a decade or more, government would simultaneously encourage efficiency improvements in new vehicles, the introduction of emissionless vehicles, higher vehicle occupancy rates, greater use of mass transit, and less driving overall.

The effects of higher fuel prices can be complemented by the adoption of road-use pricing designed to combat congestion. Road tolls on major highways, priced according to the time of day, would improve traffic flow from the moment they were phased in. The technology needed for the job—devices that can scan motor vehicles for billing purposes as they speed by—has been amply demonstrated.

The 1991 transportation bill covers a good deal of ground, but it largely overlooks pricing strategies. By ignoring the need to eliminate or reduce subsidies that have brought our mobility-prizing nation to an impasse, the federal government has failed to give Americans any reason to alter their driving habits, buy alternatively fueled vechicles, or use more efficient transportation modes.

Resuscitating the Big Three

In the U.S. auto industry these days, "business as usual" has become a rather dreary proposition: 1991 was the worst year for new car and light truck sales since 1983, with total vehicle sales 11 percent below the previous year's.[35] Collectively, the Big Three automakers lost about $5 billion in 1991. In December of that year, capping off a dismal year, General Motors announced plans to shut down 21 factories and eliminate 74,000 jobs in the United States and Canada over the next three years.[36] Meanwhile, Japan captured a greater than ever share of the American automobile market. Of the current $41-billion-a-year trade deficit with Japan, some $30 billion reflects car and auto parts sales.

These circumstances have combined to create grave concern (sometimes bordering on hysteria) in the country. In early 1992, President Bush and the heads of GM, Ford, and Chrysler made a largely fruitless—even counterproductive—trade mission to Japan in an attempt to open up Japanese markets to more U.S. cars. The economic stakes are high, to be sure, since the auto industry accounts for about 4.5 percent of America's GNP, nearly 2 million jobs, and 12.4 percent of all corporate research and development.[37]

Calling for protectionism in response to Japan's unbridled success in the automotive marketplace, as happened frequently in early 1992, may salve but can't solve U.S. manufacturers' fundamental problems—lagging productivity, inferior reliability, and a $2,000-per-car price disadvantage compared to Japanese models.

What, if anything, should be done to keep these companies from going under? And why are the U.S. automakers in such dire straits to begin with? Researchers at MIT's International Motor Vehicle Program think they have the answer after five years of studying who's ahead in the global auto wars and why. In *The Machine That Changed the World,* authors James Womack, Daniel Jones, and Daniel Roos conclude that over the past 40 years, Japanese manufacturers, led by Toyota, have evolved a totally new way of manufacturing cars, which the

authors call "lean production."[38] Compared with traditional mass production as practiced in most industries, lean production uses less of
everything: half the human effort in the factory, half the manufacturing
space, half the investment in tools, half the engineering hours to develop a new product in half the time. Lean producers also keep far less
than half the needed inventory on site, allow many fewer product defects, and put out a greater and ever-growing variety of products.

The objective of U.S. and European carmakers, the MIT authors
claim, is to make cars that are "good enough." In other words, a certain
number of defects are tolerated. They also expect to house large inventories and to produce a fairly narrow range of products. The Japanese goals, on the other hand, are continually declining costs, zero
defects, zero inventories, and endless product variety.

The MIT authors categorically conclude that in North America, "the
full implementation of lean production can eliminate the massive trade
deficit in motor vehicles." As for the obstacles to Japanese-style efficiency, don't blame the American work force—Japanese cars made in
so-called transplant factories in the United States are every bit as good
as those made in Japan. The problem lies with the Western automakers' management. "The greatest obstacle in the path of a lean world
is easy to identify: the resistance of the massive mass-production corporations that are left over from the previous era of world industry."
Many of these companies stubbornly resisted change in the 1980s. Indeed, of the Big Three in the United States, only Ford has embraced
lean production techniques wholeheartedly. (Its conversion began
nearly a decade ago, when a financial crisis threatened the company's
very existence.)

Besides fear of change and an arrogance lingering from better times,
another contributing management flaw is the lack of cooperation within
the corporations. According to Daniel Roos, one of the MIT researchers, American management teams suffer from a lack of teamwork. U.S.
managers are used to hoarding information rather than sharing it and
to competing instead of cooperating with coworkers—approaches obviously at odds with lean production.[39]

Would low-interest loans or other forms of financial assistance to
U.S. automakers give them the boost they need to compete with Japan?
No, if it means continuing the current system of built-in waste, inflex-
ibility, and inefficiency. According to the MIT study, giving "mass-

producers more money to spend on inefficient product development, inefficient factory operations, and more sophisticated equipment than they need is bound only to make things worse in the long run.''[40] Yes, if the way that U.S. automakers plan, make, and sell motor vehicles is completely reformed.

Insufficient research and development funding is not the disease that is threatening Detroit's survival. James Womack, research director of MIT's International Motor Vehicle Program, points out that the history of trying to "bribe" auto producers with R & D grants has not been encouraging. From 1969 to 1991, the federal government set aside $1 billion for contractors, inside and out of the auto industry, to promote the development of alternative concepts such as gas turbine engines and electric and hybrid vehicles. But the Department of Energy, which administered the program, was pouring money down a rathole. "It was a complete and total waste," Womack says. "The industry had no real interest in these ideas; they just took the money. Companies tend to take research and development much more seriously when they're spending their own money, especially if they're fighting to survive.''[41]

American automakers are now engaged in what might be a life-and-death struggle—a situation calling for bold action. In a letter to GM chairman Robert Stempel published in the *Washington Post*, Jessica Mathews of the World Resources Institute offered this advice: rather than trying to play catch-up with the Japanese, a game we've played rather miserably, GM should instead try to "leapfrog" ahead.

The way to do that is to figure out what consumers will want five and ten years hence. What they'll want, and what GM will give them, is a world-class "green" car. Pick your smartest, boldest, and best engineers and give them this task: Design a mass-production car from the ground up that beats every government mileage, emission, and safety standard two-, three-, or 10-fold, and that is fully recyclable. Make it stylish, comfortable, adequately peppy, and capable of freeway speeds.

It's a formidable challenge, but not impossible, Mathews says. "You are in command of a company with technical brains second to none in the world—use them!''[42]

A similar prescription comes from Ralph Nader, who rocked the industry in 1965 with his book *Unsafe at Any Speed:* "More quality control, better warranties, more fuel efficiency, better safety, better emission control, and lower repair rates. If they produce a car with that kind of quality—and they've got the engineers and talent to do so— then they won't have to worry about Japanese competition."[43]

The transportation policies and mistakes of four decades cannot be undone overnight. It has taken the nation nearly half a century to construct the road-oriented sprawl that now threatens our quality of life. It will probably take just as long to rebuild our metropolitan areas to make them livable and "user-friendly" once again.

In Washington, the federal government needs to set the technological agenda by speeding the introduction of cleaner, more efficient conventional cars—as well as more advanced, nonpolluting electric and hydrogen vehicles. Washington's other chief obligation is to get the economic signals right by removing the subsidies that will otherwise keep Americans fuming in the slow lane forever.

It's possible that the lack of vision and leadership in the federal bureaucracy will—as it has with so many other environmental and social issues—spark action and experimentation in states, counties, and communities. But we don't have to rely on dumb luck. Engineers, environmentalists, and farsighted transportation planners have already identified sound goals and crucial steps for reaching them—enough good ideas to start with and build on. But if Americans don't start acting on these ideas soon, the road to the future just may not get us there.

7

Smart Thinking

"Driving is boring," Rabbit pontificates, "but
it's what we do. Most of American life is
driving somewhere and then driving back,
wondering why the hell you went."

JOHN UPDIKE,
Rabbit at Rest

On August 25, 1916, President Woodrow Wilson signed the "Organic
Act" creating the National Park Service, to be responsible for protecting the 40 existing national parks and monuments as well as those yet
to be established. The goal, Wilson explained, was "to conserve the
scenery and the natural and historic objects and the wildlife therein,
and to provide for the enjoyment of the same in such manner and by
such means as will leave them unimpaired for the enjoyment of future
generations."[1]

There are now 50 National Parks in the United States, and the entire
system—including national recreation areas, seashores, rivers, historic
parks, and monuments—encompasses some 124,000 square miles, an
area larger than New Mexico. Although there is still more than enough
splendor to go around, the popularity of the parks has contributed to
their own undoing. And the automobile, in large measure, has served
as the agent of destruction, insulating people from the natural environment while abetting the demise of treasured wilderness areas.

In 1990, a record 258 million people drove to the parks, causing
"greenlock" on the overburdened roads. "What do you experience in
Yellowstone in the summer?" asks Teri Martin of the National Parks
and Conservation Association. "Traffic. More and more traffic. Going
to Old Faithful is like going to a huge shopping center."[2] At Yosemite,
a five-story parking garage has been proposed to accommodate the
vehicle population bomb.

Thoroughfares in the park system are swamped, explains Allen Howe
of the Conference of National Park Concessionaires, because too many

people are packed onto too few roads. His solution: pave over more wilderness areas to dilute the flow of traffic, thereby affording drivers more room to branch out.[3] Howe's reasoning is flawless except for one critical fact: the natural beauty of the land—the sole reason that people drive hundreds, if not thousands, of miles to the parks in the first place—will be sacrificed to make way for additional cars. If this mentality prevails, at some point we'll be left with places that nobody wants to visit, solving the traffic problem once and for all. This is the same sort of perverse logic that led a U.S. soldier in Vietnam to make the infamous remark "We had to destroy the village in order to save it."[4]

The lifestyle Americans have grown accustomed to cannot be supported indefinitely. "What you're doing in this country is unsustainable," José Lutzenberger, Brazil's former secretary of the environment said at a 1990 meeting of the Nature Conservancy in Washington, D.C. "If we tried to extend this orgy of wasted materials and energy to the rest of the planet, if the last person behind the last mountain somewhere in China or central Africa had as many cars as you have, we would all be dead."[5]

The influence cars exert over our lives is undeniable, as are the impacts—local, regional, and global—these vehicles have on the environment. Yet we can't blame cars (or transportation in general) for all the world's problems. Nor can we solve all the world's problems simply by focusing on transportation. When viewed from a broad perspective, our auto-related woes are merely one element of a whole range of human activities—including population growth, energy use, agriculture, forestry, industrial processes, resource consumption, and waste disposal—that are not sustainable over the long haul.

The most serious car troubles—air pollution, emissions of greenhouse gases and CFCs, and road congestion—are basically a function of numbers. The more vehicles on the roads, the worse these problems become. Cars, unlike rabbits, don't reproduce themselves. Human beings make these machines for other human beings. If the world population grows uncontrollably and auto fleets grow in step, our transportation problems will simply become unmanageable. With more and more cars clogging our streets, people will lose the freedom to come and go as they please. The air, traffic, and urban economies will stagnate. For this reason, stabilizing population growth is, in the long run, essential to resolving our transportation dilemma here at home and worldwide.

U.S. energy policy exemplifies the kind of short-term thinking we must move beyond. For decades the thrust of that policy has been expanding the development of "conventional" energy sources—an approach that has failed to meet both expectations and needs. As a result, oil imports have climbed steadily, while renewable resources and efficient energy use have been neglected. Maintaining this pattern exacts a steep economic price. The national addiction to oil now consumes a growing share of the balance of payments shortfall: the $66 billion we paid for imports in 1990 constitutes almost two thirds of our total deficit of $101 billion.[6] The tens of billions would be better spent on fuel economy improvements for motor vehicles and other energy conservation measures. Unlike the purchase of oil that is used once and discarded, these investments in the nation's future would yield dividends year after year.

It is hard to keep a steadfast gaze on problems so overwhelming in breadth. At times our attention inevitably wanders. It is tempting to put off long-term remedies for another year or two or three . . . but we are running out of time. If human beings are to survive with dignity, we must recognize that we are part of the natural world, not its owners or rulers.

Sometimes making light of the situation seems to help. Tom and Ray Magliozzi, hosts of the "Car Talk" show that airs on National Public Radio, had this to say when asked what can be done, short of human or automotive extinction, to reduce the environmental impact of our cars. "The first and best thing you can do is don't drive the stupid thing. Most people drive way too much," says Tom. "One way to minimize your driving is to have a car that doesn't run particularly well," Ray adds. "If it's a joy to drive the car, you'll be out there driving all the time. You want something that's unpleasant."[7]

Seriously, though, weaning people from decades-long habits of unrestrained driving may prove as difficult as deprogramming sports fanatics. Some observers argue that Americans drive for the same reason birds fly south for the winter and golden retrievers chase sticks—100 percent instinct. "[Americans] love to drive on the open plains," says energy secretary James Watkins. Jessica Mathews of the World Resources Institute takes issue with Watkins' claim, pointing out that "90 percent of our automobile trips are less than 10 miles long, and most are made between rows of concrete, not waving grasses. . . .We are not irrationally in love with our cars. Just the reverse. We are behaving like the most rational possible economic beings. Offered generous bonuses—hidden and direct—to drive, that's exactly what we do."[8]

If not genetically programmed to drive, Americans do learn at an early age that cars are unquestionably the preferred way of getting around. And deceptively low fuel costs, the non-Euclidian geometry of suburbia, and poor transit alternatives have made it all too convenient to use a car. As Connie Burns, a historian from Quincy, Massachusetts, puts it, "I've lived with a car and without a car. It's better to live with one."[9]

Apart from a handful of downtown areas where owning a car may be more trouble than it's worth, Burns is right. For the most part, life in America is easier if you have a car. It's only when the merits of owning vehicles are weighed on a societal rather than individual level that the drawbacks start to overshadow the benefits. But that type of assessment is rare in a nation where individualism is almost a religion. So what's to be done?

Since most Americans, understandably enough, don't want to give up cars, we've got to figure out a way to make them work *for* us, rather than against us. First and foremost, that means driving less. Ideally, this will occur voluntarily through economic incentives and the availability of good transit options, rather than through restrictions such as one-day-a-week driving bans. But changes in individual attitudes will also be needed to bring about a nationwide shift away from auto-mania. Mark Pisano, executive director of the Southern California Association of Governments, believes that only a "congestion relief ethic" will end gridlock in his region. "Just like we turn the lights off when we leave a room, or turn the shower off when we soap up, we need to make a conscious effort to reduce traffic."[10]

Changes in habits and attitudes can make a difference. Americans have modified their diets and cut back on cigarettes in response to scientific findings. Similarly, kids don't have to grow up assuming they should abandon their bikes on their 16th birthdays just because (in most

---

HOW TO DRIVE EFFICIENTLY

- Combine errands into one trip.
- Turn an engine off rather than letting it idle for more than a minute.
- Get tune-ups regularly. The car will run more smoothly and efficiently.
- Keep tires inflated to the recommended maximum pressure.
- Anticipate traffic stops.

HOW TO WASTE FUEL

- Make jackrabbit starts.
- Speed. (Traveling at 65 mph instead of 55 mph increases your fuel use by more than 15 percent.)
- Carry extra weight in the car.
- Rev the engine before shutting it off.
- Drive with the front wheels out of alignment.

---

states) they have reached the legal driving age. Taking the bus to work, likewise, doesn't have to imply a lack of imagination or money.

However, voluntary efforts alone are unlikely to change driving habits over the long run. "Voluntary measures can work for a while, but pretty soon you forget and slip back to your old ways," says MIT's James Womack. "To truly change behavior, you need a big price tag."[11]

While adjusting fuel prices to reflect economic reality, we also need to alter our perceptions about cars to reflect what might be called "transportation reality." For example, we need to question the myths propagated in movies and TV shows that continue to glamorize automobiles in the face of mounting evidence to the contrary. In the past decade, U.S. automakers have spent some $40 billion trying to entice people to buy their wares—more advertising money than has been spent on any other consumer product.[12] The TV, radio, newspaper, and magazine ads that help shape the way we look at cars and driving need to be brought up to date.

Lately there have been some encouraging signs. Public service messages that began airing in 1990 during the Middle East crisis appeared to be a step in the right direction. "Do your part, drive smart," urged the television, radio, and print advertisements sponsored by the federal government.[13] Of course the conservation-minded messages had little, if any, impact on gasoline consumption because federal efforts in that area barely extended beyond public relations.

When gasoline prices soared following Iraq's invasion of Kuwait on August 2, 1991, Cadillac advertisements began touting fuel efficiency improvements that had been made in their luxury models. But the ads were designed to have only limited influence on buying habits. "We don't want to overdo the message about fuel economy because that might cause a sense of panic or discourage people from deciding to buy a luxury car altogether," explained Peter Levin, advertising director for Cadillac.[14]

The most encouraging sign came from a 1991 Saab commercial. The camera zooms in on a house. The garage door opens, revealing a shiny new Saab. "People who care about the world they live in think before they choose their car," a voice says. "And before they use it." A man emerges from the garage riding a bicycle.

The message had already gotten through to some Americans long before this path-breaking ad hit the airwaves. Actor Ed Begley, Jr., for instance, rides his bicycle to get around town, no matter whether the town happens to be Los Angeles or New York City. When biking is impractical, he takes public transportation or drives his solar-powered car. "We have to begin doing something about the environment in our personal lives," Begley says. "You don't have to drive a 3,700-pound vehicle to pick up a dozen eggs and a loaf of bread. It's ridiculous."[15] Ben Swets, a commercial photographer from Santa Monica, regularly hauls his 30-odd pounds of camera equipment on his bicycle to his photo shoots in downtown Los Angeles. "Sitting alone in a car is sort of like a religious ritual," he says. "It promotes the notion that we have to consume. To me, the bicycle implies not taking more than your share."[16]

Of course plenty of people will gladly take as much as they can. Many are preparing for the tortuously slow rides ahead in the same way that survivalists prepare for Armageddon—by loading up their cars with the latest gadgets and accessories, anything to make the trip more bearable. This trend, called carcooning, represents a giant leap backward for humankind, encouraging people to stay in their cars at a time when efforts should be made to get them out.

It's safe to assume that most Americans will continue to drive as frequently as ever unless they are given sufficient reason—whether threats or financial inducements—to do otherwise. As far as environmental or traffic problems go, many people assume that scientists and engineers will eventually save the day. History teaches us, however, that technology alone cannot solve complex, multi-faceted problems that have intrinsic political and social dimensions. "The more solutions are taken into the realm of technology, the more people will feel that they aren't the problem as drivers," explains Deborah Gordon of the Union of Concerned Scientists.[17]

We Americans have to start taking responsibility for our actions and the havoc they unleash on the world. Like the Onondaga Nation, which plans seven generations ahead—or Woodrow Wilson, who decided to preserve part of our dwindling natural legacy before it was too late—we must consider the kind of future we want to leave for our progeny. Inspired by these examples of farsighted vision, we must adopt a new way of thinking about cars. We can no longer assume it is our God-given right to drive, alone, anywhere we please. New criteria are also needed to influence buying choices and driving behavior. Change may come in part from education, in part from pricing policies designed to reflect the new environmental realities, but the kind of farsighted thinking now needed is surely not going to come from people sitting in sealed cars, listening to the CD player blaring, the FAX machine running, and the carphone ringing.

In John Barth's novel *The End of the Road,* the narrator, Jake Horner, becomes immobilized by indecision. For every step he might take in one direction, he can think of an equally compelling reason to strike off in the opposite direction. The result is total paralysis—he can't go anywhere.[19]

America's transportation system, like Jake Horner, is approaching the end of its road. The Interstate Highway System is essentially complete, and another highway building binge seems unlikely. Such a course of action would only deepen our problems. Yet if we do nothing but pile car upon car onto already jammed streets, we could end up paralyzed, just like Barth's sorry protagonist.

To avoid that fate we must totally revamp our transportation priorities, pursuing a fresh, new strategy that lures us from the trap of deepening auto dependence. There is no real alternative. By sticking to the same old path, the U.S. could go the way of that hapless Vietnamese village. Years in the future, apologists may try to explain what happened: "We had to destroy the country in order to pave it."

Appendix **1**

Low-Impact Transport

Even as we wait for new car technologies, new fuels, and enlightened transportation policies, individual Americans can improve air quality and cut greenhouse emissions markedly *now*—if enough of us make responsible choices.

CONSIDER WALKING OR BICYCLING

Cycling and walking are obvious options for short commutes and errands, when cars are at their most polluting because a cold engine does not fire efficiently. Every time you decide to cycle or walk one mile instead of driving it alone, you keep on average 2.6 grams (0.006 pounds) of hydrocarbons, 20 grams (0.002 pounds) of carbon monoxide, and 1.6 grams of nitrogen oxides out of the atmosphere.

Americans are increasingly enthusiastic about the sport of bicycling: there are 103 million bicycles in the United States today. Yet only about 3 million Americans use a bike to get to work even though in some areas roads are so jammed with cars that two-wheelers move faster.

Part of the problem is that many of our roads and parking areas do not have space designated for bicycles. In the Netherlands, on the other hand, the Dutch government in a recent 10-year period spent some $230 million building bike paths and parking spaces and creating direct, uninterrupted bike routes. Thanks at least partly to this commitment, the share of trips made by bicycle in Dutch communities is typically between 20 and 50 percent. Here and there in the United States—mostly where it's warm and flat—there are similar success stories. Davis, California, has bike lanes on nearly one third of all streets and some 32 kilometers (20 miles) of separate cycle paths—thanks to which one in four trips is made by bicycle, according to the Worldwatch Institute.

If you do commute by bicycle, keep these safety tips in mind:

- If you're a beginner, stick to streets without too much traffic until you gain some experience.
- Keep to the right side of the road so you will be where drivers expect cyclists to be.
- Don't weave around parked cars or zigzag between lanes. Ride in a straight line. Watch for opening doors when passing parked cars.
- Obey all traffic signs and signals and lane markings.
- Use hand signals and the proper turning lanes so that drivers know when you intend to turn.
- Check behind you before changing lanes or your position within a lane.
- Ride single file when you're sharing the road with cars.
- Wear bright colors by day and reflective ones by night; be sure your headlight and taillight are working if you ride in the dark.
- Always wear a helmet. Most bikers fall from time to time, and a good helmet can save you from serious injury.

Making short trips on foot is another option—and it's cost free. It takes about 20 minutes to walk a mile at a brisk pace, so if the weather's tolerable and you're in good health, why not do it? Indeed, walking regularly can help you maintain health and vigor—and it's an activity that many can pursue for a lifetime. Think about it the next time you're tempted to drive a few blocks to the health club.

Make the destination of your walk a bus stop or a train station and your range grows exponentially. Too many city-dwellers rule out public transit unless the stop or station is within a couple blocks of home. A study of ridership on the Washington, D.C., subway system showed that trips fall off by about 2 percent for each 100-yard increase in the distance between a residential building and a subway station.

CONSIDER CARPOOLING OR MASS TRANSIT

Over half of the auto trips in the United States are made by a driver alone, but there are other options, at least for people in urban areas.

Some 19 million Americans carpool to and from work. If they all drove solo, total auto emissions of carbon monoxide and hydrocarbons would be 30 percent higher than they are now. Besides saving money on gas, maintenance, parking, and even insurance, carpoolers can save time by using designated high-occupancy vehicle (HOV) lanes. A study by the Institute of Transportation Engineers shows HOV lanes can cut rush-hour travel time by 60 percent or more.

In many urban areas, commuters also can opt for a bus, train, or ferry. Public transit now accounts for only 3 percent of all trips nationwide, though in the largest urban areas the figure rises to 19 percent for work-related trips. Unfortunately, mass transit becomes practical only where ridership is high, and in many sparsely populated regions transit is unlikely ever to displace the automobile.

IF YOU MUST DRIVE . . .

As a consumer and a civic-minded individual, you have the power to choose the *type* of car you drive, how *often* you drive, and *how* you drive.

Syndicated automotive columnist Robert Sikorsky offers more than 300 techniques for saving gasoline in his book *How to Get More Miles Per Gallon in the 1990s*. If 300 rules seem overwhelming, consider adopting the score or so that follow for starters:

Buy a car that gets at least 35 miles per gallon. The federal Corporate Average Fuel Economy (CAFE) standard for 1992 model cars was only 27.5 mpg, but at least one car on the market (the 1992 XF Geo Metro) gets more than 50 mpg, even in city driving. Buying an efficient car helps curb carbon dioxide emissions and cut the nation's appetite for imported oil, an excessive need that raises the odds that we will have more ecological disasters such as the Exxon *Valdez* oil spill in Alaska. One environmentalist puts it like this: "If you don't drive a car that gets at least 35 miles to the gallon, don't tell me how outraged you are about dead otters."

Avoid gas guzzlers. Apart from high-performance specialty cars, the 1992 leaders in this ignominious category are the BMW 850i and the BMW 750iL (both get only 12 mpg in the city), according to the Environmental Protection Agency. For each mile driven, these cars will emit nearly *four times* the carbon dioxide produced by the most fuel-efficient 1992 model, the Geo Metro XFi (53 mpg in the city). Also, think hard before buying a light truck; on average, these increasingly popular vehicles need 33 percent more fuel than the average new car does to cover the same distance.

When shopping for fuel efficiency, there is no need to sacrifice safety. Small cars can be designed to be safe. Look for such features as air bags, anti-lock brakes, traction control, padded interior, and recessed dashboard knobs. To find out how a particular model fared in federal crash tests, call the National Highway Traffic Safety Administration hotline at 1-800-424-9393 (366-0123 in Washington, D.C.) or contact the Center for Auto Safety (listed in Appendix 3).

Be selective about car accessories. Options such as air conditioning, power steering, and automatic transmissions require considerable energy—and reduce fuel economy by adding to vehicle weight. (A caveat: on the highway, air conditioning is actually more efficient than opening the windows, which increases aerodynamic drag.) Vinyl tops and sunroofs also cost you gasoline by impeding airflow over the top of the car. Finally, a light-colored car with tinted glass is more energy-efficient than a darker car with regular glass, since it requires less air conditioning.

Avoid rush hour travel when possible. Idling and stop-and-go driving waste fuel. Fuel consumption doubles when average speed drops from 30 to 10 mph, and emissions are tripled compared to the rate at 55 mph. Taking advantage of your company's flex-time policies—or pushing workplaces without such policies to adopt them, if appropriate—can save gas as well as time, tempering pollution while improving your well-being on both ends of the commute.

Don't drive faster than 55. Most cars achieve their best mileage between 35 and 45 mph, when engine efficiency is at a maximum and wind and rolling resistance are not as great, according to Robert Sikorsky. The optimal speed varies with each car; to help identify that speed, a device known as a trip computer can provide instantaneous mpg readings.

How Speed Affects Mileage

SPEED	MPG
20	13.5
30	18
40	18
50	16
60	14.5
70	13

Source: R. Sikorsky. (MPG numbers are for a large van.)

Drive smoothly, shifting gears at optimal speeds. Take it easy on those pedals: accelerate and brake smoothly. Jackrabbit starts can use 50 percent more fuel than restrained acceleration, Sikorsky says. If you have a manual transmission, consult your owner's manual for the most efficient speeds at which to shift gears. Shift into high gears as quickly as possible without straining the engine since it takes far more gasoline to travel in lower gears.

Keep your engine tuned up. An engine that runs rough burns up to 8 percent more gasoline. Dirty carburetors, clogged air filters, and worn points and spark plugs can mean higher emissions of particulates and nitrogen oxides. For some perspective here, a University of Denver study found that tuning up a small minority of rough-running cars is twice as effective (and simpler and cheaper) for controlling carbon monoxide emissions as using clean-burning oxygenated fuels throughout a given auto fleet.

Fill your gas tank properly. Patronize gas stations that have Stage II Vapor Recovery nozzles, which recapture vapors (some states require them). And don't "top off" your tank: in terms of hydrocarbon emissions, a spilled gallon of gasoline is as polluting as driving 7,500 miles.

Buy the right gasoline. So-called oxygenated gasolines, containing ethanol or the additives MTBE or ETBE, reduce carbon monoxide emissions. Other "reformulated" gasolines can reduce both carbon monoxide and hydrocarbon emissions.

Never buy high-octane gasoline unless your car requires it to prevent engine knock; no more than 10 percent of cars fall in this category, experts say. (Citizen Action estimates that Americans spend $1 billion annually on octane they don't need.) Unleaded gasolines, high-octane gas formulas especially, contain elevated levels of aromatic hydrocarbons, including the hazardous chemicals benzene, toluene, and xylene.

Use the right motor oil. Some types of oil contain additives that reduce friction and increase fuel economy by 2.7 percent or more. The cans are marked "Energy Conserving II" on the label.

Don't idle the engine for more than a minute. Idling wastes fuel and contributes to emissions of all pollutants. It takes less gasoline to restart the car than to let it idle for more than 60 seconds. Think twice about using drive-through services, which can be air pollution factories.

Combine errands into one trip. Much of the damage to air quality is done within the first few minutes of driving, when the engine is cold. In fact, the hydrocarbon emissions associated with restarting a hot engine are 80 percent less than those given off in cold starts, and cuts in carbon monoxide emissions are even more dramatic. That's a compelling argument for combining errands.

Eliminate unnecessary braking. Each time you hit the brakes momentum is lost. Regaining that momentum takes fuel. A typical driver brakes about 50 percent more often than necessary, according to Sikorsky. The alternative is to anticipate signal changes or other reasons for slowing down to allow time to decelerate by taking your foot off the gas and allowing the car to slow down in gear. (A car can get up to 100 mpg while decelerating, says Sikorsky.)

Cooperate with government emissions control programs. Have your car inspected as required by local laws. These programs test for high levels of carbon monoxide and unburned hydrocarbons. Precise limits depend on the car's age; in general, vehicles that fail have not been maintained properly. In California, drivers can monitor each other: cars that emit visible smoke exhaust for more than 10 seconds can be reported by calling 1-800-CUT-SMOG. The service gets about 8,000 reports a month.

Dispose of used motor oil and antifreeze safely. About 240 million gallons of oil are dumped into lakes and rivers and onto the ground each year by people who change their own oil, according to the EPA. (Environmental writer Jim Motavalli says the equivalent of an Exxon *Valdez* spill is dumped in this way every two weeks.) Don't dump your oil in the garbage, either—take it to a recycler, where it can be turned into fuel for ships or industrial boilers. One emerging technology can even convert it into new motor oil.

Alabama may lead the oil recycling movement: thanks to a program that includes curbside collection, about a third of the used oil in that state was recovered in 1988. To learn where you can recycle oil in your community, write to the Used Oil Coordinator, Mail Code OS 301, U.S. EPA, 401 M Street SW, Washington, D.C. 20460.

Inspect and replace filters regularly. Clogged air and oil filters can mean wasted gasoline and higher emissions, so replace these parts regularly. Oil filters should be replaced whenever the oil is changed and air filters should be checked at least once a year (more often if you drive on dusty roads).

Buy the right tires. Radial tires produce less particulate matter per mile traveled than bias-ply tires do. Radial tires also last longer and boost fuel economy 7 to 10 percent, depending on speed.

Keep tires inflated properly. With proper inflation, tires last longer, fuel economy is higher, and the car handles more safely. Fuel economy drops 1 percent for every pound of pressure below the recommended level. Sikorsky recommends inflating tires to the maximum pounds per square inch (psi) printed on the sidewall of the tires (usually 32–35 psi), regardless of what your car's owner's manual says.

Service air conditioners properly. An air-conditioned car emits about five pounds of chlorofluorocarbons (CFCs) over its life cycle, adding to destruction of the ozone layer. Leaks increase emissions further, so fix them promptly. Also, if your air conditioner needs to be recharged, take it to a mechanic who has a "vampire" machine, which recycles freon. These machines drain the coolant, purify it, and reinject it into the air conditioner.

Recycle old tires and batteries. Americans throw away 234 million tires each year—almost a tire per person—and only 12 percent are reused or recycled. Used tires can be retreaded or blended with asphalt to make road coverings. Your batteries can be recycled, too: some manufacturers and recyclers collect used batteries, salvaging the lead and acid for use in new batteries.

BEYOND DRIVING

Personal choices about transportation are not made in a vacuum. Individual differences are *not* overwhelmingly influenced, as might be expected, by income or technology. Rather, according to a study of 12 countries cited by Worldwatch Institute analyst Marcia Lowe, the decisive factors are "enlightened public policy and strong government support."

Environmentally conscious Americans have a rough road to travel: they don't get much encouragement. As *Car Trouble* shows, federal policies have not provided consistently strong support for alternatives to driving or for the development and purchase of cars that are low in emissions. A few states, most notably California, have set their own high standards for low-emission cars and the development of renewable energy resources.

You can encourage the enactment of progressive federal and state policies. As with any legislative matter, you can write to senators and representatives, both state and federal, and vote for those who are most sensitive to these issues. See Chapter 6 of this book for a discussion of some policy changes worth supporting.

Appendix 2

The Driving Force of Law

1970   **Clean Air Act Amendments of 1970**
- gave federal government more power to regulate sources of pollution, relieving state governments of total responsibility.
- established National Ambient Air Quality standards.

1973   **National highway speed limit**
- set a highway driving speed at a maximum of 55 miles per hour, saving up to 165,000 barrels of gasoline every day of that year.

1975   **Energy Policy and Conservation Act**
- set Corporate Average Fuel Efficiency (CAFE) standard at 18 mpg beginning in 1978.

1976   **Electric and Hybrid Vehicle Research, Development, and Demonstration Act**
- called for research and testing of electric vehicles.

1977   **1977 Clean Air Act Amendments**
- mandated a 96-percent reduction in hydrocarbons and carbon monoxide and a 75-percent reduction in nitrogen oxides from cars (relative to cars with no controls).

1978   **Solar Photovoltaic Research, Development, and Demonstration Act**
- called for the commercialization of photovoltaic technology.

        Energy Tax Act of 1978
- established "gas-guzzler tax," to be imposed on inefficient vehicles.
- exempted gasohol from federal gas tax.

        National Energy Conservation Policy Act
- doubled the penalty on car manufacturers who failed to meet CAFE standards.

1980   **Automobile Fuel Efficiency Act**
- made enforcement of CAFE standards less strict.

Crude Oil Windfall Profits Tax Act
- extended tax exemptions on fuel alcohol.

1986   **Department of Transportation**
- lowered CAFE standards to 26 mpg for model years 1986–1988, from 27.5, where they had been set in 1985.

1988   **Department of Transportation**
- set CAFE standards at 26.5 mpg for 1989 model year.

Motor Fuels Promotion Act
- promoted the manufacture of vehicles that run on alternative fuels, such as blends of ethanol or methanol and gasoline.

1989   **Tax Bill**
- set $0.50 per barrel tax on oil to fund oil-spill compensation plan.

Steel Quota Bill
- declared 60 million gallons per year of Carribbean ethanol, or an amount equal to 7 percent of what the United States produces each year, excise-free.

1990   **Reconciliation Bill**
- raised vehicle fuel tax by $0.05 per gallon to $.14 per gallon for gas and $.20 per gallon for diesel, to help lower the federal deficit.
- mandated a $.025-per-gallon tax on railroad fuels.
- doubled the gas-guzzler tax to $1,000 for cars that do not get 22.5 mpg and $7,700 for cars that are less efficient than 12.5 mpg.
- added 12 chemicals to the list of taxed chemicals that damage the ozone layer.

1990   **Clean Air Act Amendments**
- required cars sold in 1994 and after to have 30-percent lower hydrocarbon emissions and 60-percent lower emissions of oxides of nitrogen than cars sold previously.
- required that starting in 1993, cars will have to pass emissions control tests up to 100,000 miles (the previous limit: 50,000 miles).

- required emissions from large trucks to be restricted to 90-percent less than the unregulated levels at which 1990 model trucks operated.
- required new cars to include emission-control malfunction warning signals in the computer diagnostic system.
- required that emissions from trains, farm machinery, construction machinery, lawn mowers, and boats be controlled.
- required gas pumps to have attachments to capture vapors.
- required emissions testing to be conducted in realistic driving conditions.
- required that starting in 1996, 150,000 cars sold in California give off only half the emissions of other cars sold. By 1999, the stricter standard must be met by 300,000 new cars. In 2001, EPA will halve the emissions requirement again. (EPA maintains that car prices will not increase more than $200 per car because Clean Air Act requirements will have been phased in over 10 years.)

APPENDIX **3**

Organizations That Can Help

PUBLIC INTEREST GROUPS

American Lung Association
National Headquarters
1740 Broadway
New York, NY 20019
(212) 315-8700

The oldest nationwide voluntary health agency in the United States, the American Lung Association is dedicated to the control and prevention of all lung diseases and some of their related causes, including smoking, air pollution, and occupational lung hazards. Your local chapter is listed in the white pages of your phone directory.

Association for Commuter Transportation
808 17th Street, NW
Suite 200
Washington, DC 20006
(202) 223-9669

Provides information, education, and networking opportunities to commuter transportation professionals. An organizational membership costs $275 (student membership $55) and brings bi-monthly newsletter and newsclips. ACT provides information on commuter issues and programs and offers special rates on publications and conferences.

Bicycle Federation of America
1818 R Street, NW
Washington, DC 20009
(202) 332-6986

Promotes increased and safe use of bicycles for recreation and transportation. Regular functions include research, training, and planning, technology transfer and technical assistance, and advocacy to insure that their policies and programs contribute positively to bicycling.

Campaign for New Transportation Priorities
Harriet Parcells, Project Director
900 2nd Street, NE
Suite 308
Washington, DC 20002
(202) 408-8362

National coalition of 40 environmental, labor, religious, and local consumer groups working for greater funding for mass transit, trains, and other alternatives to solo driving. Other issues include better land-use planning and working for changes in federal tax structures that favor cars and trucks.

Center for Auto Safety
2001 S Street, NW
Suite 410
Washington, DC 20009
(202) 328-7700

Consumer advocacy group that focuses on vehicle defects, fuel economy and emissions, and auto warranties. A $15 membership brings a quarterly newsletter.

Center for Environmental Information, Inc.
46 Prince Street
Rochester, NY 14607-1016
(716) 271-3550

A private nonprofit organization that provides information on all environmental topics through publications, conferences, a library, and response to telephone and letter requests.

Environmental Action Foundation
1525 New Hampshire Avenue, NW
Washington, DC 20036
(202) 745-4870

Promotes environmental protection through research, public education, organizing, and legal action; connected to Environmental Action, Inc., a national citizens' group. Magazine subscription ($20) includes membership.

Environmental and Energy Study Institute
122 C Street, NW
Washington, DC 20001
(202) 628-1400

Works to better inform the national debate on environmental and energy issues and to generate innovative policy responses. Current work includes striving to increase automobile fuel efficiency standards within the Clean Air Act.

Environmental Defense Fund
257 Park Avenue South
New York, NY 10010
(212) 505-2100

Seeks solutions to ecological problems and enforcement of environmental standards, sometimes through litigation. Focuses on the greenhouse effect, ocean pollution, wildlife protection, recycling, rain forests, acid rain, Antarctica, and toxic waste.

Friends of the Earth
218 D Street, SE
Washington, DC 20003
(202) 544-2600

With affiliate groups in 38 countries, works to influence public policy on environmental issues. A $25 membership entails a news magazine subscription and discounts on publications.

Greenpeace
1436 U Street, NW
Washington, DC 20009
(202) 462-1177

Promotes activism and awareness of environmental issues. $30.00 membership brings quarterly newsletter; network keeps members informed of activities and letter-writing campaigns in their area.

Highway Users Federation
Public Affairs
1776 Massachusetts Avenue, NW
Washington, DC 20036
(202) 857-1200

A coalition of corporations, associations, and individuals committed to better, safer highway transportation. HUF also maintains a national membership comprising more than 20 industry groups working to develop innovative highway maintenance and improvement programs.

Motor Vehicles Manufacturing Association, Detroit
7430 2nd Avenue
Suite 300
Detroit, MI 48202
(313) 872-4311

Provides information to increase public awareness through research and statistics on the sources of economic strength in the country and the contribution of the motor vehicle to the economy and the public welfare. MVMA also appraises government, economic, and social developments that affect the industry and users.

Rails-to-Trails Conservancy
1400 16th Street, NW
Suite 300-WR
Washington, DC 20036
(202) 797-5400

A nonprofit organization devoted to converting abandoned railroad rights-of-way into trails for public use. The Conservancy works with citizen groups, public agencies, and railroads to preserve the U.S. railroad corridor system.

The Sierra Club
730 Polk Street
San Francisco, CA 94009
(415) 776-2211

Promotes conservation through public policy. A $35 annual membership ($15 for students and senior citizens) includes *Sierra* magazine and discounts on books and calendars. Publications, outings, calendars, newsletters, and national news updates available.

Transportation Alternatives
494 Broadway
New York, NY 10012
(212) 941-4600

A New York City–based activist organization that promotes bicycling and other transportation alternatives while striving to make cities far less reliant on automobiles.

1000 Friends of Oregon
534 SW 3rd Avenue, #300
Portland, OR 97204

A nonprofit organization founded in 1975 to protect Oregon's quality of life through the conservation of farm and forest lands, the protection of natural and historic resources, and the promotion of more compact and liveable cities. 1000 Friends endorses a range of transportation options, as well as urban planning that minimizes sprawl. The Oregon group has served as a model for similar organizations in Florida, Hawaii, Massachusetts, and Washington.

World Resources Institute
1709 New York Avenue, NW
Washington, DC 20006
(202) 638-6300

An independent research center focusing on resource, environment, and development issues. WRI seeks to help governments, other nonprofit organizations, businesses, and citizens find ways to meet basic human needs and nurture economic growth without degrading our planet and its resources.

Worldwatch Institute
1776 Massachusetts Avenue, NW
Washington, DC 20036
(202) 452-1999

Produces reports on a range of issues, including the environment, population, and socio-economic development.

Zero Population Growth
1400 16th Street, NW
Suite 320
Washington, DC 20036
(202) 332-2200

A nonprofit organization concerned with overpopulation and its environmental, social, and economic impacts, ZPG has an annual membership fee of $20 ($10 for senior citizens and students) that brings a bi-monthly newspaper, a quarterly newsletter, and discounts on publications and merchandise.

GOVERNMENT AGENCIES

U.S. Department of Energy—PA5
Division of Public Affairs
1000 Independence Avenue, SW
Washington, DC 20585
(202) 586-6827

Environmental Protection Agency
Public Information Center
401 M Street, SW
Washington, DC 20460
(202) 475-7751

Federal Highway Administration
Public Affairs
400 7th Street, SW
Room 4210
Washington, DC 20590
(202) 366-4570

United States Railway Association
955 L'Enfant Plaza, SW
Washington, DC 20590
(202) 488-8777

UNITED STATES CONGRESS

House of Representatives

Committee on Appropriations
Washington, DC 20515-6015

Committee on Banking, Finance, and Urban Affairs
2129 Rayburn House Office Building
Washington, DC 20515-6050

Committee on Budget
House Office Building Annex 1
300 New Jersey Avenue, SE
Washington, DC 20515-6065

Committee on Energy and Commerce
2125 Rayburn House Office Building
Washington, DC 20515-6115

Committee on Government Operations
2157 Rayburn House Office Building
Washington, DC 20515-6143

Committee on Public Works and Transportation
2165 Rayburn House Office Building
Washington, DC 20515-6256

Committee on Science, Space, and Technology
Washington, DC 20515-6301

Committee on Ways and Means
1102 Longworth House Office Building
Washington, DC 20515-6348

Senate

Committee on Appropriations
Washington, DC 20510-6025

Committee on Banking, Housing, and Urban Affairs
534 Senate Dirksen Office Building
Washington, DC 20510-6075

Committee on Budget
621 Senate Dirksen Office Building
Washington, DC 20510-6100

Committee on Commerce, Science, and Transportation
Washington, DC 20510-6125

Committee on Energy and Natural Resources
364 Senate Dirksen Office Building
Washington, DC 20510-6150

Committee on Environment and Public Works
458 Senate Dirksen Office Building
Washington, DC 20510-6175

Committee on Finance
205 Senate Dirksen Office Building
Washington, DC 20510-6200

WORLD BANK

Director of Environment
World Bank
1818 H Street, NW
Washington, DC 20043

U.S. Executive Director
World Bank
1818 H Street, NW
Washington, DC 20043

GLOSSARY

Benzene C_6H_6, a toxic, cancer-causing flammable liquid.

Carburetor A device that mixes air and gasoline in an internal combustion engine.

Catalytic converter A device attached to the exhaust system that contains an emissions-controlling chemical catalyst.

Diesel engine An engine in which fuel is ignited with the heat from the compression of a fuel-air mixture by the piston rather than with a spark, as in a gasoline engine with spark plugs.

Drag coefficient A measure of the ''slipperiness'' of a vehicle to air resistance. Designing a vehicle with a small drag coefficient makes it more streamlined, reduces its aerodynamic drag, especially at high speeds, and improves its fuel efficiency.

FHWA Federal Highway Administration, a department within the U.S. Department of Transportation.

Formaldehyde (HCHO) A colorless, strong-smelling gas that strongly promotes smog formation. It is a probable human carcinogen.

Greenhouse gases Carbon dioxide, methane, chlorofluorocarbons, nitrous oxide, and man-made ozone, all of which contribute to the ''greenhouse effect,'' or global warming.

Hydrogen (H_2) The lightest of the elements, a flammable gas without odor or color. Hydrogen is the most abundant element in the universe.

Internal combustion engine An engine powered by the heat from an explosion of a mixture of gas and air. The most common automobile engines of this type operate on four cycles: intake, compression, ignition, and exhaust.

Lean-burn engine An engine that operates on a higher air-to-fuel ratio than a standard engine does, and consequently uses less fuel.

Methane (CH_4) A colorless, odorless gaseous hydrocarbon, the principal component of natural gas. It is also a strong greenhouse gas.

Photovoltaic cell A semiconductor device that directly converts some of the sunlight falling on it into electricity. The earliest PV cells were made of selenium and were used in photographic light meters. The largest use of PV cells today is powering remote communications and navigation equipment. In the U.S. and Europe, about 15,000 vacation homes are equipped with PV systems.

Reformulated gasoline   A general term used to describe newly developed gasoline blends that produce less air pollution (such as carbon monoxide and ozone-forming compounds) than older gasoline formulas. The reformulated gasolines of different oil companies are not necessarily the same. There are, in fact, dozens of different recipes.

Solar cell   See photovoltaic cell.

Two-stroke engine   Lighter, smaller, and more efficient than a standard four-stroke engine, this type is traditionally considered more polluting. The two-stroke ignites fuel and generates power every time the piston comes to the top of its stroke, as opposed to every other time, as in the four-stroke engine. The two-stroke is currently being refined to run with significantly fewer emissions.

Turbine   An engine driven by a wheel connected to a drive shaft. Pressure from steam, air, or water turns the wheel.

NOTES

1. The Age of Invention

1. *Boston Globe*, 2/1/86, "The Motor Car as Liberator" (reprinted from *The Economist*, 1981).
2. Peter Marsh and Peter Collett, "Driving Passions," *Psychology Today*, June 1987, p. 18.
3. James Flink, *The Automobile Age* (Cambridge, Mass.: MIT Press, 1988).
4. Michael Renner, "Rethinking the Role of the Automobile," *Worldwatch Paper 84*, June 1988.
5. Ford quoted in Flink, *The Automobile Age*.
6. Fred Smith, "Autonomy," *Reason*, August/September 1990.
7. Flink, *The Automobile Age*.
8. Smith, "Autonomy."
9. Ford quoted in Nancy Shute, "Driving Beyond the Limit," *Amicus Journal*, Spring 1991, p. 10.
10. James Flink, *The Car Culture* (Cambridge, Mass.: MIT Press, 1987).
11. Flink, *The Automobile Age*.
12. Jonathan Bennett, "Who Wrecked America's Trains?" *Utne Reader*, June/July 1986.
13. Snell quoted in Leonard Arrow, "Derailing America—GM's Mark of Excellence," *Environmental Action*, 16 March 1974.
14. Dix quoted in Flink, *The Automobile Age*.
15. John Pucher, "Urban Travel Behavior as the Outcome of Public Policy," *APA Journal*, Autumn 1988.
16. Ibid.
17. Ibid.
18. King Cushman, "Exploring the Land Development and Transit Connection, in *Transit, Land Use, and Urban Form*, ed. Wayne Attoe (Austin: University of Texas, 1988).
19. Smith, "Autonomy."
20. Quoted in Flink, *The Automobile Age*.
21. Ibid.
22. Renner, "Rethinking the Role of the Automobile."
23. Motor Vehicles Manufacturers Association, *Facts & Figures '90*.
24. Dianne Dumanoski, *Boston Globe*, 9/30/90, "More Drivers Driving Gas Guzzlers."

25. Ken Zino, *Parade,* 10/7/90, "For U.S. Carmakers, the Watchword Is Quality."

26. James Womack, Daniel Jones, and Daniel Roos, *The Machine That Changed the World* (New York: Rawson Associates, 1990).

27. Steven Stark, *Boston Globe,* 8/20/90, "America's Driving Force."

28. Ivan Illich, "Energy and Equity," in *Toward a History of Needs* (Berkeley: Heyday Books, 1978).

29. *Boston Herald,* 10/12/90, "Cost to Drive in '90 Rises $533."

30. Motor Vehicles Manufacturers Association, *Facts & Figures '90.*

31. David Adams, "Bike If You're Hard Driving," *Men's Health,* February 1991, p. 32.

32. Motor Vehicles Manufacturers Association, *Facts & Figures '90.*

33. "The Lonely Commute," *Conservation Law Foundation Newsletter,* Summer 1990, p. 4.

34. Cushman, "Exploring the Land Development and Transit Connection."

35. Illich, "Energy and Equity," *Toward a History of Needs.*

36. Jeffrey Denny, "King of the Road," *Common Cause Magazine,* May/June 1991.

37. Jeremy Rifkin, *Biosphere Politics* (New York: Crown Publishers, 1991).

38. Ibid.

39. "The Automobile—An Environmental Threat," *Conservation Law Foundation Newsletter,* Summer 1990.

40. Renner, "Rethinking the Role of the Automobile."

41. Kevin Kasowski, "Sprawl! Can It Be Stopped?" *Developments,* National Growth Management Project newsletter, Summer 1991.

42. Kevin Kasowski, "Bridging the Gap," *Developments,* Spring/Summer 1990.

43. Steven Stark, *Boston Globe,* 8/20/90, "America's Driving Force."

44. Quoted in Flink, *The Automobile Age.*

45. Daniel Solomon, "Fixing Suburbia," in *The Pedestrian Pocket Book,* Doug Kelbaugh, ed. (New York: Princeton Architectural Press, 1989).

2. Dead End

1. Larry Tye, *Boston Globe,* 6/13/90, p. 23, "Ship Fire Almost Out."

2. William Coughlin, *Boston Globe,* 6/13/91, "Research Body Seeks Double-hulled Tanker."

3. Quoted by William Coughlin, *Boston Globe,* 2/25/91, p. 34, "The Other Oil Pollution Menace."

4. Ross Gelbspan, *Boston Globe,* 12/23/91, "Motor Oil Pollution of Water Uncurbed."

5. Earthworks Group, *50 Simple Things You Can Do To Save The Earth* (Berkeley: Earthworks Press, 1990).

6. Elizabeth Kolbert, *New York Times,* 7/10/90, "Mobil to Pay Millions to Clean Up Vast Pool of Oil Beneath Brooklyn."

7. Elizabeth Kolbert, *New York Times,* 7/29/90, "Ugly Reminders of the Oil That Went Underground."

8. Energy Information Administration, Department of Energy, *Annual Energy Outlook,* 1992, p. 28.

9. Motor Vehicle Manufacturers Association, *Facts & Figures '90.*

10. *Boston Globe,* 9/30/91, "Fuel Efficiency in 1992 Cars Off Slightly From Last Year."

11. Quoted in Stuart Silverstein, *Los Angeles Times,* 8/11/90, "Few Americans are Heeding Bush's Plea to Conserve Energy."

12. Office of Technology Assessment, "Improving Auto Fuel Economy," October 1991.

13. Quoted in Matthew Wald, *New York Times,* 8/16/90, p. D7, "In Cars, Muscle vs. Mileage."

14. Kasowski, "Bridging the Gap."

15. Office of Technology Assessment, "Improving Auto Fuel Economy."

16. Deborah Bleviss and Peter Walzer, "Energy for Motor Vehicles," *Scientific American,* September 1990.

17. Dianne Dumanoski, *Boston Globe,* 9/3/90, p. 33, "Risking War for Gas Guzzlers."

18. Marcia Lowe, "Alternatives to the Automobile," *Worldwatch Paper 98,* October 1990, p. 10.

19. *Boston Globe,* 5/2/90, "The '90s May Feature a Reprise of the Oil Shortages of the '70s."

20. *Boston Globe,* 10/23/91, "Oil Price Volatility."

21. Department of Energy, *Annual Energy Review,* 1990, p. 119.

22. *BP Statistical Review of World Energy,* 1991.

23. Harold Hubbard, "The Real Cost of Energy," *Science American,* April 1991, p. 36.

24. James J. MacKenzie, Roger Dower, and Donald D. T. Chen, "The Going Rate: What It Really Costs to Drive," World Resources Institute, June 1992.

25. Harold Hubbard, "The Real Cost of Energy," p. 36.

26. MacKenzie, Dower, and Chen, "The Going Rate."

27. Quoted in Patrick Lee, *Los Angeles Times,* 3/24/91, p. A20, "Addiction to Oil Still Drives U.S."

28. Mark Thompson, "Fighting for Cleaner Air," *Atlantic Monthly,* September 1988.

29. *EPA National Air Pollutant Emission Estimates 1940–1989,* Publication EPA-450/4-91-004, March 1991.

30. Dick Russell, "L.A.'s Positive Charge," *Amicus Journal,* Spring 1991.

31. Ross Gelbspan, *Boston Globe,* 5/23/91, "Environmentalist: Stop Road Work."

32. Stephanie Pollack, "Cars are Evil . . ." (internal memo), Conservation Law Foundation, 1990.

33. Michael Weisskopf, *Washington Post,* 3/26/90, "Auto-Pollution Debate Has Ring of the Past."

34. Quoted in Michael Kranish, *Boston Globe,* 4/1/90, p. 12, "U.S. Automaker Bucks Pollution Controls."

35. *New York Times,* 8/17/90, "Big Cities Lack in Clean Air."

36. Matthew Wald, *New York Times,* 3/11/90, "How Dreams of Clean Air Got Stuck in Traffic."

37. *New York Times,* 8/17/90, "Big Cities Lack in Clean Air."

38. Eliot Marshall, "Clean Air? Don't Hold Your Breath," *Science,* 5 May 1989, p. 517.

39. Richard Marini, "Commanding California's War on Smog," *Popular Science,* September 1990.

40. "The Health Costs of Air Pollution," American Lung Association, 1990.

41. "Air Pollution Is Now Threatening Health Worldwide," Worldwatch Institute news release, 12 May 1990.

42. *Boston Globe,* 3/18/92, "Mexico City Sounds Worst Pollution Alert."

43. Steve Nadis, "Mexican Cleanup," *Technology Review,* November/December 1989, p. 10.

44. Quoted in Thompson, "Fighting for Cleaner Air."

45. Quoted in Nadis, "Mexican Cleanup."

46. Quoted in Richard Levine, *New York Times,* 4/11/90, "Rise in Cars Chokes New York Area's Roads."

47. Michael Kranish, *Boston Globe,* 11/16/90, "Bush Signs Historic Clean Air Act."

48. *Electric Vehicle Progress,* vol. 14 no. 4 (2/15/92).

49. Quoted in Michael Weisskopf, *Washington Post,* 3/26/90, "Auto Pollution Debate Has Ring of the Past."

50. David Woodruff, *Business Week,* 9/4/89, p. 107, "Detroit's Big Work for the 1990s: The Greenhouse Effect."

51. *Climate Change: The IPCC Scientific Assessment,* eds. J. T. Houghton, G. J. Jenkins, and J. J. Ephraums (New York: Cambridge University Press, 1990).

52. James Anderson, Harvard University, telephone interview, 9/3/91.

53. Dianne Dumanoski, *Boston Globe,* 4/5/91, "A Bigger Hole in the Ozone."

54. "No Tech Fix for Auto Population Bomb," *Science,* 2 August 1991, p. 623.

55. Robert Silverberg, "The Greenhouse Effect: Apocalypse Now or Chicken Little?" *Omni,* July 1991, p. 88.

56. Quoted in Jeremy Rifkin, *Entropy: Into the Greenhouse World* (New York: Bantam Books, 1990), p. 144.

57. Pollack, "Cars are Evil."

58. Report of the Secretary of Transportation to the U.S. Congress, September 1991, "The Status of the Nation's Highways and Bridges" (Washington, D.C.: U.S. Government Printing Office, 1991).

59. Shawn Hubler, *Los Angeles Times,* 8/20/90, "Drivers Seeking Shortcuts . . ."

60. Carla Lazzareschi, *Los Angeles Times,* 3/30/91, "Smart Way to Unclog Roadway."

61. *USA Today,* 5/30/90, "Cities See Gridlock Around Next Corner."

62. James Hanks and Timothy Lomax, "Roadway Congestion in Major Urbanized Areas, 1982 to 1988" Research Report 1131–3, Texas Transportation Institute, July 1990.

63. Kasowski, "Bridging the Gap."

64. "Traffic Congestion: Trends, Measures, and Effects," GAO, November 1989.

65. *Boston Herald,* 2/21/92, p. 22, "A War on Cars and Drivers."

66. Roger Smith, *Vital Speeches of the Day,* 6/15/89, "Smart Cars and Smart Policies."

67. Glenn Rifkin, *New York Times,* 11/20/91, " 'Smart' Plans for Clogged Roads."

68. Ibid.

69. "Bumper to Bumper, Coast to Coast," Zero Population Growth, June 1989.

70. "California 2000: Gridlock in the Making," Assembly Office of Research, March 1988.

71. *USA Today,* 5/30/90, "Cities See Gridlock Around Next Corner."

72. Quoted by Francesca Lyman, "Rethinking Our Transportation Future," *E Magazine,* September/October 1990, p. 37.

73. *Conservation Law Foundation Newsletter,* Summer 1990, p. 2.

74. Beth Brophy, *US News & World Report,* 9/7/87, p. 22, "Jam Sessions."

75. ENO Foundation for Transportation, "Commuting in America: A National Report on Commuting Patterns and Trends," 1987, p. 38.

76. "California 2000: Gridlock in the Making," Assembly Office of Research, March 1988.

77. Robert Fishman, "Megalopolis Unbound," *Wilson Quarterly,* Winter 1990.

78. Renner, "Rethinking the Role of the Automobile."

79. "ABC World News Tonight," 6/6/90.

80. *Conservation Law Foundation Newsletter,* Summer 1990, p. 2.

81. Quoted in Matthew Wald, *New York Times,* 3/11/90, "How Dreams of Clean Air Got Stuck in Traffic."

82. Soloman, "Fixing Suburbia," *The Pedestrian Pocket Book.*

83. "Traffic Congestion: Trends, Measures, and Effects," GAO, November 1989, p. 9.

84. Stephen Koepp, *Time,* 9/12/88, p. 55, "Gridlock!"

85. Quoted in Beth Brophy, *U.S. News & World Report,* 9/7/87, "Jam Sessions."

86. Ibid.

87. Ibid.

88. "California 2000: Gridlock in the Making," Assembly Office of Research, March 1988.

89. "Driving While Automated," *Scientific American,* July 1990, p. 86.

90. Steven Morrison, *Boston Globe,* 5/14/91, "Pricing the Crowds Off the Roads."

3. The Drive for Better Cars

1. Quoted in Herb Cook, Jr., "This Man Has a Plan to Prevent World War III," *Columbus Monthly,* November 1982.

2. Sherwood Fawcett, telephone interview, 10/10/91.

3. Flink, *The Automobile Age.*

4. Sherwood Fawcett, telephone interview, 10/10/91.

5. Cook, "This Man Has a Plan to Prevent World War III."

6. Sherwood Fawcett, telephone interview, 10/10/91.

7. Jim Swain, Battelle Memorial Institute, telephone interview, 10/9/91.

8. Renner, "Rethinking the Role of the Automobile."

9. Donald Woutat, *Los Angeles Times,* 3/25/91, "Bold Designs, Exotic Fuels."

10. Renner, "Rethinking the Role of the Automobile."

11. Deborah Bleviss, "Saving Fuel," *Technology Review,* November/December 1988.

12. *Columbus Dispatch,* 9/13/91, "Nation Needs Policy to Conserve Energy."

13. ABC News, "Nightline," 10/24/91.

14. Doron Levin, *New York Times,* 10/17/91, "Honda Ready to Show a Car That Gets 100 Miles a Gallon."

15. "Improving Automobile Fuel Economy," Office of Technology Assessment, October 1991.

16. "ABC World News Tonight," American Agenda segment, 10/1/91.

17. Ibid.
18. Ibid.
19. Jacob Schlesinger, *Wall Street Journal,* 7/30/91, "Japan Car Firms Unveil Engine Lifting Mileage."
20. Karen Wright, "The Shape of Things to Go," *Scientific American,* May 1990.
21. Dan McCosh, "Carmakers Race to Produce Two-Strokes," *Popular Science,* July 1990.
22. David Woodruff, *Business Week,* 9/4/89, "Detroit's Big Worry for the 1990s: The Greenhouse Effect."
23. McCosh, "Carmakers Race to Produce Two-Strokes."
24. Gregory Patterson, *Boston Globe,* 11/10/85, "Technology Reaches Back to Move Ahead."
25. Jack Keebler, *Automotive News,* 11/5/90, "Breakthrough in Ceramics Heats Up GM Turbine Research."
26. Bleviss, "Saving Fuel."
27. World Resources Institute, *World Resources 1990–91* (New York: Oxford University Press, 1991).
28. "Improving Automobile Fuel Economy," Office of Technology Assessment, October 1991.
29. David Woodruff, *Business Week,* 9/4/89, "Detroit's Big Worry for the 1990s: The Greenhouse Effect."
30. *New York Times,* 9/11/91, "Better Valve Timing Aids Gas Mileage."
31. "Improving Automobile Fuel Economy," Office of Technology Assessment, October 1991.
32. Matthew Wald, *New York Times,* 8/16/90, "In Cars, Muscle vs. Mileage."
33. Janet Marinelli, "Cars," *Garbage,* November/December 1989.
34. Bleviss, "Saving Fuel."
35. Ibid.
36. Renner, "Rethinking the Role of the Automobile."
37. World Resources Institute, *World Resources 1990–91.*
38. "Improving Automobile Fuel Economy," Office of Technology Assessment, October 1991.
39. Bleviss, "Saving Fuel."
40. Marinelli, "Cars."
41. Renner, "Rethinking the Role of the Automobile."
42. "Improving Automobile Fuel Economy," Office of Technology Assessment, October 1991.
43. *New York Times,* 2/25/90, "Smart Tires That Read the Road."
44. Renner, "Rethinking the Role of the Automobile."
45. World Resources Institute, *World Resources 1990–91.*

46. Ibid.

47. *Boston Globe,* 6/25/91, "Opposed to Drilling? Inflate Your Car Tires."

48. Jim Luther, *Boston Globe,* 8/16/90, "Push for Conservation."

49. Deborah Gordon, *Steering a New Course* (Cambridge, Mass.: Union of Concerned Scientists, 1991).

50. GEICO Issues newsletter, June 1991.

51. Jill Abramson, *Wall Street Journal,* 9/20/91, "Car Firms Kick Lobbying Effort Into High Gear."

52. John Dillin, *Christian Science Monitor,* 4/25/91, "Safety Advocates and Efficiency Specialists Crash Over Mileage."

53. David Chandler, *Boston Globe,* 3/11/85, "Air Bags—Life-Saving and Unavailable."

54. John Dillin, *Christian Science Monitor,* 4/25/91, "The Safe Road to a Cleaner Environment."

55. John Dillin, *Christian Science Monitor,* 4/25/91, "Safety Advocates and Efficiency Specialists Crash Over Mileage."

56. Ibid.

57. Marinelli, "Cars."

58. Denny, "King of the Road."

59. Gordon, *Steering a New Course.*

60. Reed McManus, "Safe by Design," *Sierra,* November/December 1991.

61. ABC News, "Nightline," 10/24/91.

62. "Autos: Honda Lean-Burn Spurned," *Greenwire* 1, no. 90, 9/9/91

63. Quoted by Warren Brown, *Washington Post,* 8/11/91, "How Long A Wait for the Car of the Future?"

64. Steve Albu, California Air Resources Board, telephone interview, 10/23/91.

65. *Ward's Engine & Vehicle Technology Update,* 2/15/91, "Orbital 2-Stroke May Achieve ULEV Standards."

66. Steve Albu, California Air Resources Board, telephone interview, 10/23/91.

67. Nicholas Lenssen and John Young, "Filling Up In the Future," *Worldwatch,* May/June 1990.

68. Michael Weisskopf, *Washington Post,* 3/26/90, "Automobile Debate Has Ring of the Past."

69. Dianne Dumanoski, *Boston Globe,* 7/15/91, "Study: NE Must Curb Emissions."

70. Matthew Wald, *New York Times,* 3/27/91, "Researchers Act to Cut Auto Pollution Further."

71. Steve Albu, California Air Resources Board, telephone interview, 10/23/91.

72. "Automotive Newsfront," *Popular Science,* April 1992.

73. *Wall Street Journal,* 2/4/90, "More Limits Planned by EPA on Gasoline Evaporation Rate."

74. D'Vera Cohn, *Washington Post,* 3/8/90, "Gas Pump Nozzle Mandates Highlight Federal Clean Air Proposals."

75. David Woodruff, *Business Week,* 9/4/89, "Detroit's Big Worry for the 1990s: The Greenhouse Effect."

76. Frank Allen, *Wall Street Journal,* 9/27/91, "Dirty Cars Account for Much Pollution."

77. Donald Stedman, *Wall Street Journal,* 2/6/90, "Dirty Car Tune-Ups Beat Oxy-Fuels by a Mile."

78. Rick Henderson, "Going Mobile," *Reason,* August/September 1990.

79. William Chameides, Georgia Institute of Technology, telephone interview, 10/21/91.

80. Malcolm Browne, *New York Times,* 2/21/89, "New Tactics Emerge in Struggle Against Smog."

81. *Automotive News,* 3/5/90, "BMW Leads the Way."

82. Paul Eisenstein, *Chicago Tribune,* 11/25/90, "GM's Saturn Drives the Hopes of Plastic Industry."

83. Paul Eisenstein, *Christian Science Monitor,* 11/29/90, "Designers Take on Green Concerns."

84. Jack Keebler, *Automotive News,* 3/5/90, "Popular, Durable Plastic Faces Dilemma on Recycling."

85. Automotive Dismantlers and Recyclers Association, "Fact Sheet," 1991.

86. Automotive Dismantlers and Recyclers Association, "Recycled Auto and Truck Parts," 1991.

87. Ibid.

88. Jack Keebler, *Automotive News,* 3/5/90, "Popular, Durable Plastic Faces Dilemma on Recycling."

4. Weighing the Alternatives

1. Louis Wichinsky, telephone interview, 12/1/89.

2. Richard Sapienza, Brookhaven National Laboratory, telephone interview, 12/1/89.

3. L. M. Cook, *New York Times,* 2/26/91, "Oil Companies Getting After Pollution" (letter).

4. Patrick Lee, *Los Angeles Times,* 6/17/90, "Cleaner Gas: Is It Clean Enough?"

5. Matthew Wald, *New York Times,* 7/11/91, "Gasoline as Clean as Methanol Is Developed to Cut Pollution."

6. Ross Gelbspan, *Boston Globe,* 10/30/91, "States Agree to Toughest Emission Rules."

7. Quoted by Frederick Rose, *Wall Street Journal,* 7/12/91, "Arco Unveils a Low-Polluting Gasoline."

8. Quoted by Phillip Elmer-Dewitt, *Time,* 7/22/91, "Gee, Your Car Smells Terrific!"

9. Mark Ivey, *Business Week,* 4/8/91, "Big Oil Sees the Future—And It's Clean Gasoline."

10. Quoted by Patrick Lee, *Los Angeles Times,* 6/17/90, "Cleaner Gas: Is It Clean Enough?"

11. Dianne Dumanoski, *Boston Globe,* 6/18/89, "Bush's Clean-Car Air Pollution Plan."

12. Jerry Flint, *Forbes,* 5/29/89, "Fuel Fantasies."

13. Office of Technology Assessment, *Replacing Gasoline: Alternative Fuels for Light-Duty Vehicles,* September 1990.

14. General Motors, "Public Interest Report," 1991.

15. Quoted by Dianne Dumanoski, *Boston Globe,* 6/18/89, "Bush's Clean-Car Air Pollution Plan."

16. Office of Technology Assessment, *Replacing Gasoline.*

17. Henderson, "Going Mobile."

18. Jerry Flint, *Forbes,* 5/29/89, "Fuel Fantasies."

19. James J. MacKenzie, "Reducing U.S. Reliance on Imported Oil," World Resources Institute, October 1990.

20. Ibid.

21. Ibid.

22. Matthew Wald, *New York Times,* 5/9/90, "Gasohol May Cut Monoxide, But Raise Smog, Study Asserts."

23. James J. MacKenzie, "Reducing U.S. Reliance on Imported Oil."

24. Highway Users Federation, *Highway Fact Book,* 1990.

25. Lenssen and Young, "Filling Up in the Future."

26. Quoted by Matthew Wald, *New York Times,* 5/9/90, "Gasohol May Cut Monoxide, But Raise Smog, Study Asserts."

27. Ibid.

28. Office of Technology Assessment, *Replacing Gasoline.*

29. Quoted by Francesca Lyman, "Clean Cars," *Technology Review,* May/June 1990.

30. William Cook, *U.S. News & World Report,* 2/4/91, "Motoring Into the Future."

31. Patrick McGeer and Enoch Durbin, *New York Times,* 10/2/90, "Natural Gas in Cars and Step on It."

32. "Buses in Buenos Aires to Switch to Compressed Natural Gas," *International Environmental Reporter,* April 1990.

33. Elizabeth Kolbert, *New York Times,* 8/30/90, "Alternative-Fuel Vehicles for Albany."

34. John Holusha, *New York Times*, 7/29/90, "Heating, Cooking, and Now—Driving."

35. *Boston Globe*, 1/10/92, "Plan to Clean Air in Mexico City Set."

36. William Cook, *U.S. News & World Report*, 2/4/91, "Motoring Into the Future."

37. Ronald Rosenberg, *Boston Globe*, 6/29/89, "The Fuel of the Future Could Be Spelled CNG."

38. Office of Technology Assessment, *Replacing Gasoline*.

39. Patrick McGeer and Enoch Durbin, *New York Times*, 10/2/90, "Natural Gas in Cars and Step on It."

40. *Los Angeles Times*, 3/25/91, p. A15, "Methanol, Natural Gas Blends Power Many Vehicle Fleets."

41. Ronald Rosenberg, *Boston Globe*, 8/27/91, "Natural Gas-Fuel Vehicles Move to the Inside Track."

42. William Cook, *U.S. News & World Report*, 2/4/91, "Motoring Into the Future."

43. David Woodruff, *U.S. News & World Report*, 4/8/91, "The Greening of Detroit."

44. Office of Technology Assessment, *Replacing Gasoline*.

45. Dick Russell, "L.A.'s Positive Charge," *Amicus Journal*, Spring 1991.

46. Robert Reinhold, *New York Times*, 9/11/91, "Debut for an Electric Car Created for L.A."

47. "ABC World News Tonight," American Agenda segment, 10/1/91.

48. Robert Reinhold, *New York Times*, 9/11/91, "Debut for an Electric Car Created for L.A."

49. "ABC World News Tonight," American Agenda segment, 10/1/91.

50. Quoted in *Boston Globe*, 9/28/90, "California Eyes Lead Into Era of Electric Vehicles."

51. Quoted by Ross Gelbspan, *Boston Globe*, 10/20/91, "States Agree to Toughest Emission Rules."

52. Quoted by Edward Miller, *USA Today*, 10/3/91, "Drive to Cut Pollution Electrifies the Auto Industry."

53. Office of Technology Assessment, *Replacing Gasoline*.

54. California Council for Environmental and Economic Balance, "Alternative Motor Vehicle Fuels to Improve Air Quality," 1990.

55. David Woodruff, *U.S. News & World Report*, 4/8/91, "The Greening of Detroit."

56. Mark DeLuchi, "Emissions of Greenhouse Gases From the Use of Gasoline, Methanol, and Other Alternative Transportation Fuels," in *Methanol as an Alternative Fuel Choice: An Assessment*, ed. Wilfrid C. Kohl (Baltimore: Johns Hopkins University, 1990).

57. Russell, "L.A.'s Positive Charge."

58. William Cook, *U.S. News & World Report,* 2/4/91, "Motoring into the Future."

59. U.S. Department of Transportation, FHWA, "1983–1984 Nationwide Personal Transportation Study," Nov. 1986.

60. Peter Gray, "Kicking the Oil Habit," *Washington Monthly,* March 1991.

61. David Woodruff, *U.S. News & World Report,* 4/8/91, "The Greening of Detroit."

62. Office of Technology Assessment, *Replacing Gasoline.*

63. Richard Stevenson, *New York Times,* 1/4/90, "GM Displays the Impact, an Advanced Electric Car."

64. Mark Fischetti, "Electric Car Start-Ups," *Popular Science,* October 1991.

65. Quoted in Russell, "L.A.'s Positive Charge."

66. Office of Technology Assessment, *Replacing Gasoline.*

67. Russell, "L.A.'s Positive Charge."

68. Scott Pendleton, *Christian Science Monitor,* 11/4/91, "New Fuels for Cars."

69. William Stevens, *New York Times,* 8/28/90, "Alternatives to Oil Move From the Lab to the Road."

70. David Woodruff, *Business Week,* 5/14/90, "GM Drives the Electric Car Closer to Reality."

71. *Electric Vehicle Progress,* 7/15/91, "A Design Look at the TEVan."

72. Warren Brown, *Washington Post,* 3/4/92, "Chrysler, Westinghouse to Jointly Build Electric Car."

73. *USA Today,* 10/3/91, "Coming Down the Line."

74. David Swan, Center for Electrochemical Systems and Hydrogen Research, Texas A & M University, telephone interview, 11/13/91.

75. Adam Bryant, *New York Times,* 10/3/91, "A New Consumer Passion for What's Under the Hood."

76. Frederick Standish, *Boston Globe,* 8/26/91, "Nissan Has Fast-Recharge Electric Car."

77. Sharon Begley, *Newsweek,* 4/1/91, "The Power of the Voltswagon."

78. Jim George, George Consulting International, telephone interview, 11/12/91.

79. Mike Fetcenko, Ovonic Battery Company, telephone interview, 11/11/91.

80. Ibid.

81. Jim George, George Consulting International, telephone interview, 11/12/91.

82. James Worden, Solectria Corporation, telephone interview, 10/16/91.

83. Fischetti, "Electric Car Start-Ups."

84. James Worden, interview, 3/2/92.

85. David Chandler, *Boston Globe,* 5/21/91, "Futuristic Vehicles Race by the Light of the Sun."

86. Ellen Goodman, *Boston Globe,* 6/1/89, "A Scientist's Dream to be the Henry Ford of Solar Cars."

87. James Worden, telephone interview, 10/16/91.

88. Christopher Miller, *New York Times,* 7/31/91, "Park and Recharge" (letter).

89. Nick Patapoff, Southern California Edison, telephone interview, 3/6/92.

90. *Electric Vehicle Progress,* 9/15/91, "Swiss Group Developing Ultra-Light Solar-powered EV."

91. Quoted in Russell, "L.A.'s Positive Charge."

92. William Yerkes, telephone interview, 10/19/91.

93. William Yerkes, *New York Times,* 7/31/91, "Solar Cars Can't be the Size of Gas Guzzlers."

94. David Woodruff, *U.S. News & World Report,* 4/8/91, "The Greening of Detroit."

95. William Yerkes, *New York Times,* 7/31/91, "Solar Cars Can't be the Size of Gas Guzzlers."

96. Jules Verne, *Mysterious Island,* 1874.

97. Steve Nadis, "Hydrogen Dreams," *Technology Review,* August/September 1990.

98. Mike Knepper, "Fuels in Your Future," *Popular Mechanics,* November 1989.

99. John Templeman, *Business Week,* 3/4/91, "Fill 'er Up—With Hydrogen, Please."

100. Ibid.

101. Dennis Normile, "Emissionless Mission," *Popular Science,* July 1991.

102. Pennsylvania Energy Office, "Singel Introduces World's First Fuel Cell-Powered Electric Automobile" (press release), 6/19/91.

103. MacKenzie, "Reducing U.S. Reliance on Imported Oil."

104. Christopher Flavin and Nicholas Lenssen, "Here Comes the Sun," *Worldwatch,* September/October 1991.

105. Office of Technology Assessment, *Replacing Gasoline.*

106. Nadis, "Hydrogen Dreams."

107. Joan Ogden and Robert Williams, *Solar Hydrogen: Moving Beyond Fossil Fuels,* World Resources Institute, October 1989.

108. Joan Ogden, Princeton University, telephone interview, 2/8/90.

109. Nadis, "Hydrogen Dreams."

110. Michael Fetcenko, Ovonic Battery Company, telephone interview, 2/12/90.

111. David Chandler, *Boston Globe,* 10/28/91, "Dawn of an Industry: Solar/Electric Cars."

112. Quoted in Peter Hoffman, "Practical LH Cars: Maybe in 5 Years?" *The Hydrogen Letter*, August 1991.

113. Office of Technology Assessment, *Replacing Gasoline*.

114. John Templeman, *Business Week*, 3/4/91, "Fill 'er Up—With Hydrogen, Please."

115. Philip Ross, Lawrence Berkeley Laboratory, telephone interview, 2/8/90.

116. Nadis, "Hydrogen Dreams."

117. John Appleby, Center for Electrochemical Systems and Hydrogen Research, Texas A & M University, telephone interview, 1/31/90.

118. Peter Hoffman, *Business Week*, 11/28/88, "The Fuel of the Future is Making a Comeback."

119. Joan Ogden, Center for Energy and Environmental Studies, Princeton University, telephone interview, 2/8/90.

120. Quoted in David Holzman, *Insight*, 1/29/90, "A Lighter Side to Alternative Fuels."

121. Mark Fischetti, "A Shock to the System," *Omni*, November 1991.

122. Jonathan Kimmelman, Natural Resources Defense Council, telephone interview, 11/8/91.

5. The Road Not Taken

1. Naomi Bloom, *Science Digest*, March 1981.

2. Tom Dunkel, *Insight*, 1/22/90, "Sometimes a Dream Is Not Enough."

3. John Pucher, "Urban Travel Behavior as the Outcome of Public Policy," *APA Journal*, Autumn 1988.

4. Michael Repogle, "Sustainable Transportation Strategies for Third World Development," Transportation Research Board 1988 Meeting, National Research Council, Washington, D.C.

5. "Emeryville Goes Berserkeley," *Sierra*, May/June 1989, p. 27.

6. Quoted in Denise Goodman, *Boston Globe*, 8/9/90, "Worse Jams Predicted If Maine Pike Widened."

7. Ibid.

8. Peter Newman, Jeffrey Kenworthy, and T. J. Lyons, "Does Free-Flowing Traffic Save Energy and Lower Emissions in Cities?" *Search*, November 1988.

9. T. A. Heppenheimer, "Widespread Highway Deterioration," *High Technology Business*, March 1989, p. 28.

10. Ibid.

11. Charles Lockwood and Christopher Leinberger, "Los Angeles Comes of Age," *Atlantic Monthly*, January 1988, p. 54.

12. Don Phillips and Stephen Fehr, *Washington Post*, 6/6/91, "What Path Lies Ahead for U.S. Highways?"

13. Secretary of Transportation, "The Status of the Nation's Highways and Bridges: Conditions and Performance," September 1991.

14. Charles Lockwood and Christopher Leinberger, "Los Angeles Comes of Age."

15. Stephen Koepp, *Time,* 9/12/88, p. 57, "Gridlock!"

16. James Gleick, *New York Times Magazine,* 5/8/88, "National Gridlock."

17. Newman, Kenworthy, and Lyons, "Does Free-Flowing Traffic Save Energy and Lower Emissions in Cities?"

18. Quoted in James Gleick, *New York Times Magazine,* 5/8/88, "National Gridlock."

19. Office of Technology Assessment Project Staff, "Advanced Vehicle/Highway Systems and Urban Traffic Problems," September 1989.

20. Robert Dallos, *Los Angeles,* 8/14/90, "Paying As They Go, Faster."

21. *New York Times,* 8/23/90, "High-Tech Tolls and Less Pollution."

22. "By the Year 2000, 'Car Trek'," LA-TV, PBS, August 1990.

23. General Motors, *Futurama* brochure.

24. Quoted in Eric Malnic, *Los Angeles Times,* 6/26/90, "Helping Motorists Out of a Jam."

25. Quoted in Ronald Rosenberg, *Boston Globe,* 4/6/90, "Company Sees $100M in Traffic Info."

26. Elizabeth Pennisi, *Science News,* 3/21/92, "Auto(matic) Commute."

27. J. E. Ferrell, *Los Angeles Times Magazine,* 4/14/91, "The Big Fix."

28. *The Economist,* 9/24/88, p. 113, "The Boulevard of Dreams."

29. Quoted in J. E. Ferrell, *Los Angeles Times Magazine,* 4/14/91, "The Big Fix."

30. Michael Schrage, *Boston Globe,* 6/9/91, "Will 'Smart' Highways Outsmart Us?"

31. Karen Wright, "Shape of Things to Come," *Scientific American,* May 1990, p. 101.

32. Ibid.

33. Quoted in Carla Lazzareschi, *Los Angeles Times,* 3/30/91, p. A14, "Smart Way to Unclog Roadways."

34. Ronnie Lipschutz and Linda Nash, *Los Angeles Times,* 5/12/90, p. B7, "On a Highway to Nowhere."

35. Quoted in Stephen Koepp, *Time,* 9/12/88, "Gridlock!"

36. *Greenwire,* 10/31/91, "Fact of the Day."

37. Calvin Sims, *New York Times,* 11/22/91, "Motorists are Still Shunning Carpools: They Want to be Alone."

38. A. E. Pisarski, *Commuting in America* (Eno Foundation for Transportation, 1987), p. 48.

39. Calvin Sims, *New York Times,* 11/2/91, "Motorists are Still Shunning Carpools: They Want to be Alone."

40. Nancy Shute, "Driving Beyond the Limit," *Amicus Journal,* Spring 1991.

41. Ibid.

42. Richard Marini, "Commanding California's War on Smog," *Popular Science,* September 1990, p. 71.

43. Larry Tye, *Boston Globe,* 2/18/91, "New Environmental Wave."

44. Alan Weisman, *New York Times Magazine,* 7/30/89, "L.A. Fights for Breath."

45. Gordon, *Steering a New Course,* pp. 151–52.

46. Shute, "Driving Beyond the Limit."

47. J. E. Ferrell, *Los Angeles Times Magazine,* 4/14/91, "The Big Fix."

48. Beth Brophy, *U.S. News & World Report,* 9/7/87, "Jam Sessions."

49. Shute, "Driving Beyond the Limit."

50. Michael Cameron, "Transportation Efficiency: Tackling Southern California's Air Pollution and Congestion," Environmental Defense Fund and Regional Institute of Southern California, 1991.

51. "Cities to Cars: Stay Out!" *Sierra,* May/June 1989, p. 26.

52. Quoted in Marc Levinson, *Newsweek,* 6/24/91, p. 24, "Highways to Nowhere."

53. Andrew Hamilton, Conservation Law Foundation, private communication, 7/20/90.

54. Jessica Mathews, *Washington Post,* 3/31/91, "The Myth of the American Car Culture."

55. Neal Pierce, *National Journal,* 4/7/90, p. 858, "State of the States."

56. Jessica Mathews, *Washington Post,* 3/31/91, "The Myth of the American Car Culture."

57. Stephen Koepp, *Time,* 9/12/88, "Gridlock!"

58. John Pucher, "Transportation Planning," speech to the National Growth Management Leadership Conference, Airlie, Virginia, 5/18/90.

59. Jessica Mathews, *Washington Post,* 3/31/91, "The Myth of the American Car Culture."

60. Quoted in Larry Tye, *Boston Globe,* 2/18/91, "New Environmental Wave."

61. "California 2000: Gridlock in the Making," Assembly Office of Research, March 1988.

62. "Parking Subsidies and Commuter Mode Choice," Southern California Association of Governments, 7/31/91.

63. G. B. Arrington, Jr., "Light Rail and Land Use," Tri-Met, Portland, Oregon, January 1989.

64. Todd Oppenheimer, *The Independent,* 11/17–30/88, "Mass Transit for Profit."

65. Marcia Lowe, "Alternatives to the Automobile," *Worldwatch Paper 98,* October 1990.

66. Zachary Gaulkin, *FAX,* 8/7/90, p. 7, "Is Everybody Happy?"

67. Lowe, "Alternative to the Automobile."

68. Janice Perlman, "Mega-Cities," 11/17/89.

69. "Cities to Cars: Stay Out!" *Sierra.*

70. Paul Webster, 8/6/89, "War on the Car."

71. John Pucher, "Urban Travel Behavior," 1988.

72. *Boston Globe,* 12/27/91, "Italian Cities Try to Fight Pollution by Limiting Cars; Motorists Rebel."

73. Matt Moffett, *Wall Street Journal,* 3/13/90, "Mexican Driving Ban Puts a Dent in Smog."

74. Ibid.

75. Brook Lavimer, *Christian Science Monitor,* 11/28/90, "New Program Thins Smog, Streets."

76. Matt Moffett, *Wall Street Journal,* 3/13/90, "Mexico Driving Ban Puts a Dent in Smog."

77. Larry Stammer, *Los Angeles Times,* 8/1/90, "EPA Gives L.A. Basin Time to Meet Clean Air Standards."

78. Daniel Wood, *Christian Science Monitor,* 11/28/90, "Taming the L.A. Traffic Monster."

79. Shute, "Driving Beyond the Limit."

80. Richard Simon, *Los Angeles Times,* 7/18/90, "County Will Try 4-Day Work Week at Public Works."

81. Michael Alexander, *Boston Globe,* 7/20/90, "Telecommuting to Work."

82. Francesca Lyman, "Rethinking Our Transportation Future," *E Magazine,* Sept/October 1990.

83. Richard Perez-Peña, *New York Times,* 1/7/92, "For Traffic-Weary Workers, An Office That's a Long Way from the Office."

84. Fred Reid, "Real Possibilities in the Transportation Myths," in *Sustainable Communities,* ed. Sim Van der Ryn and Peter Calthorpe (San Francisco: Sierra Club Books, 1986).

85. Shute, "Driving Beyond the Limit."

86. Kevin Kasowski, "Sprawl: New Urban Growth Boundary Plans Take Shape," *Developments,* Summer 1991.

87. "California 2000: Gridlock in the Making," Assembly Office of Research, March 1988.

88. Pucher, "Transportation Planning."

89. Robert Hey, *Christian Science Monitor,* 3/18/91, "Bush and Congress Gridlock Over Transport Policy."

90. Pucher, "Transportation Planning."

91. Oppenheimer, M. and Boyle, R., *Dead Heat* (New York: Basic Books, 1990), p. 182.

92. Renner, "Rethinking the Role of the Automobile."

93. Stephen Fehr, *Washington Post,* 6/22/91, "Strapped Mass Transit Systems."

94. Flink, *The Automobile Age.*

95. Pucher, "Urban Travel Behavior."

96. Flink, *The Automobile Age.*

97. Jessica Mathews, *Washington Post,* 3/31/91, "The Myth of the American Car Culture."

98. *Boston Globe,* 3/28/91, "The Next Mass Transit Step."

99. Michael Rossmy and Steven Brown, "Congestion Management in New York," *Transportation Research Record 1237,* 1989.

100. Sam Fulwood, *Los Angeles Times,* 7/18/90, "$11 Billion in Transit Aid Sought."

101. *Boston Globe,* 7/8/91, "Flynn to Lobby for New T Line."

102. WBZ-TV, Boston, "News at 11," 7/7/91.

103. "1991 Transit Fact Book," American Public Transit Association, Washington, D.C., 1991, p. 96.

104. "Transportation Energy Data Book: Edition 11," Oak Ridge National Laboratory, January 1991, p. 2–23.

105. Matthew Wald, *New York Times,* 3/11/90, "How Dreams of Clean Air Got Stuck in Traffic."

106. Quoted in Alice Bredlin, "On Ill Health," *New York Times,* "Good Health" magazine, 10/7/90, p. 33.

107. Rich Golda, Santa Clara Light Rail, telephone interview, 12/16/91.

108. James Mills, "Light Rail Transit" (keynote address), Transportation Review Board/National Research Council *Special Report 221,* 1989.

109. Ibid.

110. Arrington, "Light Rail and Land Use."

111. John Post, "The Portland Light Rail Experience," in *Transit, Land Use, and Urban Form,* ed. Wayne Attoe (Austin: University of Texas, 1988).

112. Marcia Lowe, "Portland Bypasses Progress," *Worldwatch,* September/October 1991.

113. Arrington, "Light Rail and Land Use."

114. Kevin Kasowski, "Bridging the Gap," *Developments,* Spring/Summer 1990.

115. Alice Bredlin, "On Ill Health," *New York Times,* "Good Health" magazine, 10/7/90, p. 33.

116. Mike Tharp, *U.S. News & World Report,* 7/23/90, "California's Rush to Rail."

117. Victor Merina, *Los Angeles Times,* 8/2/90, "Free Ride is Over."

118. Quoted in Mike Tharp, *U.S. News & World Report,* 7/23/90, "California's Rush to Rail."

119. Victor Merina, *Los Angeles Times,* 8/2/90, "Free Ride is Over."

120. Penelope Lemov, "Buck Rogers Doesn't Live Here Anymore," *Governing,* November 1989.

121. Mike Tharp, *U.S. News & World Report,* 7/23/90, "California's Rush to Rail."

122. Beth Brophy, *U.S. News & World Report,* 8/7/87, "Jam Sessions."

123. Nelson Alba, Dade County Metro-Transit Agency, telephone interview, 7/12/91.

124. Lemov, "Buck Rogers Doesn't Live Here Anymore."

125. Jason DeParle, *New York Times,* 8/25/91, "West Virginia Students Still Riding Into Future."

126. Stephen Koepp, *Time,* 9/12/88, "Gridlock."

127. David Burwell and Mary Ann Wilner, *The End of the Road* (Washington, D.C.: National Wildlife Federation and Environmental Action Foundation, 1977), p. 45.

128. Lockwood and Leinberger, "Los Angeles Comes of Age."

129. Quoted in Lemov, "Buck Rogers Doesn't Live Here Anymore."

130. Highway Users Federation, "Getting Around Town."

131. Pam German, DART, telephone interview, 12/12/91.

132. Lucia Mouat, *Christian Science Monitor,* 2/7/91, "Employers Open New Routes for Workers Commuting to Suburbia."

133. Lemov, "Buck Rogers Doesn't Live Here Anymore."

134. Ibid.

135. Post, "The Portland Light Rail Experience."

136. Ross Capon, "Going Nowhere," *Utne Reader,* March/April 1989, p. 87.

137. Jeffrey Zupan, speech to the National Growth Management Leadership Conference, Airlie, Virginia, 5/19/90.

138. Elizabeth Deakin, "Land Use and Transportation Planning," *Transportation Research Record 1237,* 1989.

139. Arrington, "Light Rail and Land Use."

140. Rich Golda, Santa Clara Light Rail, telephone interview, 12/16/91.

141. Lyman, "Rethinking Our Transportation Future."

142. John Holtzclaw, "Explaining Urban Density and Transit Impacts on Auto Use," National Resources Defense Council and Sierra Club, 4/19/90.

143. John Holtzclaw, "Efficient Transportation—For Earth's Sake," Sierra Club, 8/8/90.

144. Lowe, "Alternatives to the Automobile."

145. Holtzclaw, "Explaining Urban Density and Transit Impacts on Auto Use."

146. Ibid.

147. Lowe, "Alternatives to the Automobile."

148. Ibid.

149. Marcia Lowe, "Shaping Cities: The Environmental and Human Dimensions," *Worldwatch Paper 105,* October 1991.

150. Kasowski, "Bridging the Gap."

151. Lowe, "Alternatives to the Automobile."

152. Erik Hagerman, "Small Town Thinking," *Worldwatch,* 7/8/91.

153. "ABC World News Tonight," American Agenda segment, 1/7/92.

154. Hagerman, "Small Town Thinking."

155. Philip Langdon, "A Good Place to Live," *Atlantic Monthly,* March 1988.

156. Ibid.

157. Quoted in Laura Van Truyl, *Chicago Tribune,* 8/4/90, "They Have Some Designs on Restructuring the Suburbs."

158. Andres Duany, lecture at Boston Museum of Fine Arts, 1989.

159. Quoted in Laura Van Truyl, *Chicago Tribune,* 8/4/90, "They Have Some Designs on Restructuring the Suburbs."

160. "ABC World News Tonight," American Agenda segment, 1/7/92.

161. Doug Kelbaugh, ed., *The Pedestrian Pocket Book* (New York: Princeton Architectural Press, 1989), p. 17.

162. Ibid., p. 11.

163. Quoted in Lyman, "Rethinking Our Transportation Future."

164. Kenneth Schneider, *Autokind vs. Mankind* (New York: Schocken Books, 1971).

165. James Hillman, "The Wonder of Wander," *Utne Reader,* 3/4/89.

166. Kenneth Schneider, *Autokind vs. Mankind.*

167. Pucher, "Urban Travel Behavior," p. 158.

168. Marcia Lowe, "Pedaling into the Future," *The Futurist,* March/April 1989.

169. "ABC World News Tonight," 6/6/90.

170. Marcia Lowe, "Reinventing the Wheels," *Technology Review,* May/June 1990.

171. Ibid.

172. Lowe, "Pedaling into the Future."

173. Marcia Lowe, "Pushing Pedalers," *Utne Reader,* March/April 1989.

174. Lowe, "Pedaling into the Future."

175. David Adams, "Bike If You're Hard-Driving," *Men's Health,* February 1991.

176. Cory Johnston, "Freewheeling Visionaries," *City Limits,* June/July 1991.

177. Lowe, "Reinventing the Wheels."

178. "Landmark Decision Frees Bike Lane Protesters," *City Cyclist,* May/June 1991.

179. Diane MacEachern, *Save Our Planet* (Washington, D.C.: National Wildlife Federation, 1990).

180. Dirk Johnson, *New York Times,* 5/17/91, "Stolen Bikes Join War on Pollution."

181. Quoted in Ronald Kotzch, "Replacing the Auto," *East/West Journal,* May 1981.

182. David Wilson, MIT, private communication, 7/3/90.

183. Quoted in Connie Koenenn, *Los Angeles Times,* 6/19/90, "The Converts Go by Bus or Bike."

184. Charlie Komanoff, Transportation Alternatives, telephone interview, 11/18/91.

185. Reid, "Real Possibilities in the Transportation Myths."

186. Woody Allen, "My Speech to the Graduates," *Side Effects* (New York: Ballantine, 1981).

6. Overhauling the Transportation Engine

1. Bill Moyers, "A Visit with Oren Lyons," PBS, 1991.

2. Paul Ehrlich and Robert Ornstein, *New World, New Mind: Moving Toward Conscious Evolution* (New York: Doubleday, 1989).

3. *Christian Science Monitor,* interview with Norman Cousins, 11/12/86.

4. Quoted in Jeffrey Krasner, *Boston Herald,* 9/14/90, "Save Fuel, Energy-Czar Ad Blitz Urges."

5. James M. Poterba, "Is the Gasoline Tax Regressive?" *Tax Policy and the Economy,* vol. 5, 1991. See also *Business Week,* 4/8/91, p. 16, "A Gas Tax Hike Might Not Clobber the Poor."

6. Motor Vehicle Manufacturers Association, *Facts & Figures: '90.*

7. James Womack, International Motor Vehicle Program, MIT, telephone interview, 1/9/92.

8. *Automotive News,* 3/23/92, "Cut in Japanese Quota: End of an Era."

9. See, for example, Marc Ledbetter and Marc Ross, "Light Vehicles: Policies for Reducing Their Energy Use and Environmental Impacts," *Energy and Environment,* vol. 6 (Transaction Books, 1992).

10. Motor Vehicle Manufacturers Association, *Facts & Figures: '91.*

11. "Feebates," memo by Amory B. Lovins, Rocky Mountain Institute, 7/6/91.

12. *The Energy Daily,* 10/24/91, p. 3, "DRI Says Auto Scrap Proposal More Effective Than CAFE."

13. Bernard Campbell, DRI-McGraw Hill, personal communication, 12/11/91.

14. "Reducing Greenhouse Gas Emissions With Alternative Transportation Fuels," Environmental Defense Fund, 1991.

15. Ibid.

16. *Electric Vehicle Progress,* 5/1/92.

17. *Automotive News,* 1/20/92, p. 24, "Mazda Readies Hydrogen-Powered Rotary."

18. Joan M. Ogden and Robert H. Williams, *Solar Hydrogen: Moving Beyond Fossil Fuels* (World Resources Institute, 1989).

19. "A Toolbox for Alleviating Traffic Congestion" (Washington, D.C.: Institute of Transportation Engineers, 1989).

20. Highway Users Federation, "Highway Fact Book, 1990," p. 4.

21. Keith A. Bartholomew, "Making the Land Use, Transportation, Air Quality Connection," *Developments,* Summer 1991.

22. John Holtzclaw, "Automobiles and Their Alternatives: An Agenda for the 1990s," Proceedings of Conference sponsored by the Conservation Law Foundation of New England and the Energy Foundation, 1991, p. 50.

23. Bartholomew, "Making the Land Use, Transportation, Air Quality Connection."

24. Pucher, "Urban Travel Behavior."

25. Motor Vehicle Manufacturers Association, *"Facts & Figures: '91,"* p. 82.

26. Ibid.

27. *Highway Statistics 1989,* FHWA-PL-90-003, Table HF-10.

28. Stanley Hart, "Huge City Subsidies for Autos, Trucks," *California Transit,* September 1986.

29. Pisarski, *Commuting in America,* p. 48.

30. Donald C. Shoup and Richard W. Willson, "Employer-Paid Parking: The Influence of Parking Prices on Travel Demand," Proceedings of the Commuter Parking Symposium, Seattle, Washington, 1990, p. 10.

31. See, for example, "Proceedings of the Commuter Parking Symposium," Association for Commuter Transportation and the Municipality of Metropolitan Seattle, 6–7 December 1990.

32. Donald C. Shoup and Richard W. Willson, "Employer-Paid Parking: The Problem and Proposed Solutions" (draft), July 1991.

33. Pucher, "Urban Travel Behavior," p. 514.

34. See, for example, "Proceedings of the Commuter Parking Symposium," Association for Commuter Transportation and the Municipality of Metropolitan Seattle, December 6–7, 1990.

35. Frederick Standish, *Boston Globe,* 1/6/92, "Auto Firms Eye Small Rise After Bleak Year."

36. Warren Brown, *Boston Globe,* 12/9/91, "GM to Shut 21 Plants End 74,000 Jobs."

37. Economic Strategy Institute, "The Case for Saving the Big Three," interim report, January 1992.

38. James P. Womack, Daniel T. Jones, and Daniel Roos, *The Machine That Changed the World* (New York: Rawson Associates, 1990).

39. Ibid.

40. *Automotive News,* 1/20/92, "Workers Lead Bosses in Shift to 'Lean' Ways."

41. James Womack, International Motor Vehicle Program, MIT, telephone interview, 1/9/92.

42. Jessica Mathews, *Washington Post,* 1/10/92, "Build the Green Machine" (letter).

43. Ralph Nader, on "News at 11," WBZ-TV, Boston, 1/7/92.

7. Smart Thinking

1. Mary Engels, National Park Service, Washington, D.C., telephone interview, 3/27/92.

2. Quoted in Jim Robbins, *Boston Globe,* 6/24/91, "The Crowded Outdoors."

3. Ibid.

4. Henry Allen, *Washington Post,* 10/21/90, "Driving Us Crazy."

5. Quoted in Shute, "Driving Beyond the Limit," p. 10.

6. *1991 Statistical Abstract,* p. 804.

7. "Radio's Road Scholars," Conservation Law Foundation, newsletter, Summer 1990.

8. Jessica Mathews, *Washington Post,* 3/31/91, "The Myth of the American Car Culture."

9. Connie Burns, private communication, 7/19/91.

10. Quoted in Connie Koenenn, *Los Angeles Times,* 6/19/90, "Shifting Gears."

11. James Womack, International Motor Vehicle Program, MIT, telephone interview, 1/9/92.

12. Pollack, "Cars are Evil."

13. Kim Foltz, *New York Times,* 9/14/90, "Crisis Spurs Campaign to Save Oil."

14. Quoted in Paul Judge, *New York Times,* 9/26/90, "Car Makers Push Fuel Efficiency."

15. Quoted in Connie Koenenn, *Los Angeles Times,* 6/19/90, "The Converts Go by Bus or Bike."

16. Quoted in Connie Koenenn, *Los Angeles Times,* 6/19/90, "Shifting Gears."

17. Quoted in Lyman, "Rethinking Our Transportation Future," p. 41.

About the Authors

Steve Nadis is coauthor of *Beyond the Freeze* (Beacon Press, 1982), *Energy Strategies* (Ballinger, 1980), and other books. His articles have appeared in dozens of periodicals. Formerly on the staff of the Union of Concerned Scientists, Nadis is now a contributing writer to *Technology Review* and a contributing editor at *Omni* and *The Journal of Irreproducible Results*. He lives in Cambridge, Massachusetts.

James J. MacKenzie is a senior associate in the World Resources Institute's Program in Climate, Energy, and Pollution. A physicist, Dr. MacKenzie was formerly senior staff scientist at the Union of Concerned Scientists and senior staff member for energy at the President's Council on Environmental Quality. His publications include *Driving Forces: Motor Vehicle Trends and Their Implications for Global Warming, Energy Strategies, and Transportation Planning* (WRI, 1990), *Breathing Easier: Taking Action on Climate Change, Air Pollution, and Energy Insecurity* (WRI, 1988), and, with Roger Dower, *The Going Rate: What It Really Costs to Drive* (WRI, 1992).

Laura Ost is a freelance science writer in Washington, D.C. She has written or edited a variety of projects for the National Academy of Sciences and the National Research Council and has written about science and technology for *Governing Magazine*. Previously she was a newspaper reporter, most recently for *The Orlando Sentinel*.

INDEX

About WRI

World Resources Institute (WRI) is an independent research and policy center in Washington, D.C. Since 1982, it has been helping governments, nonprofit organizations, businesses, and citizens look for ways to meet basic human needs and nurture economic growth without degrading our planet and its resources.

WRI's staff of scientists, economists, political scientists, communicators, and others collaborate in five broad research programs: climate, energy, and pollution; economics and institutions; resource and environmental information; forests, biodiversity, and sustainable agriculture; and technology and the environment. Through its Center for International Development and the Environment, WRI also offers developing countries with technical assistance in assessing, planning, and managing natural resources.

WRI's funding comes from private foundations, the United Nations, international government agencies, corporations, and concerned citizens.

World Resources Institute
1709 New York Avenue, NW
Washington, DC 20006